JAN READ'S
GUIDE TO
THE WINES OF
SPAIN

D1343856

Edited and designed by
Mitchell Beazley International Ltd
Michelin House
81 Fulham Road
London SW3 6RB

First published 1983 as *The Mitchell Beazley Pocket Guide to Spanish Wines* by Jan
Read. This edition, revised, updated and expanded, published 1992

Copyright © Mitchell Beazley International Ltd 1983, 1988, 1992
Text © Jan Read 1983, 1988, 1992

All rights reserved

No part of this publication may be reproduced or utilized in any form by any
means, electronic or mechanical, including photocopying, recording or by any
information storage and retrieval system, without the prior written permission of
the publishers

A CIP catalogue record for this book is available from the British Library

ISBN 1 85732 950 3

The author and publishers will be grateful for any information which will assist
them in keeping future editions up to date. Although all reasonable care has been
taken in the preparation of this book, neither the publishers nor the author can
accept responsibility for any consequences arising from the use thereof or from
the information contained therein

Editor: Maggie Ramsay
Art Editor: Paul Tilby
Index: Ann Barrett
Maps: Eugene Fleury
Illustrations: Madeleine David
Production: Sarah Schuman

Executive Editor: Anne Ryland
Art Director: Tim Foster

Typeset in Bembo by
Servis Filmsetting Ltd
Manchester, England
Colour reproduction by Mandarin Offset, Hong Kong
Produced by Mandarin Offset, Hong Kong
Printed and bound in Hong Kong

JAN READ'S
GUIDE TO
THE WINES OF
SPAIN

Mitchell Beazley

Key to Symbols

r	red
p	rosé
w	white
am	amber
g	*generoso*
res	*reserva*
dr	dry
s/sw	semi-sweet
sw	sweet
sp	sparkling
pt	*pétillant*

The above in parentheses means relatively unimportant
See pages 19–20 for more information

★	everyday wine
★★	above average
★★★	excellent quality, highly reputed
★★★★	grand, prestigious, expensive
★★	usually good value in its class
DO	*denominación de origen* – name and origin controlled (*see* pages 15–18)
74, 75	recommended years which may be currently available
DYA	drink the youngest available
NV	vintage not normally shown on label
HARO	name in small capitals indicates a cross-reference

Key to maps

1,000 metres
2,000 metres

Contents

Spain

The autonomous regions shown on this map are those used for the chapters of this guide. The definitive boundaries for individual wine-producing areas are shown on the regional maps at the start of each chapter.

Foreword

Some wine historian of the future, reviewing the last quarter of the 20th century, will no doubt enjoy the question of which of the leading wine countries accelerated fastest, from being a producer of wine at a fairly primitive everyday level, to highly organized quality production on the grand scale. It will be surprising if the vote does not go to Spain.

Spain has progressed in a quarter of a century from as dim a start as any land with wine in its blood to one of the world's most confident, most original and best-run producers.

Throughout this time an English film writer and scholar with a passion for Spain has been more than just passively observing the revolution. He has been a much-valued commentator and critic at the heart of it.

Jan Read and his wife Maite (and their son Carlos, too) have been both interpreters and ambassadors for Spain, and at the same time creative inspiration at *bodega*-floor level.

To its maker, good wine is a very personal thing. It is not just anybody he takes into his confidence. Jan, above all, has been one of the people winemakers can trust – to give them a frank opinion, technical advice, encouragement and friendship.

And he has been the same to other writers studying Spanish wine. My own most rewarding journeys in this most rewarding of countries have been with Jan as a guide, philosopher and friend.

This book condenses more experience than any other writer can claim, of one of the most exciting wine countries on earth. Can we ask for more?

Hugh Johnson

Introduction

Since the time of Sir Francis Drake's rape of the barrels in Cádiz (*see* page 204), Spain has been known first and foremost for a single wine: sherry. The sweet dessert Málagas achieved a certain vogue in England in Victorian times, but the better beverage wines have been slow to establish themselves in foreign markets, and until recently the image was of sturdy (though often drinkable) 'plonk'.

The reasons for this are to be found in the drinking habits of the Spanish themselves. What Richard Ford wrote in his *Gatherings from Spain* in 1846 long remained true: 'The Spaniard himself is neither curious in port, nor particular in Madeira; he much prefers quantity to quality and loves flavour less than he hates trouble . . .'

When I first began drinking Spanish wine some 40 years ago, the custom was to take an empty bottle to the wine shop and to fill it from a cask marked with the alcoholic degree and some such terse description as *tinto* (full-bodied red), *clarete* (light red), *blanco* (white), Moscatel or so on. It is true, of course, that better wines were available, sometimes of excellent quality, like those from the Rioja, which had been bottling its fine wines since the end of the 19th century. They were not, however, much drunk except on special occasions and at the more expensive restaurants.

Various factors have contributed to a remarkable improvement in quality over the last few decades. One of the achievements of General Franco in his latter years was a marked rise in living standards and the creation of a middle class with more sophisticated tastes and the money to indulge them; at the same time the millions of tourists who started to flood across the Pyrenees began asking for the better wines, and liked what they found.

Hand in hand with this, and starting with the Rioja in 1926, the Ministry of Agriculture began the demarcation of the different winemaking areas, laying down strict regulations for the production of better quality wines sold under a *denominación de origen* (DO) and modernizing the cooperatives.

Over the last ten years there has been an increasing realization among the younger and more enlightened *bodegueros* that Spain's future as a wine producer lies in quality rather than quantity. While the bulk of the wine produced in the vast central plateau is cooperative-made and acceptable enough for everyday drinking, it and dozens of other regions are now producing characterful and individual growths, and perhaps no other country in Europe makes wine in such a variety of styles: there are the *pétillant* young wines of the north and northwest; a whole gamut of reds, whites and rosés; excellent sparkling wines produced in larger quantity than champagne; apéritif and dessert wines such as sherry, Montilla and Málaga; and a cupboard-full of vermouths and liqueurs.

Exports of the better table wines have soared in recent years. For example, shipments of Rioja to the UK have increased from 20,000 cases in 1970 to some 400,000 today, and are still increasing; and the story is much the same in the USA and northern Europe, indicating the growing appreciation of outstanding value, particularly in the medium-price bracket.

A–Z listings in this volume are arranged within broad geographical areas. This reflects the fact that in Spain individual labels and house styles are generally of greater significance than minor geographical areas, and the smaller producers tend not to bottle their wine but to sell to larger concerns or direct to local restaurants.

In preparing this new edition I have been helped by *bodegueros* up and down Spain too numerous to mention individually, but should particularly like to thank that brilliant oenologist and leading exponent of Spanish wines, Don Miguel Torres Riera. Mr Jeremy Watson of Wines from Spain (London) has kindly made suggestions for updating the book, and my wife, Maite Manjón, has made a major contribution to the sections on *Wine and Food*, which I hope will add to the enjoyment of visitors to Spain.

How to Read an Entry

Entries are generally of two types: those descriptive of a region, and those relating to individual producers (*bodegas*) and their wines.

The top line of entries referring to producers generally gives the following information:

1. The name of the producer

2. Whether the wine is bottled with a *denominación de origen* (DO). *See* Laws and Labels

3. The types of wines made by the producer, for example red, rosé, white, sparkling (abbreviated to r, p, w, sp – *see* Key to Symbols, page 4)

4. Their general standing as to quality, a necessarily rough and ready guide based on the following ascending scale:
   - ★ everyday wine
   - ★★ above average
   - ★★★ excellent quality, highly reputed
   - ★★★★ grand, prestigious, expensive

   So much is more or less objective. Additionally there is a subjective rating; a box round the stars of a wine which is in my experience particularly good value within its price range, be it luxury or everyday.

   Stars have not been used in the sections on Málaga, Montilla-Moriles, Sherry, Sparkling Wines and Spirits, Aromatic Wines and Liqueurs. Here the producers often make such a vast range of wines or spirits that general judgements become more or less meaningless: one of a sherry house's *finos* may deserve three stars, while its *oloroso* is of merely two-star quality, and vice versa. Guidance to the quality of such wines will be found in the descriptive notes on each producer.

5. Vintage information: which were the more successful of the recent vintages that *may* still be available and which of the

younger are ready for drinking and will probably improve with keeping. A consistent climate and Spanish bottling practice place less importance on vintages than with French wines, and vintages are not given for wines which are made for current consumption.

The second line of each of these entries begins with:

1   The town or village in which the *bodega* is located

2   The province, in parentheses

3   Where a *bodega* makes demarcated wines, the DO is specified, eg DO Penedès. This is not repeated for the many wines of Rioja and the sherry region, which all fall under their respective single DOs.

The information under *Wine and Food* at the end of each section is primarily intended for visitors, and the dishes which are briefly described are those typical of the region. 'International cooking' proliferates in the tourist resorts and large cities. *Nouvelle cuisine* and its developments have left their mark on Spain as elsewhere – often to the good in lightening overheavy dishes. The current trend among sophisticated chefs is to revive traditional dishes and to cook the best prime ingredients in such a way as to bring out their individual flavours to the full.

Where wines are coupled with particular dishes, they are examples of what I myself might choose; but I do not believe in hard and fast rules about which wine goes with which dish, and suggest that all readers follow their individual preference.

The names of recommended hotels appear under the towns listed in the A–Z listing, and suggestions for travelling to and within the regions are made in the introductory paragraphs.

Anatomy of Spanish Wine

Spain has more land under vines than any other country in Europe, but comes third, after Italy and France, in terms of production. The reasons for the low yield are various: much of the soil is barren; many of the vines are old and in need of replacement; and the vineyards are often split up among smallholders with few resources or technical expertise.

Crisscrossed by great chains of mountains, Spain is a country of wide geographical contrasts, ranging from the wet and mountainous north to the arid central plateau, with its bitter winters and hot summers, and Andalucía in the south, mild in winter and sun-baked for the rest of the year. It is a pattern giving rise to wines in great variety, and almost every region, apart from the Atlantic coast in the north, produces wines of sorts.

The best of the world's table wines are produced along a belt lying between 30° and 50° latitude in both hemispheres, and the best Spanish table wines come from the Rioja, Penedès, Ribera del Duero and Galicia lying towards the centre of this zone but somewhat cooler than average because of their altitude. The Rioja and Ribera del Duero are predominantly producers of red wines; the Penedès makes both red and white (together with a great deal of sparkling wine), but is better known for its white; Galicia produces elegant and flowery whites. When faced with an unfamiliar Spanish wine list, it is usually a safe bet to order a red Rioja or white Penedès.

The great central plateau of La Mancha, which produces a massive 35 percent of Spain's wines, is classified as semi-arid and much of the wine is cooperative-made and sold in bulk. Ninety percent is white and the introduction of cold fermentation has resulted in fresher, lighter wines. The best of the reds are from Valdepeñas, where some are now matured in oak.

The coastal region of the Levante (the Valencian area and Murcia), bordering the Mediterranean to the east of La Mancha, has traditionally produced earthy, full-bodied wines high in alcohol, both red and white, of which the most attractive are the light and fresh rosés from Utiel-Requena. Here, sweeping improvements in technology have resulted in the large-scale elaboration of lighter and very drinkable wines for export.

Andalucía is more or less exclusively a producer of apéritif and dessert wines made in *solera* (*see* page 233) by the progressive blending of older and younger wines. Apart from sherry, the best known are the very similar wines from Montilla–Moriles and the classical dessert Málagas.

The future looks bright for the Spanish wine industry. As regards exports, the emphasis has for too long been on quantity rather than quality. This has largely been because the heat of the long summers in the central and southerly parts of the country produces very large amounts of sugar in the grapes, and traditional methods of fermentation have led to robust wines overstrong in alcohol. With the introduction of earlier picking and stainless steel vats, permitting fermentation at lower and controlled temperatures, the picture is changing; and the Mediterranean countries (after all the cradle of winemaking in Europe) may yet be at an advantage over the wetter and colder areas of northern Europe.

Further progress will depend on improvement of the vines, either by the cloning of the best native varieties – always with a view to quality rather than quantity – or by the acclimatization of noble varieties, such as Cabernet Sauvignon and Chardonnay, from abroad. Again a great deal remains to be done, for example by denser planting of the vines and the provision of supports, so as to afford more shade and conservation of water in the soil.

These are matters which are being actively tackled. Certainly there is an awareness among winemakers of the importance of quality. Important steps have already been taken and the Spanish wine industry can look forward to a promising future.

Grape Varieties

It would be a herculean task to list all the grape varieties used in the production of the wines named in this book. In Galicia alone there are 136 recognized types of vine. To add to the confusion, the same grape often goes under a different name in different regions of Spain: the Riojan Tempranillo is the Ull de Llebre in Cataluña, and the Cencibel in Valdepeñas. The main grape varieties of each region are discussed in the general introductions, and the entry for each DO zone names the grapes used for those wines.

Laws and Labels

Since Spain joined the EC, its wine law has been modified to meet the regulations laid down for European wine-producing countries in general. The Community recognizes two broad categories: table wine and quality wine. In Spain, as in France, Germany and Italy, these have been subdivided and are, in ascending order of quality: for Spanish table wines, *vino de mesa* and *vino de la tierra*; and for quality wines, *denominación de origen* (DO) and *denominación de origen calificada* (DOCa). *Vino de mesa* is wine made from grapes grown in unclassified vineyards or blended, and *vino de la tierra* (corresponding to the French *vin de pays*) is local wine from a defined area not qualifying for DO. As far as comparisons can be made, Spanish DO wines correspond in quality to either the French VDQS (*vin délimité de qualité supérieure*) or AOC (*appellation d'origine contrôlée*), and to the Italian *denominazione di origine controllata* (DOC). Only Rioja has as yet qualified for the DOCa, corresponding to the Italian DOCG (*denominazione di origine controllata e garantita*).

The first regions to be demarcated were the Rioja in 1926, Jerez in 1933 and Málaga in 1937. The complete list of DOs now runs to:

Alella	La Mancha
Alicante	Málaga
Almansa	Méntrida
Ampurdán-Costa Brava	Montilla-Moriles
Bierzo	Navarra
Binissalem	Penedès
Calatayud	Priorato
Campo de Borja	Rías Baixas
Cariñena	Ribeiro
Cava	Ribera del Duero
Chacolí/Txacoli	Rioja
Cigales	Rueda
Conca de Barberà	Somontano
Condado de Huelva	Tacoronte-Acentejo
Costers del Segre	Tarragona
Jerez/Xérès/Sherry	Tierra Alta
Jumilla	Toro

Utiel-Requena   Valencia
Valdeorras   Vinos de Madrid
Valdepeñas   Yecla

Each of these denominations is controlled by a Consejo Regulador, a regulatory body under the presidency and vice-presidency of delegates appointed by the Ministries of Agriculture and Commerce and including representatives of the growers, the *bodegas* (winemakers) and shippers. In 1972 the Ministry of Agriculture set up a central body, the Instituto Nacional de Denominaciones de Origen (INDO), to coordinate and to control the activities of the Consejos Reguladores in the field. After the death of General Franco and the restoration of local autonomy to the four provinces of Cataluña between 1978 and 1980, INDO transferred its functions in Cataluña to an agency of the revived Generalitat, the Institut Català de Vi (INCAVI).

All Spanish wines must conform to the procedures and standards laid down in the *Estatuto de la Viña, del Vino y de los Alcoholes*, a lengthy government decree first promulgated in 1970 and applying to Spain as a whole. It defines the different types of wine and spirits and lays down rules for acceptable and unacceptable methods of viticulture and vinification, for chemical composition, and for the transport, distribution, sale and export of wines.

In addition to complying with the *Estatuto*, wines with *denominación de origen* must also be made in accordance with the further detailed provisions of a *reglamento* issued by the appropriate Consejo Regulador. Briefly, this defines the geographical area within which a demarcated wine may be made and grown, the permitted grape varieties and the density of plantation; and also sets limits on the amount of must that may be extracted from the grapes. Further regulations relate to viticulture; pruning; the vinification and maturation of the wine; and to its chemical composition, limits being set for alcoholic degree, volatile acidity, sugar content, dry extract and other elements.

The Consejos maintain control laboratories in the different regions, and when a wine has satisfied its inspectorate there and in the field, the Consejo authorizes the printing of labels to cover the amount involved. Its guarantee often appears on the label in the form of a small emblem or stamp, some of which are shown.

Official seals denoting Denominación de Origen

Alella

Alicante

Almansa

Ampurdán-
Costa Brava

Campo de Borja

Cariñena

Condado
de Huelva

Jerez-Xeres-Sherry
and Manzanilla-
Sanlúcar de Barrameda

Jumilla

La Mancha

Málaga

Méntrida

Montilla-Moriles

Navarra

Penedès

Priorato

Ribeiro

Rioja

Rueda

Tarragona

Utiel-Requena

Valdeorras

Valdepeñas

Valencia

Yecla

To begin with, *cava* (sparkling wine made by the champagne method) was the subject of a *denominación específica* relating only to quality and the way in which it was made. In addition to this, the DO Cava, like the others, now defines the areas in which it may be made, in its case in several different regions of Spain (*see* Sparkling Wines, page 253). In similar fashion a *denominación específica* for wines made with the Albariño grape has been replaced by the DO Rías Baixas, demarcating the three principal areas where the Albariño is grown (*see* Galicia, page 124).

Standards of excellence in the different demarcated regions vary greatly, and the largest production of quality wines is in those like the Rioja, Jerez and the Penedès with a long-established reputation for making fine wines. At the other end of the scale, no one could possibly maintain that the wines from the DO Méntrida are in any way comparable with French VDQS or AOC wines. Indeed, the authoritative *Guide to the Wines of Spain* published by the Club de Gourmets of Madrid is of opinion that 'this is the most inexplicable of Spanish denominations of origin' and that 'given the current rigorous criteria ... Méntrida would never have qualified.' Again, it would seem that some other regions, such as Costers del Segre and Binissalem, have recently been granted DO status on the strength of a single prestigious producer. Decisions have clearly been taken with the future potential of the region in mind – and the grant of a provisional DO has often induced producers to modernize equipment and improve their wines – but the magic phrase DO on a label is currently not a reliable yardstick of quality for the consumer. At one time the famous firm of Miguel Torres was debarred from labelling wines made with acclimatized foreign grapes with the DO Penedès, yet the name 'Torres' is the best possible guarantee of quality. The name and reputation of the producer is, in fact, at least as important as DO – and often more so.

Within Spain light wine is sometimes labelled not with the vintage year, but with a description such as *3° año* or *5° año*, meaning that it was bottled during the third or fifth calendar year after the harvest and *not*, as commonly stated abroad, that the wine is three or five years old. Many *2° año* wines, bottled during the calendar year following the harvest (the 'second') are not, in fact, even a year old.

Spanish wine terms commonly appearing on labels are listed in the glossary which follows.

Glossary

Words used on wine labels

abocado semi-sweet table wine

amontillado a style of sherry made by ageing the *fino* wine

amoroso a light dessert sherry

añejo, añejado por old, aged by

(4)°ano bottled in the (fourth) year after the harvest (*see* page 18). A description much used in the past, but now being discontinued

blanco white

bodega literally, a wine cellar, but used to describe a concern which may have grown, made, shipped or sold the wine. Without further qualification it normally means that the *bodega* has made and shipped the wine

brut extra-dry, used only of sparkling wine

cava a) an establishment making sparkling wines
b) a term used to describe such wines made by the champagne method, now the subject of the DO Cava

cepa literally, a vine. Its use on labels is not precise, though the word is sometimes coupled with the name of a grape

clarete light red table wine. The description is no longer permitted on labels

con crianza used on the back label, this indicates that the wine has been aged in oak and bottle in accordance with the *reglamento* of the Consejo

Regulador (local regulatory body) for a minimum of two years unless otherwise indicated

cosecha vintage, for example Cosecha 1976

cream a sweet sherry or Montilla

criado por matured and/or blended by

denominación de origen (DO) the guarantee of the Consejo Regulador (regulatory body) for a demarcated area, often printed on the label in the form of a small stamp or drawing

dulce sweet

elaborado por matured and/or blended by

embotellado por bottled by

espumoso sparkling wine

fino a pale, dry and delicate sherry or Montilla

generoso a fortified apéritif or dessert wine

gran reserva wine of good quality, aged in the case of *tinto* for at least two years in oak cask, followed by a minimum of three in bottle. White or rosé *gran reservas* must be aged for a minimum period of four years, with at least six months in oak

gran-vas sparkling wine made by the *cuve close* method (*see* page 260)

manzanilla one of the driest of sherries, made at Sanlúcar de Barrameda

método tradicional replaces the term '*méthode champenoise*' as from 31 August 1994

oloroso a dark, fragrant, full-bodied sherry or Montilla

palo cortado a rare and superior sherry or Montilla, with the nose of an *amontillado* and the body of an *oloroso*

pasada, pasado used to describe old and superior *fino* and *amontillado* sherries

raya a) term used in classifying musts for sherry
b) a sherry or Montilla resembling *oloroso*, but not of the same quality

reserva wine of good quality, aged in the case of *tinto* for at least three years in total in oak cask and bottle (and usually for longer) with a minimum of one year in cask. White and rosé *reservas* must be aged for at least two years in total in oak

cask and bottle, with a minimum of six months in oak

rosado rosé

seco dry

semi-seco semi-dry

sin crianza used of a young wine with little or no maturation in cask

solera this denotes (or should denote) that the wine has been aged in a series of butts containing progressively older wine of different vintages (*see* Sherry, page 233)

tinto red wine

vendimia vintage, for example Vendimia 1976

viña, vinedo vineyard. Used rather loosely; the name 'Viña Zaco' does *not* necessarily mean that the wine originated exclusively from a vineyard of this name

vino wine (*see also* Miscellaneous, below)

Miscellaneous

agua water

agua de soda soda water

agua mineral mineral water:
  con gas sparkling
  sin gas still

aguardiente a) alcohol of not more than 80 degrees strength distilled from vegetable materials
b) colloquial name for *aguardiente de orujo*, akin to the French *marc*

anís aniseed-flavoured liqueur

resembling anisette

barrica small cask (usually 225 litres) used for maturing wine

bodeguero the person who owns or runs the *bodega*

café coffee

cerveza beer

chacolí a green (young) wine from the Biscay coast. Now the subject of the DO Chacolí (*see* Navarra, page 155)

cold fermentation fermentation in stainless steel vats over long periods at low temperatures (see Anatomy of Spanish Wine, page 14)

comarca subdistrict

coñac used colloquially of Spanish brandy

crema liqueur:
    de cacao cocoa-based
    de café coffee-based
    de menta crème de menthe
    de naranja Curaçao

flor a film of yeasts which grows on the surface of some wines during maturation in *solera* (see Sherry, page 233)

ginebra gin

hielo ice

horchata milky-looking, non-alcoholic drink made from *chufas* or earth-nuts

leche milk

licor liqueur

limonada lemonade (fizzy)

orujo slang name for *aguardiente*

parador state tourist hotel of a good standard, often housed in a building of historic interest

ponche a herbalized brandy (see page 279)

queimada a punch made from *aguardiente* (see page 280)

ron rum

SA Sociedad Anónima, an indication of a public company's limited liability, equivalent to Ltd, plc or Inc

SAT private company which was formerly a cooperative

sangría cold wine-cup, made by adding sliced orange and lemon, together with ice and a dash of brandy, to red wine

sidra cider

sifón soda water

socio a member of a wine cooperative

té tea

vermut vermouth

vino wine:
    corriente inexpensive everyday wine
    de aguja slightly sparkling, *pétillant*
    de Jerez sherry
    de la tierra table wine of superior quality made in a demarcated region without DO
    de lágrima sweet wine made from the juice which has emerged from the grapes without mechanical crushing
    de mesa table wine
    de pasto an ordinary table wine, often light
    embotellado a better wine, bottled at the *bodega*
    gaseoso cheap, carbonated sparkling wine
    generoso an apéritif or dessert wine, such as sherry or Málaga
    joven young wine for immediate drinking, bottled after fining and without ageing in wood
    rancio an old white wine, maderized and sometimes fortified
    verde young wine, white or red, with a slight sparkle or *pétillance*

zumo fruit juice:
    de naranja natural juice from freshly crushed oranges

Ordering wines and drinks

May I see the wine list?

La carta de vinos, por favor

I should like a bottle/half-bottle of
. . ./a carafe/half-carafe of your
house wine

**Por favor traiga una botella/
media botella de . . ./una
jarra/media jarra de vino de
la casa**

Where does your house wine
come from?

¿De dónde es el vino de la casa?

Can you recommend a good local
wine?

**¿Puede usted recomendar un
vino bueno de la región?**

Yes, I would like a bottle

Sí, me gustaría una botella

I should like to drink a red/dry
white/sweet white wine

**Me gustaría beber un vino
tinto/vino blanco seco/vino
blanco dulce**

Can you please chill the wine?

**¿Por favor puede usted enfriar
el vino?**

*The waiter, too, will have something to say, and will probably begin by asking
if you would like an apéritif:*
¿Quieren ustedes un apéritivo?

Depending upon whether you would like one or not, the answer is:

Yes, I should like a . . . and the
lady a . . .

**Sí, por favor, un . . . para mí y
un . . . para la señora**

No, thank you

No gracias

*After you have ordered the wine, he will ask you whether, as is usual in
Spain, you want mineral water:*
¿Quieren ustedes agua mineral?

Yes, I should like a bottle/half-
bottle of still/sparkling

**Sí, por favor. Me gustaría una
botella/media botella sin
gas/con gas**

At the end of the meal the waiter will ask you if you want coffee:
¿Quieren tomar café?

Yes, I/we would like black coffee/
    white coffee/coffee with a little
    milk

**Sí, por favor, me/nos gustaría
café solo/café con leche/café
cortado**

*Except in expensive restaurants, if you want brandy or a liqueur at the table,
you should ask for it:*

I/we should like a brandy/liqueur.
    What sorts do you have?

**Me/nos gustaría tomar un
coñac/licor. Qué marcas
tienen?**

And to ask for the bill:

La cuenta, por favor

The saleroom at the Cellers de Scala Dei

Aragón

With some 82,000 hectares of land under vines and an average annual production of some 75 million litres of wine, Aragón ranks fifth in order of area and tenth of the Spanish autonomies as regards production. In the past it has been known for sturdy wine high in alcohol and extract, much of it sold outside the area for everyday drinking or blending. There have, however, been marked changes in recent years, beginning with the demarcation of new regions and the accompanying modernization of the cooperatives, the planting of new vine varieties, earlier picking of the grapes so as to lighten the wines, and the emergence of small, sophisticated private firms.

In the early 19th century, the best known of the regions, Cariñena, made one of the most sought-after of Spanish wines and later, at the height of the phylloxera epidemic, the Bordeaux firm of Violet maintained a large establishment for shipping them to France. With the land lying mostly between 450 and 650 metres and in the harsh climatic conditions of freezing winters, hot summers and strong winds, the vine that does best, and by far the most prevalent, is the sturdy black Garnacha, though Tempranillo is increasingly being planted for better quality, oak-aged red wines, and there are also small quantities of white grapes such as the Viura, Garnacha Blanca and Alcañón (native to Somontano). Oddly enough, the black Cariñena is much more widely grown in Cataluña (also in France as the Carignan). As elsewhere in Spain, small amounts of Cabernet Sauvignon and Chardonnay have been introduced on an experimental scale.

Aragón has four DO zones: Cariñena; the more recently demarcated Campo de Borja and Somontano to the north; and to the west Calatayud, demarcated only in 1990.

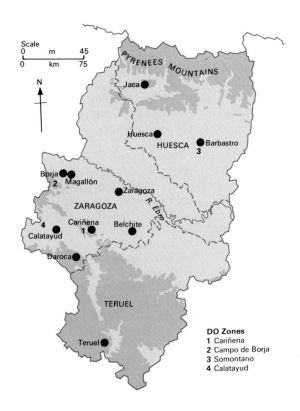

Scale
0   m   45
0   km   75

N

PYRENEES MOUNTAINS

Jaca●

Huesca●
HUESCA   ●Barbastro
      3

Borja●●
2 Magallón
        ●Zaragoza
ZARAGOZA
       R. Ebro
4   Cariñena●   Belchite●
Calatayud●   1

Daroca●

TERUEL

DO Zones
1 Cariñena
2 Campo de Borja
3 Somontano
4 Calatayud

Teruel●

Aragonesas, Bodegas
See San Juan Bautísta

Belchite r w dr ★
Small area east of CARIÑENA making sturdy reds and whites.

Bordejé, Bodegas DO r (w g) ★★ 89
Ainzón (Zaragoza). DO Campo de Borja. A family concern dating from 1770 and growing all its own grapes on 100 hectares of vineyards. It is best known for its cherry red Abuelo Nicolás, made by carbonic maceration, not shipped abroad but entirely delicious when drunk young

and on the spot. It also produces a luscious and intensely fruity dessert Moscatel.

Borruel, Bodegas DO r w dr ★★ 85, 89

Ponzano (Huesca). DO Somontano. Small, old-established (1903) *bodega* with 14 hectares of vineyards. Best of its wines is the characterful red Barón de Eroles *reserva* made with a blend of Moristel and Garnacha.

Calatayud DO r p ★

Newly demarcated area in the west of Aragón making honest enough wine for everyday drinking. The best are the rosés made with 100 percent Garnacha.

Campo de Borja DO r ★

The region takes its name from the small town of Borja in the Ebro valley west of Zaragoza, the ancestral home of the Borgia family, whose castle still survives. Demarcated in 1977, it embraces 9,889 hectares of vineyards. Made mainly from the Garnacha Tinta grape, the traditional wine was a very full-bodied red, more astringent and acidic than the wine from CARIÑENA and containing an average 15–16 percent alcohol, but sometimes a hefty 18 percent. For this reason it was often used for blending with less robust growths from other regions, much of it being sold in bulk to concerns in the Rioja and Cataluña. Lighter rosés and better oak-aged Tempranillo reds are now being produced.

Cariñena DO r (w dr sw g) ★→★★

A little to the south of Zaragoza, Cariñena, with 21,674 hectares under vines, is the most important wine-producing area in Aragón. The vines grow in calcareous clays, and the most predominant varieties are the black Garnacha Tinta (60 percent) and white Viura (21 percent). The typical wine of Cariñena is the red, of a purplish ruby colour with a bouquet of violets, 13–17 percent in strength, full-bodied and deep in flavour, slightly astringent when young, but becoming smoother and silkier when aged in cask. Cariñena also produces some everyday white wine from the Viura and Garnacha Blanca, and a fortified dessert wine made like Málaga (*see* page 133).

Daroca r ★
Undemarcated area in the far south of Aragón on the borders of Teruel, producing sturdy red wines with 13–16 percent alcohol.

Lalanne, Bodegas DO r p w dr res ★★
Torre de San Marcos, Barbastro (Huesca). DO Somontano. Small *bodega*, founded by a French family at the time of the phylloxera epidemic in the 19th century, and growing 12 vine varieties on its 22 hectares of vineyards. Among its highly individual oak-aged wines are Viña San Marcos rosé and Laura Lalanne red.

San Juan Bautísta, Cooperativa del Campo DO r p w dr g ★→★★
Fuendejalón (Zaragoza). DO Campo de Borja. Large cooperative making and exporting worthwhile wines, some of them aged in oak, including young red, white and rosé Crucillón; red Don Ramón, Duque de Sevilla and Mosen Cleto *reservas*, all made with 100 percent Garnacha.

San Valero, Bodega Cooperativa DO r (p w dr) ★→★★
83, 85, 86, 88, 89
Cariñena (Zaragoza). DO Cariñena. Large cooperative on the Zaragoza–Teruel road in the village of CARIÑENA; makers of the young Don Mendo white, red and rosé; the cold-fermented Perçebal rosé; and oak-aged Monte Ducay *crianza* and *reservas*.

Somontano DO r p w dr ★→★★
This very recently demarcated region in the province of Huesca in the foothills of the Pyrenees produces wines completely different from the others of Aragón. Made from a profusion of grape varieties, including the Alcañón, Macabeo (Viura), Garnacha Tinta, Mazuelo and Parraleta, they are traditionally ruby-coloured, faintly perfumed, light

on the palate and slightly acid, with some 11–13 percent alcohol. At the turn of the century they were popular in France, and one of the best of the area's wineries, Bodegas LALANNE in Barbastro, is of French origin. It is a region where a dramatic improvement in standards is under way.

Somontano, Compañía Vitivinícola del DO r w dr ★★→★★★

88, 89

Barbastro (Huesca). DO Somontano. Founded in 1986, the firm possesses a sizable 515 hectares of vineyards and state-of-the-art winery. The first vintages of its wines, sold under the label Viñas del Vero, augur well for the future. They embrace a lively 100 percent Chardonnay and excellent red wines made with 100 percent Cabernet Sauvignon, and a 50/50 blend of Tempranillo and Moristel.

Somontano de Sobrarbe, Bodega Cooperativa Comarcal

DO r p w ★★ 84, 85

Barbastro (Huesca). DO Somontano. Since 1980 this large cooperative has been modernized and re-equipped and is making quality wines, sold under the labels Montesierra, Monasterio and Señorío de Lazán. Some of the oak-aged reds are first rate.

Valdejalón r ★

Large area just west of Zaragoza. The predominant grape variety, the Garnacha Tinta, produces wines high in alcohol and extract, more resembling those of CAMPO DE BORJA than of CARIÑENA.

Zaragoza

Capital of the medieval kingdom of Aragón, Zaragoza is rich in historic remains from Roman times onwards, including the Moorish Aljafería with its figured plasterwork and beautiful *artesonado* ceilings; but the city is dominated by the many-domed Basílica del Pilar, looming above the bridge across the Ebro, which contains the oldest Marian sanctuary in Europe. The festival of El Pilar in October is the most important date in Spain's religious calendar.

The best hotels are the five-star Meliá Zaragoza Corona and the four-star Gran Hotel and Palafox.

Wine and Food

Aragón is sometimes called the *zona de los chilindrones*, in recognition of the famous sauce made with onions, tomatoes and peppers, and served with chicken and lamb. The young lamb from the mountains is excellent, and south of Zaragoza in the direction of Teruel the miles of gardens and orchards produce some of the best fruit in Spain: peaches, plums, apricots, apples, cherries and strawberries. The vegetables, too, including the white Aragonese cabbage and cardoon, are first rate.

The sturdy red wines go well with simple dishes and country fare, and with a more sophisticated meal try one of the new, lighter growths from Somontano.

Bacalao al ajoarriero Dried salted cod with garlic, paprika and chopped parsley.

Migas de pastor Breadcrumbs fried until crisp in olive oil, often served as a starter or side dish. Some devotees eat them with hot chocolate or with grapes.

Pollo al chilindrón Chicken with *chilindrón* sauce, made from olive oil, garlic, tomatoes and peppers.

Sopas de ajo Garlic soups with bread, eggs and a piquant *sofrito* base are a great speciality of Aragón.

Teresicas Small pastries made with butter, flour and yeast and fried in olive oil.

Ternasco asado Roast baby lamb cooked with white wine, lemon and garlic.

Restaurants

Huesca *Navas* (apple salad with goose foie gras); *Venta del Sotón* (at Esquedas on the Tarragona road).

Zaragoza *La Casa del Ventero* (sophisticated regional and Lyonnais dishes); *Los Borrachos* (elegant and comfortable, good fish and game); *Mesón del Carmen* (typically Aragonese).

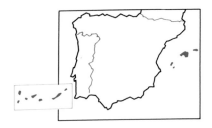

Balearics and Canaries

Both these groups of islands, the green and fertile Balearics with their mild Mediterranean climate and sandy beaches, and the volcanic Canaries in the wastes of the Atlantic off the coast of North Africa, are favourite tourist resorts for sun-starved northern Europeans. On balance they consume more wine than they make, so that familiar names from the mainland figure more on their wine lists than the local growths.

Before the devastations of phylloxera there were about 27,000 hectares under vines in Mallorca, the main producer in the Balearics, but in the principal vineyard areas of Binissalem and Felanitx the area has now shrunk to 2,589 hectares. Tourism aggravated this decline – it proved more profitable to sell the land for holiday villas, and the young people left the villages to work in the hotels of Palma and Pollensa.

The soils of the Balearics are mainly ferruginous clays, and the vines are grown in small plots interspersed with olives and almonds. Most of the grapes are native to Mallorca, the typical varieties being the Manto Negro, Callet, Fogoneu and Fogoneu Francés. Apart from the superior growths of José L Ferrer, most of the wines are reds or rosés made by the cooperatives or small proprietors for current consumption.

In the Canaries, famous for sack in the 16th century, wine production is now mainly confined to the islands of Tenerife, La Palma and Lanzarote. The soils are volcanic, and the principal grape varieties are the white Listán Blanco and Malvasía (Malmsey), and the red Listán and Negramoll. The wines are acceptable enough for holiday drinking, but because demand exceeds supply there is an unfortunate tendency to blend them with wine from the mainland.

Until recently the few wines with real character were the white Malvasías from Bodegas El Grifo and Bodegas Mozaga, halfway to a dessert wine, but with the introduction of stainless steel and cold fermentation a new generation of fresh young wines for early drinking is appearing.

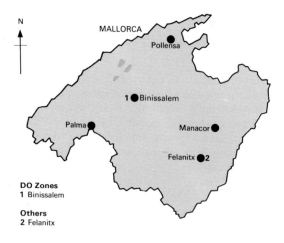

N

MALLORCA

Pollensa

1 Binissalem

Palma

Manacor

Felanitx **2**

DO Zones
1 Binissalem

Others
2 Felanitx

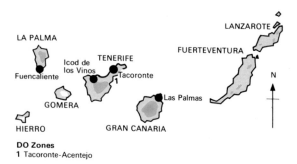

LANZAROTE

LA PALMA

FUERTEVENTURA

Icod de
los Vinos

TENERIFE

Fuencaliente

Tacoronte

1

N

GOMERA

Las Palmas

HIERRO

GRAN CANARIA

DO Zones
1 Tacoronte-Acentejo

Binissalem DO r (w dr) ★→★★★

With some 400 hectares under vines, the newly demarcated Binissalem is the producer of the best Mallorcan wines, although the area under cultivation has shrunk to a fraction of its former size. The principal red grape is the Manto Negro, producing full-bodied reds of 14–16 percent with pronounced bouquet and a high amount of extract; also recommended is the native Callet, while the new regulations additionally permit use of the Tempranillo and Monastrell. The main grape for white wines, made in much smaller amounts, is the Moll, or Prensal Blanco.

El Grifo, Bodegas r p w dr g ★→★★

La Geria (Lanzarote). Old-established *bodega*; with Bodegas MOZAGA, one of the best in the Canaries. It has long been famous for its Malvasía El Grifo, of 14·5 percent strength, but is now making fresh young red and white wines by cold fermentation.

Felanitx p ★

In the southeast of the island, Felanitx, with some 2,000 hectares under vines, is the largest of the Mallorcan wine areas, although not, except in a couple of very small *bodegas*, producing a wine to match those of José L FERRER in BINISSALEM. The typical grape is the Fogoneu, usually vinified so as to give rosés of 9–11 percent. Much of the wine is made in the cooperative at Felanitx serving the small proprietors; the cooperative has, however, been on the point of bankruptcy. There are also distilleries in the town producing grape spirit and alcohol.

Ferrer, Bodegas José L DO r (w dr p) res ★★→★★★ 84, 85, 86

Binissalem (Mallorca). DO Binissalem. José L Ferrer, an enthusiastic and informed oenologist, and owner of one of the best hotels in Palma, owns 150 hectares of vineyards planted mainly with the Manto Negro and Callet, and makes practically the only wines of distinction from the Balearics; his is the name to look for on local wine lists. The wines include a Blanc de Blancs; the young, fresh and fruity red Autentico; and red *reservas*, such as the exceptional 1970, deep in nose and flavour and of remarkable quality. The wines are readily obtainable in shops and restaurants in

Palma – where waiters recommend them as 'better than Rioja' – and small amounts are exported.

Flores, Bodegas DO r ★★ 89

La Matanza (Tenerife). DO Tacoronte-Acentejo. Makers of a young, fruity and deceptively smooth and velvety wine, made with the native Listán Negro, Negramoll and Listán Blanco and containing some 13 percent alcohol.

Fuencaliente r ★

The main production area in the Canary island of La Palma. The principal vines, which were unaffected by phylloxera and are grown ungrafted, are the Listán Blanco and Negra, Vijiriego and Negramoll, and the typical wine is a dry and full-bodied *clarete*. Winemaking is on the decline, however, and there are now only 500 hectares under vines.

Geria, La am ★

The principal vine-growing area in Lanzarote, the most desolate of the Canary islands with its 300 volcanoes, blazing volcanic sands and torrid winds from the Sahara. The vines are grown under difficulties, being sunk into deep pits and surrounded by stone walls to protect them from the wind. The typical wines which result from all this effort are made from a blend of the white Malvasía and Listán and are amber-coloured and high in alcohol.

Icod w dr ★

Icod, in the island of Tenerife, has 520 hectares of vineyards planted with the Listán Blanco and Malvasía. It makes wines of 11–13 percent with good aroma but little fruit.

Las Palmas

The largest town in the Canaries, with a population of 350,000, Las Palmas is dramatically situated on Gran Canaria beneath an extinct volcano, and possesses good beaches, a colourful promenade and a bustling port with regular ferry services to the other islands. Of its many hotels, serving a thriving tourist industry, the best are the four-star Santa Catalina, Reina Isabel, Meliá Las Palmas and Sol Iberia.

Manacor p ★

Sizable vine-growing area near FELANITX in Mallorca, making very similar rosé wines from the Fogoneu grape.

Mesquida, Jaume r w dr p ★★ 82, 83, 85

Porreras (Mallorca). Together with José L FERRER and Miguel OLIVER, Jaume Mesquida is the third maker of quality wines in Mallorca. Unlike his colleagues, he believes the future of Mallorcan wines lies with acclimatizing foreign vine varieties and makes good Cabernet Sauvignons and Pinot Noirs.

Monje, Bodegas DO r w dr ★★ 89

El Sauzal (Tenerife). DO Tacoronte-Acentejo. The young red Monje, made from 80 percent Listán Negro with a little Listán Blanco and Negramoll, is smooth, full-bodied and fruity: a *vino joven* for early consumption.

Mozaga, Bodegas w sw g ★→★★

La Geria (Lanzarote). Maker of one of the best wines from the Canary island of Lanzarote, the Malvasía Seco. The grapes are picked when well ripe, lightly crushed and aged in oak for two to three months after vinification. The wine is further aged in bottle in cellars excavated beneath the lava. Also a good Moscatel Mozaga of 17 percent strength.

Oliver, Miguel r w dr p ★★ 84

Petra (Mallorca). Miguel Oliver is one of the very few producers to be making worthwhile wines in the Balearics. He believes in the native vines, and his fruity, oak-aged red Mont Ferrutx is made from a blend of Callet, Manto Negro and Guefarro. Also a good Muscat made with 100 percent Moscatel.

Orotava, Valle de la w dr ★

Small vine-growing area situated between TACORONTE and ICOD in the island of Tenerife. It produces dry white wines very similar to those of Icod.

Palma de Mallorca

Palma is one of the most beautiful cities of the Mediterranean, with its wide bay and surrounding beaches and the 13th-century cathedral dominating the port. The narrow streets in the centre are full of elegant shops, good restaurants and old houses with secret, shaded patios. Nowhere in Mallorca is very far from Palma, so it is a good base for visiting the wine areas. There are dozens of hotels, from the luxurious Valparaiso Palace, Meliá Victoria and Sol Palas Atenea to more modest establishments.

Tacoronte–Acentejo DO r (w dr p) DYA

Tacoronte, which has just (1992) been demarcated, is the most intensely cultivated wine area in Tenerife. The 2,492 hectares, of which only 390 qualify for DO, lie on the mountain slopes to the west of the island and are planted mainly with the red Listán Negro and Negramoll. Since the installation of stainless steel in some of the *bodegas*, they are beginning to make fresh and lighter red wines in the modern style, all of them at the moment young.

Viticultores del Norte de Tenerife DO r w dr ★★ 89

Tacoronte (Tenerife). DO Tacoronte-Acentejo. Former cooperative selling the wines produced individually by 71 farmers from the region, under the general name of Viña Norte. One of the best is the fresh and fruity young red *vino joven* from Marcos Guimerá Ravina.

Wine and Food

The Balearics, famous for the invention of mayonnaise (from Port Mahón), have a varied regional repertoire. As might be expected, they excel in seafood and rich fish soups. The appetizing *coca mallorquina*, traditionally made in outdoor ovens fired by wood, much resembles the Italian pizza; *tumbet* is a variation on ratatouille; most typical of the excellent charcuterie are the delicate white *butifarra* and soft red *sobrasada*; there is a good Mahón cheese; and do not miss the fluffy *ensaimadas*, halfway between bun and pastry, for breakfast. Although the Canaries have a few regional specialities, these do not amount to a cuisine; like the Canary wines, you may find it difficult to find them in holiday hotels, where the menus and wine lists are mainland Spanish, if not the international style provided for tourists. Apart from basic cooperative-made wine, the local label to look for in the Balearics is that of José L Ferrer.

Balearics

Acelgas con pasas y piñones Spanish variety of spinach, paler in colour and sweeter than the English, boiled and served with *sofrito*, a sauce made with pine kernels, raisins, toasted bread and garlic.

Berenjenas rellenas estilo balear Aubergines stuffed with ground beef, chopped ham, onions, eggs, breadcrumbs and garlic.

Butifarra A delicate white pork sausage, eaten uncooked, or in a stew with *mongetes* (haricot beans).

Caldereta de dátiles de mar Chowder made with small, dark brown mussels, fished off the coast.

Caracoles con sobrasada Snails cooked with ham, onions, tomatoes, garlic, olive oil, milk, brandy and white wine. They are served with *sobrasada*, the soft and spicy Mallorcan pepper sausage, and green vegetables.

Coca mallorquina The Mallorcan version of pizza, often containing onion, peppers, tomatoes, anchovies and sardines.

Sopa de pescador Formentor Rich fish soup made with garlic, onions, tomatoes, olive oil and parsley.

Tumbet A Mallorcan egg and vegetable pie made with potatoes, red peppers, onions, courgettes and tomato sauce.

Canaries

Buñuelos de dátiles Sweet fritters made with flour, orange juice, Cointreau, sugar, eggs and dates.

Gofio Popular form of bread eaten all over the Canaries in country districts and made in the shape of a big ball from a mixture of flour with water or milk.

Mojo colorado Sauce prepared with olive oil, vinegar, hot paprika, cumin seeds and chillis.

Papas arrugadas New potatoes, boiled in their skins in sea water or much-salted water, then baked in a hot oven and served with *mojo* sauce.

Platanos canarios fritos Fried bananas, Canary style.

Restaurants

Felanitx, Mallorca *Violet* (isolated, but worth the visit).
Inca, near Binissalem, Mallorca *Celler C'an Amer* (one of the best for typical Mallorcan dishes).
Las Palmas, Gran Canaria *Acuario* (best in the city, fresh shellfish from a tank).
Palma de Mallorca *Ancora* (local ingredients imaginatively prepared).
Tacoronte, Tenerife *Las Cuevas de Tacoronte* (good local food and wines).
Teguise, Lanzarote *Las Salinas* (international food, local dishes in the buffet).

Castilla–La Mancha

Between them, the two Castiles occupy the wide central plateau of Spain. Old Castile, so called because it was the first part of the area to be reconquered from the Moors, stretches north from Madrid. South of the capital the landscape becomes increasingly arid, and the central and southern parts of New Castile are known as La Mancha. What was New Castile is now substantially the autonomy of Castilla–La Mancha, and Old Castile (less Cantabria) the autonomy of Castilla–León (*see* page 53). Madrid, though listed in this section, is an autonomy in its own right.

The climate is of the Mediterranean type, with long, very hot summers and low rainfall; for this reason the grapes contain large amounts of sugar and have traditionally produced earthy wines with a high content of alcohol and little acid, though cold fermentation and earlier picking of the grapes are changing the picture. Since the land, though lying between 500 and 800 metres, is mainly flat, the vineyards extend in unbroken expanses – in reality a patchwork of holdings belonging to small proprietors.

This is *par excellence* the land of the cooperatives, of which there are no less than 485 in the central region as a whole. Because of its huge size and despite a low yield of about 16–18 hectolitres per hectare, the region supplies about 35 percent of the country's output of wine, much of it going to other less prolific areas for blending and the surplus being used for distillation.

The typical grape is the white Airén (or Lairén), its thick skin affording some protection against the beating sunshine, of which, on average, there are 200 days in the year. It is a favourite with the small proprietors because it produces proportionately three times as much must as the other most important grape of the region, the black Cencibel (known in the Rioja as the Tempranillo and in Cataluña as the Ull de Llebre or Ojo de Liebre).

Some 90 percent of the wine from the central area is white; but perhaps the best is the red Valdepeñas from the extreme south of La Mancha bordering Andalucía, made with a proportion of the black Cencibel and famous since the days of the Holy Roman Emperor Charles V (King Charles I of Spain), who had them sent across Europe on mule-back during his military campaigns in the Low Countries in the 16th century.

Apart from Valdepeñas, the other DO regions of the area are Almansa, La Mancha, Méntrida and Vinos de Madrid.

Abellan, Sucesores de Alfonso DO r p ★→★★ 73, 82, 85
Almansa (Albacete). DO Almansa. One of the three *bodegas* in the DO Almansa to bottle its wines, which are labelled as Señorío de Almansa. The reds are made from 100 percent Monastrell and some are aged in oak.

Almansa DO r w ★

Bordering the Levante and just north of the DO zones of Yecla and Jumilla (*see* Valencia and Murcia, page 240), the region centres on the town of Almansa with its story-book castle. The soils are chalky, and in its 7,600 hectares of vineyards the predominant grape variety is the black Monastrell (43·5 percent); the Garnacha Tinta and Tintorera account for another 33 percent and there is also some white Forcallat, Airén and Bobal. Since the area was little affected by phylloxera, 83 percent of the vines are ungrafted and produce wines high in alcohol and extract.

The typical wines are deep in colour, full-bodied with little acid and with 12–15 percent of alcohol. Their quality depends on the proportion of Monastrell, but most are sold in bulk for blending. Only three concerns in the region bottle the wines: Hijos de Miguel CARRION, Sucesores de Alfonso ABELLAN and Bodegas PIQUERAS. Those from Bodegas Piqueras are outstanding.

Aloque r dr ★★

The lightest style of VALDEPEÑAS, made with a blend of black and white grapes, usually ten percent Cencibel and 90 percent Airén, dry, deep in colour and of some 13–15 percent alcohol. Considering their strength, the wines are surprisingly light and fresh in taste, and much drunk in the bars and restaurants of Madrid.

Arganda DO r w dr ★★→★★★

One of the subzones of the DO VINOS DE MADRID to the south of the capital. The principal grape varieties are the black Tinto Madrid and Tempranillo, and white Malvar and Jaén; when blended they produce smooth red wines. The district also makes a pleasant straw-coloured white of 12–13·5 percent strength.

The wines were at their most popular during the 17th century, when the Court transferred from Valladolid to Madrid. At that time the present airport of Barajas was a flourishing vineyard, producing white wines reputedly more fragant and delicate than those of Rueda, while

Carabanchel, now the site of the great prison, made a luscious Moscatel. Today, the best wines from the area are made by Jesús DIAZ E HIJOS.

Ayuso Roig, Fermín DO r p w dr ★★ 78, 82, 88
Villarrobledo (Albacete). DO La Mancha. Large, well-equipped *bodega*, selling the best of its wines under the Estola label. Red Estola, made with 100 percent Cencibel, is available as *crianza, reserva* and *gran reserva*.

Calatrava, Campo de DO
Subdivision of the DO LA MANCHA, bordering the DO VALDEPEÑAS in the direction of CIUDAD REAL.

Carrión, Hijos de Miguel DO r ★→★★
Alpera (Albacete). DO Almansa. Small family firm making the smooth and fragrant red Cueva de la Vieja, and ageing it for three to four years in large oak vats.

Casa de la Viña DO r p w dr ★★ 82, 85
La Solana (Ciudad Real). DO Valdepeñas. The firm belongs to Bodegas y Bebidas (formerly Savin, *see* page 174) and sells its pleasant white, rosé and red wines under the labels Vega de Moriz and Casa de la Viña, ageing its 100 percent Cencibel *reservas* in oak.

Castillo de Alhambra
Reliable and inexpensive red, white and rosé wines from the VINICOLA DE CASTILLA.

Ciudad Real
Important winemaking town and capital of the province of the same name in LA MANCHA.

Cueva del Granero DO r p w dr ★★ 87, 88
Los Hinojosos (Cuenca). DO La Mancha. The firm owns a sizable 600 hectares of vineyards, growing Airén, Cencibel, Garnacha and Cabernet Sauvignon. The wines are sold under the label Cueva del Granero, one of the most

successful being the 1987 Cencibel, intense in nose and flavour, complex and long.

Diaz e Hijos, Jesús DO r ★★→★★★
Colmenar de Oreja (Madrid). DO Vinos de Madrid. The red wines from this *bodega* were 'discovered' by CLUVE (Club de Selección de Vinos) and have since been rated with those of the Rioja and Cataluña.

La Invencible, Cooperativa DO r p w dr ★→★★
Valdepeñas (Ciudad Real). DO Valdepeñas. Best of the cooperatives in VALDEPEÑAS. Its light red is particularly attractive.

López Tello, Rafael DO r w dr ★→★★
Valdepeñas (Ciudad Real). DO Valdepeñas. One of the oldest *bodegas* in VALDEPEÑAS, making typical wines by thoroughly traditional methods in clay TINAJAS.

Los Llanos, Bodegas DO r (p w dr) res ★★→★★★ 75, 77, 78, 81, 82, 84
Valdepeñas (Ciudad Real). DO Valdepeñas. Founded as Bodegas Cervantes in 1875, this was the first concern in Valdepeñas to mature its wines in oak, and Cosecheros Abastecedores, who acquired it in 1972, scored another first in bottling their wines. The *bodega* is equipped with stainless steel fermentation tanks and possesses no less than 12,000 American oak *barricas*; its mature and fruity Señorío de los Llanos red *reservas* and *gran reservas* are fine wines which will surprise those used to the traditional Valdepeñas made for early drinking. The younger wines, white, rosé and red, are sold as Don Opas.

Madrid
Madrid lies at the centre of the DO VINOS DE MADRID, a vine-growing district of some interest; and in view of the dearth of accommodation in the wide plains of La Mancha, a stopover in the capital is in any case more or less obligatory for a visit to this region. Nevertheless, its main

interest on a wine tour is that, between them, its hundreds of restaurants offer the widest possible spectrum of regional wines and cooking from the length and breadth of Spain. Apart from wines, if there for the first time one could hardly leave without visiting the magnificent Prado gallery, the arcaded 16th-century Plaza Mayor or the Palacio Real. The Ritz Hotel is one of the most perfect in Europe; the best guide to Madrid's countless other hotels and to its restaurants is the red Michelin for Spain and Portugal.

Mancha, La DO (r) w dr ★→★★

La Mancha, embracing the province of Ciudad Real and parts of those of Toledo, Albacete and Cuenca, comprises the larger part of the great central *meseta* of Spain and extends at an average height of some 700 metres from the River Tagus in the north to the Sierra Morena, dividing it from Andalucía, in the south. This is Don Quixote country, an arid, treeless expanse, bitingly cold in winter and mercilessly hot in summer, clothed with unbroken expanses of wheat, olives or vines.

The DO La Mancha, at the centre of the area, is by far the largest in Spain, with 142,910 hectares under vines and an output in 1990 of 74·5 million litres of wine, most of it made in cooperatives. The subsoil is chalky with a layer of clay above, and by far the most predominant grape, amounting to some 90 percent, is the white Airén (or Lairén). The typical wines are light yellow in colour, with a pleasant enough nose but without much fruit, containing very little acid and of 13–14 percent strength. Because of their somewhat neutral character, they are supplied in vast quantities to other regions for blending and further huge amounts are distilled. More recently, earlier picking and cold fermentation have resulted in crisper, fruitier wines.

Manchuela

It was always a puzzle why Manchuela, lying to the east of the DO LA MANCHA and producing bulk wines of no very marked character, was demarcated. Sensibly the *denominación de origen* has been revoked.

Vineyards of La Mancha

Marqués de Griñon r ★★★→★★★★

Malpica de Tajo (Toledo). At the suggestion of Professor Amerine of Davis University, California, the adventurous Carlos Falcó, Marqués de Griñon, embarked on the plantation of Cabernet Sauvignon and Merlot on his estate near Toledo, and with advice from the redoubtable Professor Peynaud and Alexis Lichine is making a Bordeaux-style Cabernet, the like of which has never been seen in La Mancha. If the wine first attracted attention because the former Marquesa was the glamorous Isabel Preysler, it has long since triumphed in its own right and gone from strength to strength since the first vintage in 1981. The 1985 loses nothing by comparison with good Bordeaux. *See also* Castilla la Vieja, page 56.

Megía, Luis DO r p w ★→★★

Valdepeñas (Ciudad Real). DO Valdepeñas. A *bodega* notable for its size and the modernity of its equipment, including plant for continuous vinification and huge nitrogen-capped *depósitos* of 1·5 million litres capacity. Best wine is the superior red Duque de Estrada, made with 80 percent Cencibel.

Méntrida DO r p ★

Méntrida, with 32,820 hectares under vines and an average output of 45 million litres, lies southwest of Madrid in the north of the province of Toledo. The grapes are predominantly (85 percent) Garnacha Tinta, producing robust red wines, deep in colour and of 14–15 percent strength. The bulk go for blending, and the quality is so nondescript that in Spain itself it has been suggested that the DO be suspended. With a decline in the demand for bulk wines, exports from the region fell to zero from 1987.

Navalcarnero DO r ★

A little to the south of the capital, this is a subdivision of the DO VINOS DE MADRID. Its dark red and slightly astringent wines have a following locally and in Madrid, but are apt to oxidize rapidly and lose their freshness because of the high content of Garnacha.

Nuestra Señora de Manjavacas, Cooperativa DO r p w dr ★→★★

Mota del Cuervo (Cuenca). DO La Mancha. Large cooperative producing improved and fresh young wines under the label of Zagarrón by temperature-controlled fermentation in stainless steel.

Nuestro Padre Jesús del Perdón, Cooperativa DO (r p) w dr ★→★★ 85, 86

Manzanares (Ciudad Real). DO La Mancha. A cooperative with a capacity of 40 million litres, bottling its wines under the names of Lazarillo and Yuntero: good dry whites, and reds made with 100 percent Cencibel, some cask-aged.

Piqueras, Bodegas DO r res ★★→★★★ 81, 82, 83
Almansa (Albacete). DO Almansa. This small family *bodega* makes some of the best red wines from La Mancha, using Cencibel, Monastrell and Garnacha grapes. They include the Castillo de Almansa *crianza* and *reserva*, and Marius *gran reserva*.

Rodriguez y Berger DO w dr sw (r p) ★
Cinco Casas (Ciudad Real). DO La Mancha. Large private firm making fresh young wines by temperature-controlled fermentation in stainless steel. Former suppliers of white Don Cortez to Grants of St James's.

San Martín de Valdeiglesias DO r ★
Subzone of the DO VINOS DE MADRID lying between MENTRIDA and Cebreros (*see* Castilla-Léon, page 56). Its sturdy red wines, made from a blend of Garnacha Tinta, Tinto Navalcarnero and white Albillo grapes, resemble those from Cebreros.

Sánchez Rustarazo, Bodegas DO r ★★
Valdepeñas (Ciudad Real). DO Valdepeñas. Founded in 1900, this family concern makes some of the most honest VALDEPEÑAS, fermenting the wine in the traditional clay TINAJAS and ageing some of them, like its Solar de Hinojosa, in oak casks.

Solís, Bodegas Félix DO r res w ★★ 83, 88
Valdepeñas (Ciudad Real). DO Valdepeñas. Best known for its sturdy red wines, aged in oak and made with 100 percent Cencibel.

Tinajas
These large amphora-shaped vessels, made of the local clay and derived from the Roman *orcae*, some 3 metres high and of about 1,600 litres capacity, have traditionally been used in LA MANCHA, Málaga and Montilla-Moriles for fermenting the wines. In VALDEPEÑAS they are also used for maturing it. They are progressively being replaced by much larger

cylindrical receptacles of cement reinforced with steel rods, and by stainless steel tanks.

Toledo

Rising dramatically above the River Tagus, Toledo, with its superb medieval cathedral and collections of paintings by its adopted son, El Greco, is by far the most interesting place in LA MANCHA. It is also the only one with any choice of comfortable hotels: the three-star Carlos V, Alfonso VI and Hostal del Cardenal, and the four-star Parador Nacional Conde de Orgaz, poised on a hill above the city.

Valdepeñas

Town in the south of the province of Ciudad Real long famous for its red wines, which has given its name to the local DO and is the headquarters of the Consejo Regulador. There are *bodegas* in almost every street, in the form of courtyards with a high, blank wall pierced by a high arch and double doors. Many are now disused, but the town still boasts establishments of all sizes currently making wine. It is an unpretentious place of low houses and sunbaked streets, and the most comfortable place to stay is at the three-star Meliá El Hidalgo outside the town to the north, on the N IV towards Madrid.

Valdepeñas DO r (w dr) ★★

The demarcated region lies in the most southerly part of the province of Ciudad Real and possesses 34,700 hectares of vineyards, which produced some 70 million litres of wine in 1989. The soil is a mixture of gravel, clay and chalk, and average annual rainfall is only 400 millimetres. Although the typical wines are red, some 93 percent of the grapes are white Airén, the balance consisting of the black Cencibel (or Tempranillo) and Garnacha Tintorera. The wines are vinified with 90 percent Airén, but such is the amount of colour and extract in the black grapes that they emerge a deep ruby colour. The tradition has been to make and mature the wines in earthenware TINAJAS, from which they were usually sold young in their first or second year. The *tinajas* have very largely been replaced by stainless steel tanks allowing for temperature-controlled fermentation. Again, it was not normal practice to age the wines in oak, because Airén musts oxidize easily and until recently little wine was made with a large proportion of the scarcer and more expensive Cencibel. There are now a number of *bodegas*, notably CASA DE LA VIÑA, LOS LLANOS and Félix SOLIS, making red *crianza* and *reserva* wines from 100 percent Cencibel and successfully ageing them in 225-litre oak *barricas*.

The Airén contributes a fragrant nose to the finished wine, but is also responsible for low acidity; and the colour, body and fruity flavour derive from the Cencibel. Alcoholic strength lies between 12·5 and 14 percent. Valdepeñas also makes white wines similar to those of the DO LA MANCHA.

Of the 104 *bodegas* in the DO Valdepeñas, increasing numbers bottle their wine – but it must be said that some of the best and freshest comes unnamed from the jugs of bars and restaurants in Madrid.

Villarrobledo

Villarrobledo, off the road from MADRID to Albacete, was the source of much of the clay for making TINAJAS.

Viña Albali r ★★

Well-known red, white and rosé wines from Félix SOLIS.

Vinícola de Castilla DO r p w dr sw ★★→★★★ 81, 82, 83, 85

Manzanares (Ciudad Real). DO La Mancha. This huge, ultra-modern *bodega* with a storage capacity of 15 million litres was one of the showpieces of the dispossessed RUMASA group (*see page 230*). The *bodega* is well known for its well-made and reasonably priced Gran Verdad, Castillo de Manza and Castillo de Alhambra wines (red, white and rosé). It also makes very superior Señorío de Guadianeja 100 percent Cencibel and 100 percent Cabernet Sauvignon *gran reservas* from grapes grown in its own vineyards.

Vinos de Madrid DO r ★→★★

New DO in the immediate vicinity of Madrid, long known for its sturdy red wines. It comprises the subzones of SAN MARTIN DE VALDEIGLESIAS, NAVALCARNERO and ARGANDA.

Visán DO r (w dr) ★★ 82, 85, 86

Santa Cruz de Mudela, Valdepeñas (Ciudad Real). DO Valdepeñas. The firm makes pleasant white and red wines, selling them under the labels of Castillo de Calatrava, Castillo de la Mancha and Castillo de Mudela. Some of the reds are aged in oak.

Wine and Food

With its roasts, its nourishing *potajes* (thick soups) and *cocidos* or *ollas* (stews), the cooking of New Castile is in many ways similar to that of Old, though, because of its more limited resources, more austere.

Drink a good red Valdepeñas with meat dishes (or, if the dish deserves it, treat yourself to a bottle of the Marqués de Griñon's Cabernet Sauvignon) and a La Mancha white with lighter fare.

Atascaburras Rabbit stewed with garlic.

Bizcochos borrachos Sponge cakes in the shape of rings soaked in wine or liqueur.

Caldereta de cordero Lamb ragout with tomatoes and peppers.

Callos a la madrileña Tripe Madrid style, highy spiced and a model to other countries' tripe dishes.

Ensalada manchega Salad containing dried cod, tuna, hard-boiled egg, olives and onions.

Espárragos de Aranjuéz Aranjuéz, with its royal palace, south of Madrid, produces some of the most luscious fresh asparagus (and the best strawberries) in Spain.

Gallina en pepitoria Stewed fowl with almonds.

Lágrimas de aldea A stew of pork, potatoes, black pudding or *chorizo*.

Marmita de verduras A vegetable hot-pot.

Miel con hojuelas Pancakes with honey.

Migas Fried breadcrumbs, often served with fried eggs.

Mojete A vegetable dish resembling ratatouille.

Morteruelo Highly spiced regional version of liver pâté.

Perdices estofadas Partridge stewed in white wine with chopped ham and seasoning.

Pisto manchego A vegetable dish rather like ratatouille with scrambled eggs.

Queso frito Wedges of cheese, dredged in egg and breadcrumbs and fried.

Queso manchego Best known of Spanish cheeses, made in large rounds from ewes' milk.

Tortilla a la magra An omelette made with strips of cooked fillet of pork.

Tortilla española Thick potato omelette, sometimes with added onion.

Restaurants

Almagro *Parador de Almagro* (historic *parador* in a fascinating old town. Try aubergines in spicy sauce; rabbit stewed in white wine).

Madrid A vast range. For the ultimate in sophisticated cooking and wines, *Zalacaín* and *Jockey* are outstanding. Among the others, a few personal favourites are: *El Cenador del Prado; Café de Oriente; Valentín* (popular with actors, bullfighters and visitors, long wine list); *Lhardy* (one of the oldest and most traditional); and *Luarqués* (simple food well cooked, excellent value).

Manzanares *Parador Nacional de Manzanares* (a gastronomic oasis).

Toledo *Hostal del Cardenal; Venta de Aires.*

Castilla-León

Old Castile and the ancient Kingdom of León, united in 1230, are the very heart of Catholic Spain. It was their monarchs who planned and carried through the counter-offensive against the Moors; and the very names of their cities – Avila, Segovia, Salamanca, Burgos, Valladolid and León – seem to echo the 'slow old tunes of Spain'. They now form the autonomous region of Castilla-León. (The former province of Santander is now the autonomy of Cantabria, *see* page 154.)

Apart from the enclave of Cebreros in the Sierra de Gredos near Avila, it is only the northern area, especially around the basin of the River Duero, which produces wines in any quantity. The land is often bleak and arid, bitterly cold in winter and fierily hot in summer; and in areas such as Toro the annual rainfall amounts to only a meagre 300 millimetres. In some districts, once famous for their wines, production has declined disastrously because of the difficulty of cultivating the vines in such cruel conditions.

Nevertheless, Castilla-León produces worthwhile wines in great variety, notably the stylish reds from the Ribera del Duero, the refreshing whites from Rueda and the light reds of Cigales and Bierzo; while the wines from León and Toro have improved notably with modern methods.

There is a profusion of vine varieties, but among the best and most typical are the black Tinto Fino or Tinto Aragonés, a variant of the Tempranillo grown in the Ribera del Duero; the white Verdejo, native to Rueda; and the Prieto Picudo, a black grape with a white pulp, used for making rosés in León. The white 'Jerez' or Palomino is also widely grown, but its musts are not of the same quality as in its native habitat in the south of Spain. In one remote district of León there are even hybrids resulting from the direct crossing of American and native vines, but they are frowned upon by the authorities as containing a toxic alkaloid, the ill-famed *malvina*, and wines of this type may not be exported.

As in most parts of Spain, a great deal of the wine is made in cooperatives; but perhaps nowhere have small proprietors making wine for consumption in the immediate vicinity survived in greater numbers. In districts such as Los Oteros and Valdevimbre near León, the serried peasant *bodegas*, dug deep into the ground with a mounded earth roof, look like prehistoric earthworks. There are five *denominaciones de origen*: Rueda, instituted in 1980, Ribera del Duero (1982), Toro (1987), and the even more recently demarcated Bierzo and Cigales.

DO Zones
1 Rueda
2 Ribera del Duero
3 Toro
4 Bierzo
5 Cigales

Others
6 Valdevimbre, Los Oteros
7 Fermoselle
8 Cebreros

Agrícola Castellana Sociedad Cooperativa DO w dr am

★→★★

La Seca (Valladolid). DO Rueda. This large and well-run cooperative in the TIERRA DE MEDINA was founded in 1935 and now has a storage capacity of eight million litres. It makes both the traditional *flor*-growing RUEDA from a blend of Verdejo and Palomino, ageing it either in *solera* or in glass carboys in the open, and also fresh young wines made from 100 percent Verdejo. Typical of the first type are the Campo Grande *fino* and Dorado 61, both sherry-like in flavour and of about 15 percent strength. The Cuatro Rayas, made from 100 percent Verdejo, light greenish in colour, dry, fragrant, fruity and pleasantly astringent, is of 12·5 percent strength and is a good example of the fresh young wines now being made in the area.

Bañeza, La r ★

An area to the west of the city of León and part of the undemarcated Comarca de LEON. It was formerly widely known for its *claretes de aguja* (light red wines with slight sparkle), but little wine is now made except in primitive subterranean cellars for local consumption.

Barrigón Tovar, Pablo DO r ★→★★

Cigales (Valladolid). DO Cigales. One of the only two private firms to make a genuine *clarete* from CIGALES, a wine with a long and honorable tradition. Apart from a three-year-old red, San Pablo, it bottles *claretes* (which must now unhelpfully be described as either *tintos* or *rosados*) in four styles: three-year-old San Pablo; six-year-old Barrigón; eight-year-old Viña Solana and Viña Cigaleña *reserva*. The older wines, matured in oak, are best.

Benavente r ★

Like LA BAÑEZA, Benavente once made good *claretes* with a slight sparkle, but many of its vineyards have now been abandoned. The *parador*, housed in the 12th-century castle of Fernando II of León, is an attractive base from which to visit RUEDA, CIGALES and TORO.

Bierzo DO r w p ★→★★★

Bierzo, in the northwest corner of the province of León bordering Galicia, of which the new DO Bierzo forms part, is ideally suited for the production of quality wines. In its 3,000 hectares of vineyards the climate is halfway between the dry heat of Castilla-León and the rain and humidity more typical of Galicia.

Vines are thickest on the ground around Villafranca and Ponferrada, and the most predominant vine varieties are the black Mencía and Alicante, and the white Palomino.

The fragrant and fruity red wines age well in cask, developing a good ruby colour, and are smooth and silky with not more than 12 percent alcohol. The whites, averaging 10·5–11·5 percent, are fruity, flowery on the nose and better balanced than the somewhat acidic wines of Galicia. There are also excellent rosés, made mainly with the Mencía and with a refreshing residual acidity.

The temptation has always been to sell the wines to Galicia and Asturias, where they find a ready market. The cooperatives of Cacabelos and Villafranquina bottle worthwhile and representative wines (*see* Vinos del Bierzo); but the most sophisticated wines from the region are those of the PALACIO DE ARGANZA and VALDEOBISPO.

Casar de Valdaiga DO r p w dr ★★

Label for the wines made by Pérez Carames in the DO BIERZO. The fruity red is well worth looking out for.

Castilla la Vieja, Bodega de Crianza DO r w p ★★

Rueda (Valladolid). DO Rueda. Founded by a group of local growers to elaborate their wines in the best possible fashion, ageing some of them in oak. Its best-known wine is the fresh young white Marqués de Griñon, made from Verdejo. *See also* Castilla-La Mancha, page 45.

Cebreros r p ★

Situated in the province of Avila in the Sierra de Gredos west of Madrid, Cebreros produces wines from the black Garnacha and Tinto Aragonés and the white Albillo.

Robust and heady *tintos* and *rosados* with a minimum of 13 percent alcohol, they are much in demand for everyday drinking in Madrid and the surrounding area. A delightful place to stay is the Parador de Gredos, a former hunting lodge of King Alfonso XIII, set high in the mountains among pine forests.

Cigales DO r ★→★★

The 5,315 hectares of vineyards of the newly demarcated Cigales are planted with the white Palomino, Verdejo and Albillo, and the black Garnacha, Tinto del País and Tinto Madrid. Its *claretes*, famous since medieval times, may no longer be labelled as such thanks to the wisdom of Brussels; they are made by mixing the black and white grapes, destalking them and fermenting them *en blanc*. It was light red wines of this type which from time immemorial were the most popular in the taverns of Valladolid, but what now passes for a light red Cigales is more likely to be a blend of red wine from Zamora with a white from the central plains of La Mancha.

The fact that much of the wine is made in archaic subterranean *bodegas* for local consumption, and that the production of good quality Cigales is now more or less in the hands of only two sizable private concerns, those of Pablo BARRIGON TOVAR and Bodegas FRUTOS VILLAR, delayed the demarcation of this small region.

Fariña, Bodegas DO r res ★★→★★★ 82, 85, 86

Casaseca de las Chanas (Zamora). DO Toro. Best-known *bodega* of the newly demarcated TORO, making dark, spicy reds with heavy fruit: Colegiata is unoaked and Gran Colegiata is aged in cask.

Fermoselle r ★

Fermoselle lies between the basins of the Rivers Duero and Tormes in the southwest corner of the province of Zamora, almost within a stone's throw of the Portuguese border. Its granitic and schistous soils, and its blistering summers and low rainfall, resemble those of the Upper Douro; that its wines, though in some ways resembling the Portuguese, are not their equal, is probably because the predominant grape, the Juan García, is not of the same quality as the varieties grown in Portugal.

During the 18th century, Fermoselle produced an annual one million litres of wine, and the place is hollow with disused cellars hewn from the granite; but it is now difficult to find the authentic full-bodied red wine, with its strange, resinous but not unattractive nose and flavour, most of it being sold in bulk for blending.

Fernández, Alejandro DO r res ★★★★ 82, 83, 84, 85, 86, 87
Pesquera de Duero (Valladolid). DO Ribera del Duero. The *bodega* was founded in 1970. Its wines, intensely fruity in the best manner of the RIBERA DEL DUERO, have improved dramatically since the installation of stainless steel and new oak barrels. Since the PESQUERA wines were 'discovered' by the foreign press and Robert Parker put them on a par with those of Château Pétrus, prices, prestige and exports have leapt. The Janus *gran reserva* is made only in exceptional years, the last two vintages being 1982 and 1985.

Frutos Villar, Bodegas DO r p w dr ★→★★
Cigales (Valladolid). DO Cigales. One of the two major concerns in Cigales, making the white Viña Cansina, which suffers from spending too long in oak, and the reliable Viña Calderona *rosado*.

Grupo Sindical de Colonización No 795 r (p w dr) ★→★★
Cebreros (Avila). Makers of El Galayo, available in different styles and perhaps the best of these sturdy wines.

León
Situated high on the Castilian plateau, the old city of León, capital of the medieval kingdom, is the centre of an increasingly important wine-producing area. The Gothic cathedral with its airy flying buttresses and magnificent stained glass windows is one of the finest in Spain; and you need stir no further than the memorable Parador San

Marcos, housed in a splendid 16th-century monastery, to sample a good range of wines from the Comarca de LEON and BIERZO in its sophisticated restaurant.

León, Comarca de r p w dr ★→★★

The name used to describe the wine-producing area to the southeast of the city of León. It comprises, in order of importance, the following subdivisions: VALDEVIMBRE, LOS OTEROS, LA BAÑEZA, León, Tierra de Campos, VALDERAS, La Antigua, Payuelos and RIBERA ALTA DEL CEA.

Oenologist at work at Vega Sicilia

Los Arcos, Bodegas DO r p w dr ★★
León. DO Bierzo. Small private *bodega* making good
BIERZO wines, of which one of the best is Santos Rosado.

Los Curros, SAT DO w dr r ★★→★★★
Rueda (Valladolid). DO Rueda. Former cooperative
making the fresh and flowery Viña Cantosán from 100
percent Verdejo – the house white at Madrid's famous
Zalacaín restaurant. The *bodega* also bottles the rich and
oaky YLLERA made by a sister establishment in Boada de
Roa in RIBERA DEL DUERO.

Marqués de Riscal
See Vinos Blancos de Castilla

Mauro, Bodegas r res ★★→★★★ 81, 87
Tudela de Duero (Valladolid). Small private *bodega* making
round and fruity red wines from the Tinto Fino. They do
not currently carry the DO RIBERA DEL DUERO, since they
are vinified in Rueda, but are none the worse for it.

Nava del Rey
Largest of the townships in the TIERRA DE MEDINA southwest
of Valladolid and part of the DO RUEDA.

Oteros, Los r p w dr ★→★★
With 3,077 hectares under vines, Los Oteros, to the east of
the road from León to BENAVENTE, is second in importance
of the subdivisions of the Comarca de LEON. The most
important of the grapes is the Prieto Picudo, grown in clay
soils. Much of the wine is made in tiny peasant *bodegas*,
constructed by digging deep into the ground, installing the
simplest of beam presses, mounding up the soil on top and
leaving a chimney for the escape of carbon dioxide. The
typical wine made in these primitive cellars is a *clarete*
(which may no longer be described as such under EC
regulations) of 10–13·5 percent, but methods are so archaic
that on occasion the volatile acidity is so high the wine
tastes of raspberry vinegar. *See also* Valdevimbre.

Palacio de Arganza DO r p w dr res ★★→★★★ 74, 75, 76, 80, 83, 85

Villafranca del Bierzo (León). DO Bierzo. Installed in the 15th-century palace of the Dukes of Arganza, the *bodega* was founded in 1805 and has for long been the most famous in BIERZO. A disastrous fire in 1979 destroyed much of the *bodega*, but most of its oak casks and old *reservas* survived unharmed. Its wines are sometimes confused with the better-known Viña Ardanza from Bodegas La Rioja Alta, but are entirely different in style. The clean, fragrant white wines are labelled Palacio de Arganza and the characterful reds, made with 100 percent Mencía, may be sold as Palacio de Arganza or Señorío de Arganza.

Peñafiel

Township in RIBERA DEL DUERO surmounted by a magnificent 12th-century castle, beneath which the Bodega RIBERA DUERO maintains cellars for maturing its wines; another medieval survival is the extraordinary jousting ground and the houses surrounding it.

Peñalba López, Bodegas DO r (p) ★★→★★★ 76, 79, 81, 82, 83, 86, 89

Aranda de Duero (Burgos). DO Ribera del Duero. Small firm with its own vineyards making and ageing in oak good fruity TORREMILANOS reds from the Tinto Fino grape.

Pérez Pascuas, Bodega Hermanos DO r (p) res ★★★ 81, 83, 86, 89

Pedrosa de Duero (Burgos). DO Ribera del Duero. Tiny, scrupulously kept family *bodega* making fruity and complex VIÑA PEDROSA red wines currently rated by *Club de Gourmets* magazine as among the 100 best in Spain.

Pesquera r ★★★ 83, 84, 85, 87

Label of the now-famous red wine produced by Alejandro FERNANDEZ in the RIBERA DEL DUERO.

Protos r ★★→★★★ 70, 76, 79, 80, 85

The *gran reserva* with long age in cask from the Bodega RIBERA DUERO.

Ribera Alta del Cea r

Small winemaking area between León and Palencia producing red wines from hybrids obtained by the direct crossing of European and American vines. Since the wines contain small amounts of a toxic alkaloid, the so-called *malvina*, they are blended with others from the area. The district also produces pleasant light red wines made from a blend of Mencía, Prieto Picudo and Palomino.

Ribera de Burgos DO r ★→★★

Part of the DO RIBERA DEL DUERO, centring on Aranda de Duero. The predominant grape varieties are the Tinto del País, Tinto Madrid, Jaén, Valenciano, Albillo, Tinto Aragonés and Tempranillo. The area's typical wines are the light reds formerly known as *claretes* or '*claros*', most of them made by small proprietors or in cooperatives. Some of the best are produced by the Bodega Cooperativa Santa Eulalia de la Horra and bottled as Conde de Siruela.

Ribera del Duero DO r ★★→★★★

Demarcated in 1982, the region, which produces some of the best wine in Spain outside the Rioja and Cataluña, borders the River Duero for a distance of some 110 kilometres, with a maximum width of 30 kilometres from Tudela de Duero near Valladolid to just east of El Burgo de Osma. The larger and central part of the region lies within the province of Burgos; there are small areas within the provinces of Soria to the east and Segovia to the south, but the best of the wines are made around Peñafiel and Valbuena in the province of Valladolid. Here the vines grow on chalky, pine-fringed slopes bordering the Duero, and the predominant grape is the Tinto Fino or Tinto Aragonés, a variant of the Riojan Tempranillo, whose musts are particularly suitable for maturation in oak. This area is famous for the legendary VEGA SICILIA but many excellent *bodegas*, such as Alejandro FERNANDEZ and PEREZ PASCUAS, have now come to the fore.

Ribera Duero, Bodega DO r (p) ★★→★★★

Peñafiel (Valladolid). DO Ribera del Duero. Formerly a cooperative and one of the first in Spain to age its wines in oak, its storage capacity runs to 1·2 million litres and 2,000 American oak casks for maturing the wines, which average 11·5–12·5 percent alcohol. The youngest wine is the two-year-old Ribera Duero, a deep plummy colour, fresh and tasting of blackberries. The Ribera Duero *reserva* spends two years in oak *barricas*; and there are also PROTOS *gran reservas*, aged for much longer in cask and bottle. The wines, which are now shipped to the UK, have been much admired by connoisseurs for their clean fruity nose, deep flavour and long finish.

Rueda DO w dr am ★★

This small region to the southwest of VALLADOLID, long known as the TIERRA DE MEDINA, takes its name from the village of Rueda, which, with NAVA DEL REY, LA SECA and SERRADA, is a main centre for making the wines. The predominant grape varieties are the native Verdejo and more recently introduced Palomino, grown in calcareous clays. The district makes nothing but white wine, for which it has been famous since the 17th century. The traditional Rueda, amber-coloured and of some 15 percent strength, is a *flor*-growing white matured either in loosely stoppered glass carboys or in *solera*, and tasting like a rough sherry. More recently, and following the lead of the Marqués de Riscal, which has built a large modern winery near Rueda, the region has been producing fresh and attractive young white wines, made mainly with the Verdejo.

Sanz, Vinos DO r p w dr am res ★→★★

Rueda (Valladolid). DO Rueda. Large family *bodega* founded in 1900. It makes wines in various styles, including white Vinos Sanz Rueda and Vinos Sanz Rueda Superior, and also undertakes the vinification and maturation of wines for a variety of other concerns.

Seca, La

Small village and winemaking centre in the DO RUEDA.

Serrada

Another of the winemaking villages of the DO RUEDA; much of the house wine in the bars and restaurants of Valladolid is sold as 'Serrada'.

Tierra de Medina

Traditional name for what is now the DO RUEDA. Before the phylloxera epidemic of 1909 there were some 90,000 hectares under vines, but this is now reduced to 24,000 hectares, of which the DO Rueda occupies 6,900 hectares.

Tierra del Vino

Vine-growing area near TORO, once famous for its strong red wines, but now virtually abandoned.

Toro DO r ★

This newly demarcated region to the east of Zamora, with 15,290 hectares under vines, of which 3,200 qualify for DO, is one of the most parched in Spain with an annual rainfall of only 300 millimetres. In strength and body its red wines are rivalled only by those from Priorato (*see* Cataluña, page 93), Jumilla and Yecla (*see* Valencia and Murcia, pages 245 and 249) and were formerly among the most prized in Spain, being much drunk by the students and academics of Salamanca University. The principal vine varieties are the Tinta de Toro and Tinto de Madrid, together with some Garnacha. Until recently, winemaking methods were primitive and the wines overstrong, but something of a revolution is under way, spearheaded by concerns such as Bodegas FARIÑA.

A pleasant stopping place, especially if you are en route for Galicia, is the Parador de los Condes de Alba y Aliste, with its magnificent Renaissance courtyard, in the historic old town of Zamora.

Torremilanos r ★★ → ★★★ 81, 82, 83

Name of the light, well-made red wines from Bodegas PEÑALBA LOPEZ in the RIBERA DEL DUERO.

Valdeobispo r p w dr ★★→★★★ 76, 79, 82, 86

Well-known wine from the DO BIERZO made by Viñas y Bodegas del Bierzo. The good red *reservas* and *gran reservas* are made with 100 percent Mencía.

Valderas r p ★

As in the neighbouring small area of RIBERA ALTA DEL CEA, most of the vines are hybrids; the wines are similar in style.

Valdevimbre r ★→★★

With 4,861 hectares under vines, Valdevimbre is the largest of the subdistricts of the Comarca de LEON. It borders LOS OTEROS and at their best its light red wines, traditionally known as *claretes*, are aromatic, light and fruity. They are traditionally made by adding whole bunches of Prieto Picudo to the must during secondary fermentation, so prolonging it and giving the wine a refreshing 'prickle'. In some of the more primitive *bodegas*, the proprietors try for the same result by adding fizzy lemonade!

Some of the best of the wine is bottled by the Cooperativa Vinícola Comarcal under the label of San Tirso. *See also* Vinos de León.

Valladolid

The home of a famous university and once the capital of Spain, Valladolid is a good base for visiting the wine areas of RIBERA DEL DUERO, RUEDA, TORO, BIERZO and CIGALES. When there, do not miss the 15th-century Colegio de San Gregorio, which houses the National Museum of Polychrome Sculpture, with its outstanding collections both of sculpture and painting. The best hotels are the four-star Olid Meliá, Meliá Parque and the somewhat old-fashioned Felipe IV.

Vega de la Reina, Vinos r (w dr) res ★★★ 78, 80, 81, 82

Rueda (Valladolid). Only the white wine rates DO, because the region is not demarcated for reds. However, the *bodega* is famous for its red wines, which are complex and oaky in the style of Rioja *gran reservas* of once upon a time.

VINO FINO
DE MESA

VEGA-SICILIA "UNICO"

COSECHA 1966

Número de embotellador 9342

Tirado alcohólico 13.5°

Medalla de Oro y Gran Diploma de Honor
Feria de Navidad de Madrid de 1927
Medalla de Oro y Gran Diploma de Honor
Exposición Hotelera de Barcelona de 1927
Gran Premio de Honor
Exposición Internacional de Barcelona 1929-30

Esta cosecha se ha escogido para ser embotellada este año y consta de 96.000 botellas.

El número de esta botella es el   Nº   45574

BODEGAS VEGA SICILIA, S. A.
El Presidente

VALBUENA DE DUERO (Valladolid)

Vega Sicilia, Bodegas DO r ★★★→★★★★ 60, 62, 65, 68, 73, 75, 80, *Reserva Especial*

Valbuena de Duero (Valladolid). DO Ribera del Duero. Vega Sicilia is a name to conjure with in Spain, where its wines, all of them red, are strictly rationed and supplied only for state functions and to the best hotels and restaurants. The estate of some 900 hectares borders the river in the RIBERA DEL DUERO, east of Valladolid, at a height of 765 metres. As long ago as 1864, select French vines were acquired from Bordeaux and acclimatized in its chalky, pine-fringed vineyards. They have recently been replanted with the same three varieties, Cabernet Sauvignon, Merlot and Malbec, whose musts are blended with those of the native Tinto Aragonés, Garnacha and white Albillo. The *bodega* believes in vinifying and maturing its wines very slowly; only the must which separates naturally after light crushing is used, and after vinification the Vega Sicilia is matured for not less than ten years in oak with a further two in bottle. The *bodega* also makes a three-year-old and five-year-old red Valbuena.

The wines, of 13·5 percent alcohol or more, are full-bodied, deep in colour, complex and intensely fruity, with a fragrant nose, compounded of oak and fruit, and long finish. Some experts criticize Vega Sicilia for the degree of volatile acidity, preferring the Valbuena with its shorter period in cask.

Viña Pedrosa r ★★★ 81, 83, 85, 86, 88

The intensely fruity red RIBERA DEL DUERO from Bodega Hermanos PEREZ PASCUAS.

Vinos del Bierzo, Bodega Comarcal Cooperativa DO r res (p) ★★→★★★ 80, 81, 85

Cacabelos (León). DO Bierzo. The red Guerra *reservas* from this large cooperative, made with 100 percent Mencía and aged in oak, are soft and well-balanced with hints of coffee and spices.

Vinos Blancos de Castilla DO w dr ★★→★★★ DYA

Rueda (Valladolid). DO Rueda. The *bodega* was constructed some years ago, with advice from Professor Peynaud of Bordeaux University, by the Rioja firm of the Marqués de Riscal, which did not at the time market a white wine. It has a capacity of two million litres, and the wines are cold fermented in stainless steel tanks. They are made with some 90 percent Verdejo, but Professor Peynaud considered that they were improved by blending a little Viura and also by maturing them for a few months in oak casks. Fresh and fruity, they are sold under the label of the Marqués de Riscal, most of the output going for export. More recently the *bodega* has introduced a fresh young wine made with 100 percent Sauvignon Blanc and a first-rate, characterful Marqués de Riscal Limousin, matured in oak.

Vinos de León, Bodegas r p w dr ★→★★ 82, 86, 87
Armunia (León). For long known as VILE, a somewhat unfortunate abbreviation, this large private consortium owns a modern winery with a capacity of 12 million litres and 2,500 casks for maturing the wines. The group has vineyards of its own, but buys most of the grapes, mainly Prieto Picudo, Tempranillo and Mencía for the red and rosé wines, and Verdejo and Palomino for the white, from independent proprietors in VALDEVIMBRE and LOS OTEROS.

Its crisp young red and white wines have proved very popular in the UK. Among its more select and older wines are the Palacio de Los Guzmanes in various styles and the good, full-bodied red Don Suero *reservas*.

Yllera r ★★ 86
Good value RIBERA DEL DUERO red from LOS CURROS, but not DO because it is bottled in Rueda.

Wine and Food

If one had to name a single type of dish most typical of Castilla-León, it would be the roasts, of lamb, sucking pig and kid; and the baby milk-fed lamb or *lechazo* is at its best around Valladolid. However, the region has much else to offer: partridge from the mountains, trout from the cold streams, and the rib-warming *cocidos* made from chickpeas and local varieties of pork sausage.

Arroz con cordero Rice with tomato sauce and stewed lamb, finished in the oven to crisp the top. A light red or rosé with a little residual acidity, such as Vinos de León's Castillo de Coyanza or Calderona from Cigales.

Besugo al ajoarriero Sea bream in a sauce made with olive oil, garlic, onions, parsley and vinegar. A fresh young Rueda, for example Verdejo Palido.

Cabrito asado Roast kid.

Cachelada leonesa Potatoes boiled with seasoning and *chorizo* sausage, from which they take the cheerful orange colour and spicy flavour.

Cochinillo asado Roast milk-fed sucking pig of a tenderness and succulence rarely found in Britain or the USA, where the piglets are killed older. A good red *reserva* such as Valbuena, Pesquera or Vega Sicilia, if you can find it.

Cocido castellano A substantial stew of chickpeas, brisket, marrow bones, ham bones, black pudding, pork, potatoes and green vegetables. Go the whole hog and wash it down with a sturdy Cebreros!

Cordero asado/lechazo Roast lamb/milk-fed baby lamb, often cooked in a baker's oven. A good red, such as Torremilanos.

Jamón de Guijuelo Cured *pata negra* ham, made from semi-wild pigs.

Judías blancas a la castellana Stew of haricot beans, fresh tomatoes, onions, garlic and seasoning. Try the local red house wine.

Leche frita Squares of a stiff custard, dredged in beaten egg and breadcrumbs and fried crisp in hot olive oil.

Lentejas zamoranas Lentils stewed with black pudding, onions, paprika, garlic, parsley and seasoning.

Liebre en su salsa Hare, marinated in white wine and garlic, then cooked in an earthenware dish with onions, carrots, turnips, nutmeg and red wine. The sauce is thickened with the liver. A good red, such as Gran Colegiata from Bodegas Fariña.

Mantecadas Small cakes made with butter, flour and eggs and baked in paper cups.

Olla podrida *See* Cocido

Pantortillas de Reinosa Fluffy pancakes made from puff pastry flavoured with *anís* and eaten cold.

Pisto castellano A vegetable dish resembling ratatouille, with potatoes, bacon and, often, eggs.

Rebozos zamoranos Small cakes made with flour, eggs and lemon.

Ropa vieja Meat from a *cocido* served with a sauce made with fresh peppers, aubergines and tomatoes.

Tomates rellenos Tomatoes stuffed with olives, anchovies, rice and peppers.

Truchas a la montañesa Trout cooked in white wine with bay leaves and onions. A white wine with a hint of oak, such as Marqués de Riscal.

Restaurants

Aranda de Duero *Mesón de la Villa* (good charcuterie and regional dishes).

León *Independencia*; *Parador San Marcos* (regional dishes and selection of local wines); *Regia* (local fare and Bierzo wines in a 13th-century house near the cathedral).

Palencia *Lorenzo*; *Casa Damián* (both restaurants, run by the same family, are worth the stop when approaching Valladolid from Burgos or Santander).

Peñafiel *Asador Mauro* (roast sucking pig and baby lamb, regional wines).

Valladolid *Mesón Panero*; *Asón*; *Mesón La Fragua* (all offer well-cooked Castilian dishes and regional wines).

Cataluña

The resourceful and industrious Catalans claim that they make wines in a greater variety of styles than any other region of Spain, instancing the fine table wines from the Penedès; its sparkling wines (separately described under Sparkling Wines, page 253) which account for 90 percent of Spanish production; the maderized *rancio*; and the old *solera*-made dessert wines of Tarragona, so much resembling Málaga or sweet *oloroso* sherry. All these, plus some of the best brandy in the country and a gamut of vermouths and liqueurs, both indigenous varieties and foreign brands made under licence, give substance to that claim.

Comprising the provinces of Gerona (Girona), Barcelona, Lérida (Lleida) and Tarragona, with an area about the size of the Netherlands or Belgium, Cataluña's landscape is rugged and broken – it has been described as a flight of stairs rising from the coastal plain of the Mediterranean towards the peaks of the Pyrenees and its associated spurs to the south. In the more mountainous areas the slopes must be terraced to allow a foothold for the vines, a system still employed in upland areas such as Priorato, and you need not leave the *autopista* from Barcelona through the Penedès to see disused terraces, constructed during the late 19th century when every available patch of ground was pressed into service to supply wine to a France desolated by phylloxera, the epidemic not at that time having reached Spain.

Patterns of agriculture date from the times of the Kingdom of Aragón, among the most powerful medieval states of the Mediterranean, when James the Conqueror (1213–76) made over the territories recaptured from the Moors to working farmers, instead of handing over large estates to the nobility, as happened in

Castile. The tradition of the small peasant farmer was reinforced by the institution of the *Rabassa Morta*, which provided for a landowner to lease part of his land to smallholders for the plantation of vineyards in exchange for half of the produce. To this day, the great bulk of the wine is made in cooperatives from fruit supplied to them by small farmers, and even the large and well-known private firms buy more grapes than they grow in their own vineyards, and purchase large amounts of cooperative-made wine for further elaboration in their *bodegas*.

Until recent decades the emphasis was on bulk rather than quality, and the emergence of wines rivalling those of the Rioja in quality is a comparatively new phenomenon. This has largely been a matter of climate. Vineyards are thickest on the ground in the coastal regions of the Penedès and Tarragona, with their Mediterranean climate and hot summers. When the grapes were fermented by traditional means, temperatures often rose to 30°C or more, and much of the fruity nose and flavour were lost during a fast and furiously tumultuous fermentation. The first stainless steel vats with provision for cooling were introduced about 1960, and they are now widely and increasingly used. This has revolutionized the Catalan wine industry. Given suitable soils and the excellent quality of the fruit, there is now nothing to prevent the production of wines as good as those from more northerly regions; and, indeed, Cataluña is at one advantage vis-à-vis the traditional producers of fine wines such as Bordeaux, Burgundy and the Rhine, namely the reliability of its weather conditions. In Cataluña, the winters are not too severe and the summers uniformly sunny and hot, although still tempered by breezes from the Mediterranean, and in fact harvests are good in 90 percent of the years.

Grape Varieties

Although Torres and other *bodegas* have very successfully experimented with the acclimatization of noble vines from France and Germany, most of the wine is made from native grapes. The most important varieties are:

DO Zones
1 Ampurdán-Costa Brava
2 Alella
3 Penedès
4 Tarragona
5 Priorato
6 Terra Alta
7 Conca de Barberà
8 Costers del Segre

White

Macabeo Also known as the Viura in the Rioja and widely grown in Spain as a whole, the Macabeo produces pale-coloured, fruity and well-balanced wines, resistant to oxidation and well suited to cold fermentation.

Xarel-lo A native of Cataluña, known in Alella as the Pansa Blanca, its wines are of medium alcoholic strength, though over-acid in the relatively rare years when it does not fully ripen. It is one of the grapes much used for making sparkling wines in the Penedès.

Parellada (or Montonec) Grown exclusively in the higher areas

of the Penedès Superior and Conca de Barberà, its musts are
low in alcohol (9–11 percent) and high in acidity. Again
much used for making sparkling wines, it is the Parellada
which gives the exceptionally fresh and fruity bouquet to
still wines such as the Torres Viña Sol.

Garnacha Blanca Also grown in the Rioja, it is extensively
cultivated in Terra Alta and the Camp de Tarragona,
yielding wines high in alcohol with little acid.

Malvasía This is the well-known Malmsey, of Greek origin but
grown for centuries in Spain. Its musts are fruity and of
medium strength and (as also in Madeira, where Malmsey is
the name given to the sweetest wine) when fortified and
aged give rise to dessert wines like those of Sitges.

Pansé Grown in the Camp de Tarragona, Conca de Barberà
and Ribera d'Ebre, it matures late and prolifically, but the
wines are coarse and high in alcohol.

Pedro Ximénez Much grown in Andalucía, where it is used
for sweet wines, and in Montilla, where it makes dry, the
Pedro Ximénez is grown in small amounts in Priorato and
Terra Alta, where its musts are mixed with those from
other varieties.

Black

Cariñena Originally a native of Aragón, the Cariñena produces
wines of 11–12 percent strength, robust, rich in colour and
extract, but without a very distinctive nose.

Garnacha Peluda A mutant of the Garnacha Tinta, cropping
more regularly and with similar characteristics.

Garnacha Tinta Another native Spanish grape, very widely
grown in the Rioja and other parts of Spain. Its wines are
high in alcohol (11–14 percent), full-bodied, fruity and deep

in colour, but oxidize rapidly, soon turning a brick-red when aged in wood.

Monastrell A native grape, also widely grown in the central regions of Spain. The yield is small, but its wines are deep in colour, of considerable elegance, and mature well.

Ull de Llebre (Ojo de Liebre) This is the well-known Tempranillo of the Rioja or Cencibel of Valdepeñas, which produces wines of 11–13 percent with good acid balance, distinctive fruity nose and good ageing properties.

Sumoll Once widely cultivated in the Penedès, the Sumoll, which produces aromatic but very tart wines, is now being phased out.

In addition to these native grapes, the plantation of Cabernet Sauvignon, Chardonnay and other foreign grapes, increasingly grown in the area, has been authorized by the Consejo Regulador.

Cataluña now possesses eight *denominaciones de origen*, of which control has passed from INDO (Instituto Nacional de Denominaciones de Origen) to INCAVI (Institut Català de Vi), an agency of the Generalitat, the autonomous governing body of Cataluña. The areas, with average annual production figures, are: Penedès (170 million litres); Alella (472,000 litres); Tarragona (40 million litres); Priorato (1·2 million litres); Ampurdán-Costa Brava (9 million litres); Conca de Barberà (19 million litres); Terra Alta (8 million litres); and Costers del Segre (4·6 million litres).

Vintages, as has been explained, are remarkably consistent, and the only really poor one in recent years was in 1972. The following chart for the Penedès gives some idea of the variation:

Year	Red wines	White wines
1974	*good*	*fair to good*
1975	*good*	*very good*
1976	*very good*	*good to very good*
1977	*good to very good*	*very good*
1978	*very good*	*good*

1979	*fair to good*	*good*
1980	*good*	*good*
1981	*excellent*	*very good*
1982	*very good*	*very good*
1983	*good*	*good*
1984	*excellent*	*good*
1985	*good*	*good*
1986	*fair*	*good*
1987	*excellent*	*good*
1988	*very good*	*fair to good*
1989		*excellent*

Provided you have a car, it is not difficult to plan a visit to the Catalan winemaking areas, since four of them (Ampurdán-Costa Brava, Alella, Penedès and Tarragona) lie along the axis of the A17 *autopista* from the French border to Barcelona and its southward extension (the A7) to Tarragona and Valencia. The newly demarcated Costers del Segre is near Lérida (Lleida). Conca de Barberà, Priorato and Terra Alta, in the hills of the hinterland, are less easy of access and require fairly time-consuming side trips, but there are notable consolations in the rugged and well-wooded countryside, the hill-top castles and in the great monasteries of Montserrat and Poblet, so closely associated with the development of viticulture in the region. Cataluña also boasts the pleasant coastal resorts and the splendid cliff scenery of the Costa Brava; and it would be a single-minded devotee of wines who did not pause in Barcelona to visit Gaudí's astonishing cathedral of La Sagrada Familia or its magnificent museums and galleries, or in Tarragona to see the remarkable Roman remains.

Large *bodegas*, such as Torres, welcome visitors without appointment, arranging guided tours and instructive tastings of their wines; and even in the smallest cooperative you will be able to taste and buy the wine, and will receive a friendly welcome – if you can muster enough Spanish to communicate. If in doubt about your reception, ask the porter at the hotel to telephone beforehand.

Catalan food is interesting and varied, though sometimes more than substantial in country hotels and restaurants. The names of hotels in or near the winemaking areas are given in the A–Z listing.

The Catalans take their regained autonomy seriously. Under

Franco it was forbidden to speak in Catalan – now it is a point of pride to do so. Most signs and place names are now in Catalan, which is a separate language and not a dialect, though the Castilian equivalent is generally added, and often looks similar, so it is not impossible to work out. This also applies to menus, although these sometimes appear exclusively in Catalan in smaller restaurants. The waiter or proprietor will, however, always explain in Castilian.

Alella DO (r p am) w dr sw ★★→★★★

The tradition of winemaking in this small region dates from Roman times, but it is now threatened by urban expansion from Barcelona to its south, and, despite a surprising extension of the DO zone in 1989, of the 1,400 hectares under vines in 1967 only 560 survive, producing mostly white wine. The grape varieties approved by the Consejo Regulador are: for the white wines, Xarel-lo (or Pansa Blanca), Pansa Rosada, Garnacha Blanca, Chardonnay and Chenin Blanc; and for the reds, Tempranillo (Ull de Llebre), Garnacha Tinta and Garnacha Peluda. Many of the vineyards, all of them small and few exceeding 1·5 hectares, are owned by professional people dedicated to preserving the wine industry. The vines are planted on granitic slopes sheltered from the prevailing east wind, one of which, with a northerly aspect, produces wine of high acidity; the wine from the other, more southerly, slope is rather sweeter and lower in acidity.

Alella Vinícola, Cooperativa DO (r p am) w dr sw ★→★★
Alella (Barcelona). DO Alella. This well-equipped
cooperative, founded in 1906, makes much of the wine
from ALELLA. It is sold as Alella Legítima in hock-type
bottles under the brand name of Marfil ('ivory'), and the
wines range in alcohol content from 11·5–13·5 percent. The
semi-dry Marfil Blanco, aged in oak in the traditional
fashion, has been criticized for lack of freshness. The red
Marfil Tinto is soft and fruity.

Altar wine
Altar wine, made without chemical additives especially for
the celebration of Holy Communion, is a speciality of
Tarragona and particularly of DE MULLER, suppliers to Popes
Pius X, Benedict XV, Pius XI, Pius XII and John XXIII. It
is often made with the Macabeo from the CAMP DE
TARRAGONA, alcohol being added to the musts so as to
produce a sweet white *generoso* of some 15 percent.
Recently De Muller, which runs to a special *bodega* with
stained glass windows, has been making drier wines, more
to the taste of a younger generation of priests. It is exported
all over the world in resin-coated steel drums.

Ampurdán, Cavas del DO r p w res sp ★→★★
Perelada (Girona). DO Ampurdán-Costa Brava. Situated in
the village of Perelada near Figueres, on the verges of the
Pyrenees, this is the sister ship of the well-known sparkling
wine concern of the Castillo de Perelada (*see* page 264). Its
worthwhile still wines include the three-year-old red Tinto
Cazador, Perelada Rosado, and a good red Reserva Don
Miguel, aged for one and a half years in cask and five to six
in bottle. The dry and *pétillant* white Pescador is made in
cuves closes pressurized to only a quarter of the normal
extent; and the *bodega* also produces a *cuve close* sparkler, the
subject in 1960 of the famous 'Spanish champagne' case,
brought by the French champagne companies in England
and known in France at the time as 'the Second Battle of
the Marne'.

Ampurdán-Costa Brava DO r p w dr ★→★★

Known as Empordà-Costa Brava in Catalan, this is one of the more recently demarcated regions, abutting the Pyrenees in the province of Girona and inland from the holiday coast. A problem for the growers is the prevailing north wind, the *tramontana*, which blows for some 100 days in the year, at velocities of up to hurricane force. For this reason the vines are staked. The area under vines is 3,060 hectares, and the main vine varieties are the black Garnacha Tinta and Cariñena, and the white Macabeo and Xarel-lo. Some 60 percent of the wine, made mostly in cooperatives, is rosé, but the region is now producing a fresh young *vi novell* in the manner of Beaujolais Nouveau.

l'Anoia, Comarca de r (p)

Undemarcated area bordering the PENEDES to the west.

d'Artes (Bages), Comarca (w dr) sp

Undemarcated area to the northwest of Barcelona.

Bach, Masía DO r p w dr sw res ★★→★★★ 83, 84, 85

Sant Esteve Sesrovires (Barcelona). DO Penedès. Shortly after World War I a couple of elderly bachelor brothers from Barcelona, who had made a fortune by supplying uniforms to the Allied armies, built themselves a flamboyant Florentine-style mansion in the PENEDES and started a small winery. It grew, like Topsy, and when it was taken over by the great sparkling wine firm of Codorníu (*see* page 257), embraced vast cellars and 8,500 oak casks with a total capacity of 3·1 million litres. The *bodega* maintains its high reputation, and makes good red Viña Extrísima wines including a velvety *reserva*; a fresh, young Extrísimo Seco white; but the wine for which it is best known is the luscious and oaky Extrísimo, one of the best white dessert wines from Spain.

Baix Ebre-Montsià, Comarca de (r) w dr

Undemarcated area in the extreme south of the province of Tarragona, bordering the Ebro delta.

Baixa Segarra (Les Garrigues), Comarca de la r w dr
Undemarcated area to the north of the demarcated region
of CONCA DE BARBERA.

Balada, Celler Ramón DO w dr (r) ★★★ DYA
Sant Martí Sarroca (Barcelona). DO Penedès. This tiny hi-
tech family *bodega* specializes in Viña Toña varietal whites
made from Xarel-lo, Macabeo and Parellada. All three are
aromatic and fruity with fresh acidity and green finish. Also
a pleasant 100 percent Cabernet Sauvignon Vinya Sibil-la.

Barcelona
Barcelona, the capital of Cataluña and second city of Spain,
takes its name from the Carthaginian general Hamilcar
Barca, but was founded long before his time, probably by
the Phoenicians. Apart from being an excellent base for
visits to the wine areas of Cataluña, it is a city of
outstanding interest. Do not miss the old city, with its
Roman remains, its Gothic cathedral, the Palace of the
Generalitat (the governing body of Cataluña), and the
flower-decked Ramblas; or again, the many buildings by
that master of Art Nouveau, Antonio Gaudí, foremost
among them the extraordinary unfinished cathedral of La
Sagrada Familia. There are many museums and galleries,
including those devoted to Primitive Art, Picasso and Miró.
    Once every two years, in mid–March, Barcelona is of
special interest to gastronomes, when it mounts the Salón
Internacional de la Alimentaria, one of the largest
international wine and food fairs, with exhibits from every
Spanish wine firm of consequence. It is a city long famous
for its high culinary standards, and in recent years its
restaurateurs have been leading exponents of the *nouvelle
cuisine*. Of its many comfortable hotels, reasonably priced
establishments with high standards are the Colón, near the
cathedral, the Regente, the old-fashioned and thoroughly
traditional Oriente and new Rivoli in the Ramblas.

Barril, Masía DO r (g) ★★→★★★ 87, 88
Bellmunt del Priorat (Tarragona). DO Priorato. The tiny

family firm makes authentic Priorato wines, dense in colour and concentrated in fruit and alcohol, by strictly traditional methods; also a herbal white apéritif wine and delicious sweet RANCIO.

A quiet corner in Falset

Bombonas

These large, loosely stoppered pear-shaped glass carboys are used for making the traditional, sherry-like Catalan RANCIO (*rancî*) wine in an open-air CAMPO DE AÑEJAMIENTO.

Camp de Tarragona DO r w dr sw ★

Large subdenomination of the DO TARRAGONA occupying much of the centre of the province and embracing the towns of REUS, Valls, and TARRAGONA itself. Its vineyards are the most extensive of the Tarragona region, but in recent years farmers have found that hazelnuts are a more profitable crop, and the plantations, amounting to some 70 percent of arable land in some areas, have been making severe inroads. Most of the wines are sturdy whites made from the Macabeo (Viura) and Xarel-lo, known locally as the Cartuxà, but the Cooperativa de Valls makes small quantities of a smooth, ruby-coloured wine from the Ull de Llebre (Tempranillo) and Trepat – however, the whole production is pre-empted by the Mossos d'Esquadra, the security force of the Catalan Generalitat.

Campo de añejamiento

Name given to the open-air plots where the maderized RANCIO, known in Catalan as *vi rancí*, is made in BOMBONAS by a method corresponding to that of a rough and ready *solera* (*see* Sherry, page 233). *Campos de añejamiento* are also to be found in other parts of Spain, as in La Seca near Valladolid (*see* Castilla-León, page 64).

Can Ràfols dels Caus DO r w dr ★★★ 84, 85, 86

Avinyonet del Penedès (Barcelona). DO Penedès. This small, recently established firm is already making first-rate wines – its 1984 Gran Caus Tinto came fifth among the Cabernets at the 1986 Vinexpo in Bordeaux. Made from Cabernet Sauvignon, Cabernet Franc and Merlot, it spends seven months in cask and 20 in bottle, and is a big, fruity wine with masses of extract. The white Gran Caus Blanco, a blend of Chardonnay, Chenin Blanc and Xarel-lo, is clean and buttery.

Castell del Remei r p w dr res ★★→★★★

Penelles (Lleida). Old-established firm with its own
vineyards in the undemarcated *comarca* (subdistrict) of
Penelles-La Noguera in the extreme west of Cataluña near
Lleida. It has for long grown small amounts of Cabernet
Sauvignon and Semillon, and its wines, which have won
many medals in international exhibitions, are matured for
long periods in oak casks. They include a Reserva Blanco,
Reserva Tinto, a younger Castell del Remei Rosado and the
Extra Cep Semillon 1920 and Extra Cep Cabernet 1921.

Conca de Barberà (r p) w dr

This hilly region, bordering the Penedès to the west, was
first demarcated by INCAVI (Institut Català de Vi), and
recently by INDO (Instituto Nacional de Denominaciones
de Origen). Its 7,600 hectares of vineyards produce an
annual average of 18·6 million litres of wine, most of it
white and for everyday drinking – though standards are
improving with the construction of hi-tech wineries – made
from Parellada and Macabeo (Viura) grapes. Its Parellada
grapes are also much in demand for making sparkling wines
in the *cavas* of SAN SADURNI DE NOYA. A little red and rosé is
also made from the Ull de Llebre, Sumoll and Trepat, but
until recently the only concern to bottle any wine (in REUS,
outside the region) was the great cooperative combine, the
UNIO AGRARIA COOPERATIVA.

An interesting development in the region has been the
purchase of the 12th-century castle of Milmanda and its
surrounding vineyards by Miguel TORRES, after investigation
had shown that the soils were exceptionally well suited for
growing Cabernet Sauvignon and Pinot Noir; the
plantations also supply Chardonnay for the exceptional
MILMANDA, vinified and matured in cask.

Conca de Tremp, Comarca de la r w dr (p)

Undemarcated area to the far northwest of Cataluña in the
province of Lleida, better known for its hydroelectric
schemes than its wine. The better wines are made by
Bodegas Valeri Vila – red, white and rosé Castell d'Orcau.

Conde de Caralt DO r p w dr sw res ★★→★★★
Sant Sadurní d'Anoia (Barcelona). DO Penedès. Long
known for its sparkling wines made by the champagne
method, this old family firm is now part of the FREIXENET
group, sharing premises with Segura Viudas (*see* Sparkling
Wines, page 266) and RENE BARBIER. Apart from sparkling
wine, it now produces a range of sound still wines, Conde
de Caralt Tinto, Rosado, Blanco Seco, Blanco Suave. The
light and soft red *reservas*, containing a proportion of
Cabernet Sauvignon and with a hint of cedarwood at the
end, are wines of considerable sophistication. *See also*
Sparkling Wines, page 258.

Costers del Segre DO r p w dr res sp ★★★
Demarcated in 1988, the region comprises four small
separate subzones around the city of Lleida: Artesa to the
northeast, Valls de Riu Corb and Les Garrigues to the
southeast and Raimat to the west. It was undoubtedly
because of the successful development of the 3000-hectare
estate of RAIMAT by the Raventós family of Codorníu and
the growing prestige of its wines, inside and outside Spain,
that the region was demarcated. The total area under vines
is 3,647 hectares and average production of wine 460,000
litres. A large amount of the grapes goes to Raimat and to
SAN SADURNI DE NOYA for making *cava*, and the only sizable

winery in the region apart from Raimat is the Cooperativa del Campo de Artesa.

Dalmau Hermanos DO r w dr sw am gen ★→★★

Tarragona. DO Tarragona. The firm began blending and exporting wines as long ago as 1830, and like many of the large houses in Tarragona it is mainly concerned with bulk shipments abroad. It does, however, bottle some of its better wines exclusively for the home market, notably the Selecto Blanco Seco, Costa Dorada Blanco Suave and Añejo Selecto Tinto.

De Muller DO r p w dr sw am gen ★→★★★★

Tarragona. DO Tarragona, Priorato. This is the most prestigious wine firm in Tarragona. Founded in 1851, it is still in family hands, its President being the Marqués de Muller y de Abadal. Its picturesque old cellars in the port area of Tarragona have a total capacity of four million litres and house more oak casks than all the other concerns in Tarragona put together; it was also the first firm in Spain to use refrigeration techniques. If its Tarragona table wines, sold under the label of Solimar, are not up to PENEDES standards, its fortified and *solera*-made wines, reminiscent of very old and round *olorosos* and Málagas, are outstanding. They include the Moscatel Añejo, Aureo, Moscatel Rancio, Pajarete and others. De Muller has for long been a principal supplier of ALTAR WINE to the Vatican and until recently maintained a small *bodega* in SCALA DEI, producing several fortified wines of note including a velvety, full-bodied Priorato de Muller, used as a basis for the splendid dry Priorato Dom Juan Fort Solera 1865 and the sweet Priorato Dulce Solera 1918.

Falset, Comarca de DO r w dr ★

Subdenomination of the DO TARRAGONA to the southwest of the region. Its cooperative-made wines are high in alcohol, the reds velvety and with agreeable astringency, and the sturdy whites soon tending towards maderization.

Freixedas, Bodegas J DO r p w dr res sp ★→★★

Vilafranca del Penedès (Barcelona). DO Penedès. Founded
in 1897, this exporter buys in its grapes and wine. Apart
from sparkling wine, it makes the red, white and rosé Santa
Marta and a five-year-old *reserva*.

Freixenet DO r p w dr sp ★★

Sant Sadurní d'Anoia (Barcelona). DO Penedès. Much
better known for its sparkling wines (*see* page 258),
Freixenet has recently begun making fresh white, rosé and
red wines labelled as Vinã Carossa and now owns CONDE DE
CARALT and RENE BARBIER.

Gandesa, Cooperativa Agrícola DO (r) w dr sw res ★→★★

Gandesa (Tarragona). DO Terra Alta. Founded in 1919, this
is the oldest of the cooperatives in the recently demarcated
region of TERRA ALTA and now has a capacity of 2·8 million
litres. It bottles 25 percent of its wines, of which the best are
the robust but characterful Gandesa Blanc Gran Reserva and
Gandesa Blanc Especial. In 1938, during the Spanish Civil
War, the cooperative found itself in the firing line, but this
was not allowed to interfere with production, and a year
later the remains of two of General Franco's Moorish
guards were found in one of its vats!

Gran Coronas Black Label Mas La Plana DO res ★★★★ 83,
84, 85, 87

The famous varietal from Miguel TORRES, which in its 1970
vintage was declared the best Cabernet Sauvignon in the
world at the 1979 Gault-Millau 'Olympiad'.

Gran Magdala DO res ★★★★ 85

This magnificent 100 percent Pinot Noir from Miguel
TORRES outclassed all the Burgundy wines at the Gault-
Millau 'Olympiad' of 1988.

Hill, Cavas DO r p w dr s/sw sw res sp ★★→★★★

Moja-Vilafranca del Penedès (Barcelona). DO Penedès. The
Hill family emigrated from England in 1660, planting a

small vineyard and establishing a *bodega* much expanded by
Don José Hill Ros in 1884. The firm now makes wines by
the champagne process and a large range of still wines,
including the good whites Blanc Brut and Blanc Cru; the
semi-sweet Oro Penedès; and excellent red Gran Civet and
Gran Toc *reservas*. *See also* Sparkling Wines, page 260.

INCAVI

Following the death of General Franco and the restoration
of local autonomy to the four provinces of Cataluña,
between 1978 and 1980 the Instituto Nacional de
Denominaciones de Origen (INDO) transferred control of
the demarcated regions and oenological stations in Cataluña
to an agency of the revived Generalitat, the Institut Català
de Vi. Under the energetic direction of the late Jaume
Ciurana, it has since demarcated the new regions of CONCA
DE BARBARA, TERRA ALTA and COSTERS DEL SEGRE and
subdivided the DO TARRAGONA.

León, Jean r w dr res ★★★ 77, 78, 79, 80, 81, 82, 83, 84
Plá del Penedès (Barcelona). Owned by a Los Angeles
restaurateur of Spanish descent, this tiny *bodega* was one of
the first to plant foreign vines in the Penedès and, unusually
for Spain, grows all its own grapes. The vineyards now
extend to 158 hectares planted mainly with Chardonnay
and Cabernet Sauvignon. Annual production amounts to
10,000 bottles of Chardonnay and 200,000 of Cabernet
Sauvignon, the bulk of them exported to the USA, though
a little is available in Spain. Both are excellent wines: the
Chardonnay, fermented in cask, is round and buttery, while
the reds are huge, fruity, tannic wines, of which Hugh
Johnson has remarked that 'a decade or more has not yet
resolved the intense flavour of the 1974 and 1975, while the
1978 and 1979 in 1986 are still children.' They have since
been somewhat lightened in style.

Marqués de Alella DO ★★→★★★ 86, 87, 88, 89 DYA
Fresh and elegant white Alella wines from PARXET.

Marqués de Monistrol DO r dr sw p w pt dr sw res ★★→★★★
75, 77, 78, 80, 82

Sant Sadurní d'Anoia (Barcelona). DO Penedès. This old family concern has been taken over by Martini & Rossi. It has been making excellent sparkling wine since 1882 and still wines since 1974. The best are the refreshing and incipiently *pétillant* young Vin Natur Blanc de Blancs, made with 60 percent Parellada and 40 percent Xarel-lo, bottled only two months after the grapes are picked; the Vin Natur Blanc en Noirs; a fruity rosé; and a smooth, velvety red *reserva*, aged for two years in oak *barrica* and three in bottle. *See also* Sparkling Wines, page 261.

Mascaró, Cavas DO r w dr ★★ 85

Vilafranca del Penedès (Barcelona). DO Penedès. Makers of a lemony, fresh Viña Franca white and a good (1985) Anima Cabernet Sauvignon. *See also* Sparkling Wines, page 262, and Spirits, Aromatic Wines and Liqueurs, page 278.

Milmanda DO w dr ★★★★ 86, 88, 89

This beautiful Chardonnay from Miguel TORRES takes its name from the castle of Milmanda below the monastery of POBLET, where the grapes are grown. Vinified and matured in small oak casks, it is one of Spain's best white wines.

Mollet de Perelada, Cooperativa de DO r p w dr gen ★→★★

Perelada (Girona). DO Ampurdán-Costa Brava. Simón Serra, the French-trained oenologist of this sizable cooperative with a storage capacity of some 2·8 million litres, is making very fresh red, white and rosé *vi novell* after the style of Beaujolais Nouveau, of which the most attractive is perhaps the red. The cooperative also makes a very full and fruity dessert wine from Garnacha Blanca grapes, fermented with their skins for a few days before addition of grape spirit, and small quantities of a good sparkling wine.

Montserrat, Monastery of

On the northwest fringe of the PENEDES, the monastery of

Montserrat is an essential stop for any visitor to the area. The precipitous hill to which it clings, with its massive outcrops of rounded, weatherworn rock, is so extraordinary as to have inspired Wagner's *Parsifal*, and appropriately enough the splendid boys' choir is the oldest musical conservatory in Europe. In medieval times its vineyards, along with those of POBLET, were among the most important in Cataluña. The Virgin of Montserrat, whose blackened wooden image is preserved in the monastery, is the patron saint of Cataluña, and the monastery, founded in the 11th century, is the object of mass pilgrimages; its huge restaurants have panoramic views across the Penedès.

Parxet DO w dr ★★→★★★ 86, 87, 88, 89 DYA
Santa María de Martorelles (Barcelona). DO Alella. Founded in 1981, this young concern owns 45 hectares of vineyards, mostly Pansa, and makes its new-style white wines by cold fermentation in stainless steel without ageing them in oak. Its MARQUES DE ALELLA, made from 100 percent Pansa Blanca, is light and clean with delicate fruit. Even more attractive are the very fruity Marqués de Alella Seco, made with the addition of Macabeo and Chenin Blanc, and a light and delicious Marqués de Alella Chardonnay. *See also* Sparkling Wines, page 263.

Penedès DO r p w dr s/sw sw am g res ★→★★★★
The Penedès, with its 25,730 hectares of vineyards, is a limestone region southwest of Barcelona best known for its sparkling wines, but the best of its still wines rival those of the Rioja.

The region slopes upwards from the Mediterranean coast to a height of some 700 metres in the hills of the interior. The temperate climate and adequate rainfall are ideal for growing grapes. There are three subregions: the hotter Bajo Penedès near the coast is best suited for black grapes; the Medio Penedès, at an average altitude of 200 metres, produces some 60 percent of the wine from the area as a whole, much of it made from the white Xarel-lo and Macabeo and used for sparkling wines; and the typical grape of the cooler and hillier Penedès Superior is the white Parellada, used both for the dry, fragrant and refreshing white wines and also for sparkling *cava* wines, widely produced in the area (*see* page 253).

The Consejo Regulador, the official regulatory body, whose standards are rigorous, approves the following types of native grape: the white Macabeo (or Viura), Xarel-lo, Parellada (or Montonec) and Subirat-Parent; and the black Cariñena, Monastrell, Garnacha Tinta, Samsó, Ull de Llebre (or Tempranillo) and Cabernet Sauvignon. In addition to these, a variety of foreign noble grapes, first acclimatized by Miguel TORRES, are permitted.

Owing to the favourable climate, vintages are remarkably consistent, the best of the last decade being, for the white wines, 1978, 1981, 1982, 1984, 1985, 1986, 1987 and 1989; and for the reds, 1978, 1981, 1982, 1984, 1985, 1987 and 1988. The only really disastrous year during the last two decades was 1972.

The best base for visiting the Penedès is VILAFRANCA DEL PENEDES where there is one of the best wine museums in the world. Many visitors prefer to stay in one of the comfortable hotels of the pleasant coastal resort of SITGES, half-an-hour's drive from Vilafranca, or in BARCELONA, an hour away by the *autopista*.

Penelles (La Noguera), Comarca de r w dr sp ★→★★
Tiny undemarcated area in the west of Cataluña near Lleida, best known for the wines of the CASTELL DEL REMEI.

Pinord, Bodegas DO r p w dr sw g ★→★★
Vilafranca del Penedès (Barcelona). DO Penedès. Family firm making a large range of wines which are marketed under labels including La Nansa, Reynal and Chateldon.

Poblet, Monastery of
Famous Cistercian monastery dating from the 12th century in the hills of CONCA DE BARBERA, and the burial place of the Kings of Aragón and Cataluña. During the Middle Ages it was the abbeys and monasteries which fostered viticulture,

and along with those of the monastery of MONTSERRAT, the vineyards of Poblet were important in keeping winemaking traditions alive in Cataluña. Today an interesting feature of Poblet is the magnificent arched wine cellars.

Pontons

Vineyard area at a height of 700 metres in the PENEDES Superior, developed by Miguel TORRES for growing the native Parellada and also the Riesling, Gewürztraminer and Chardonnay vines from the cooler climes of northern Europe. Hailstorms, so damaging to vines, are dispersed by rockets charged with silver iodide, and the results are so promising that other producers are moving into the area.

Porrón (Catalan **Porró**)

This conical-shaped glass drinking vessel with spout and handle, now sold in debased form in souvenir shops up and down Spain, has been used for centuries in Cataluña. When in use, the spout does not touch the lips, so that the *porrón* serves the practical purpose of enabling a party of drinkers to enjoy their wine without the need for glasses.

Priorato (Catalan **Priorat**) DO r (w dr) am ★→★★

A small, mountainous enclave, with 1,860 hectares of vineyards and its own DO, within the much larger DO TARRAGONA. The name means 'priory' and derives from that of the ruined monastery of SCALA DEI.

The grapes are grown in small plots or on terraces in the volcanic soils of the steep hillsides, a decayed lava with high silica content, which, in combination with the hot summer sun, produces good, very fully bodied wines with high alcohol content. Authorized grapes for the red wines are the Garnacha Tinta, Garnacha Peluda and Cariñena; and for the whites, the Garnacha Blanca, Macabeo (Viura) and Pedro Ximénez.

The most typical wine is red, almost black in colour with a huge amount of extract, containing up to 18 percent alcohol and much in demand for blending. The other speciality is a golden yellow RANCIO.

Apart from the Cellers de SCALA DEI, DE MULLER and Masía BARRIL, there is only one producer which bottles and labels its wines: the UNIO AGRARIA COOPERATIVA (cooperative union) with cellars in Reus outside the demarcated area.

The best base for visiting Priorato is the city of TARRAGONA on the coast.

Rabassa Morta

The historic form of land tenure in Cataluña, according to which a proprietor leased land to a farmer on condition that he planted it with vines, and that the landowner should share the produce with the farmer, whose right to cultivate the land expired only with the death of the first-planted vines. After the onset of phylloxera in 1876 and replanting with grafts, the life of the vines became much shorter, and the institution fell into disuse. It is now usual for small farmers to own their land.

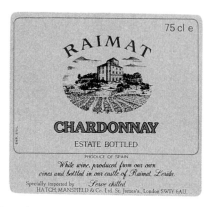

Raimat DO w dr r res ★★★→★★★★ 82, 86, 87, 88
Raimat (Lleida). DO Costers del Segre. Winemaking in the area had declined until the sparkling wine company of Codorníu (*see* page 257) bought the castle of Raimat and its 3,000-hectare estate. With advice from Davis University in California, 1,300 hectares have been irrigated and planted with selected native vines, together with Cabernet

Sauvignon and Chardonnay. A brand new winery has been built into the side of a hill, and as a result Raimat is now making some of the most attractive wines from Spain. They include white Raimat Clos Casal and Raimat Chardonnay; a red Clos Abadía; a 100 percent Tempranillo; a 100 percent Pinot Noir; and, perhaps most attractive of all, a Raimat Cabernet Sauvignon made with 85 percent Cabernet Sauvignon and 15 percent Merlot, aged in oak and bottle, with strong varietal characteristics and overtones of coffee and tobacco.

Rancio (Catalan **Rancí**)

A maderized or oxidized white wine, popular in various parts of Spain, but particularly so in Cataluña. *Rancios* vary enormously in character and quality from the tart and sour product of a peasant *bodega* or local cooperative, where the wine is left to oxidize without sufficient hygiene, to the perfected wines of DE MULLER in Tarragona. These are sweetened with *mistela* (a must in which fermentation has been checked by the addition of alcohol) or *arrope* (boiled-down must), and aged in *solera* (*see* Sherry, page 233). They can be magnificent, resembling in their different styles very round and old *oloroso* sherries. Another type is made in large glass carboys, known as BOMBONAS, and left partially unstoppered and open to the sun and wind, as at Miguel TORRES, whose fortified Dry Solera is very palatable and distinctly sherry-like. What all *rancios* have in common is a deep golden yellow colour, a sherry-like nose, more or less marked, and a high degree of alcohol.

René Barbier r p w dr sw res ★★→★★★

This company, like the CONDE DE CARALT, with which it shares cellars at the *cavas* of the sparkling wine firm of Segura Viudas near Sant Sadurní d'Anoia in the PENEDES, is now part of the FREIXENET group. Its Kraliner is a lively and fresh young white wine, and there are good red wines made with a blend of Tempranillo, Garnacha and Monastrell. The *bodega*, which has invested heavily in new oak, also makes a 100 percent Cabernet Sauvignon.

Reus

Important wine town of some 80,000 inhabitants west of
TARRAGONA. It is here that the great cooperative combine
the UNIO AGRARIA COOPERATIVA maintains its central
establishment for blending, maturing and bottling wines
from outlying cooperatives. There are also many private
firms engaged in elaborating both wines and vermouth.

Ribera d'Ebre, Comarca Vitícola Especial r w dr ★

Subdenomination of the DO TARRAGONA adjoining the DO
TERRA ALTA in the extreme southwest of the province of
Tarragona. The wines resemble those of FALSET but are
rather more acid. It makes some good dessert wines,
especially those from its leading *bodega*, Pedro ROVIRA.

Robert, Cellers g ★★

Sitges (Barcelona). One of the few small *bodegas* still
making the classical white dessert SITGES from Malvasía and
Moscatel grapes.

Rovira, Pedro DO r p w dr sw g res ★→★★

Old-established firm with cellars at Móra la Nova in the
Ribera d'Ebre, a *comarca* (subdistrict) of the DO TARRAGONA,
and at Gandesa in the DO TERRA ALTA. Among its wines are
a dry white Viña Montalt, a fruity Viña Mater red *reserva*, a
characterful old Gran Vino Tinto, aged for 18 months in
cask and five years in bottle, and a seductive dessert Vino
de Lágrima.

San Miguel de las Viñas, Cofradía de

Catalan order of *tastevins*, celebrating its functions at the
historic old castle of San Martí near Vilafranca del Penedès.
Its lighthearted inauguration ceremony, conducted to the
strains of a band in traditional costume, includes drinking
from a PORRON and distinguishing blindfold between a
white and a rosé wine – much more difficult than it sounds
– on pain of continuing the tasting indefinitely.

San Sadurní de Noya (Sant Sadurní d'Anoia)

Township in the east of the PENEDES towards Montserrat,
where most of the *cavas* making sparkling wines are
situated. Now that firms such as MARQUES DE MONISTROL,
CONDE DE CARALT, RENE BARBIER and FREIXENET are
diversifying, it has also become a centre for making still
wines. *See also* Sparkling Wines, page 265.

Sant Cugat del Vallés, Monastery of

Between Barcelona and MONTSERRAT, Sant Cugat, with its
beautiful Romanesque cloisters, was one of the great
religious houses which did so much to foster viticulture.
Among its muniments is a deed recording the gift of a
vineyard to the monastery in 927.

Santamaría, Cellers DO r (p) res $\boxed{\star\star \to \star\star\star}$ 78, 83

Capmany (Girona). DO Ampurdán-Costa Brava. Made
with a blend of Cariñena and Garnacha, the Gran Recosind
is ruby in colour, full-bodied, soft, fruity and long in finish.

Scala Dei, Cellers de DO r res (w dr p) $\star\star \to \star\star\star$ 85, 87, 88

Scala Dei (Tarragona). DO Priorato. Housed in an old
stone building near the ruined monastery and belonging to
a consortium of Barcelona families growing their own
grapes, the Cellers are equipped with stainless steel
fermentation vats, underground *depósitos* coated with epoxy
resin, oak *barricas* and a modern bottling line allowing for
the topping up of bottles with carbon dioxide. The *bodega*
makes a fresh but alcoholic rosé, a young Negre Scala Dei
red, and a superb Cartoixa Scala Dei, aged in oak and
bottle, deep and complex in flavour and of some 13·8
percent alcohol.

Scala Dei, Monastery of

When visiting the *bodega*, it is worth walking the ten
minutes to the great roofless monastery, choked with trees
and aromatic vegetation, a victim of Mendizábal's anti-
clerical reforms of about 1830. According to legend, it was
founded when angels were seen ascending and descending a

ladder into the heavens, and the theme of the ladder is embodied in the seal of the Consejo Regulador for PRIORATO.

Serra, Jaume DO r w dr (p) res ★★→★★★

Vilanova i la Geltrú (Barcelona). DO Penedès. Formerly one of the only three producers in ALELLA, the firm has transferred to the Penedès, where it makes fresh young white wines and good reds from blends of Tempranillo, Cabernet Sauvignon and Merlot.

Sitges

The Subur of the Romans, Sitges, on the coast south of Barcelona, is now a pleasant and relatively unspoilt seaside resort with a palm-fringed promenade, though bursting at the seams in summer. Its famous dessert wine, made by allowing Malvasía and Moscatel grapes to wrinkle on the branch before picking, the addition of grape spirit to the must and long maturation in oak, is now made only in minuscule amounts.

Sitges celebrates a picturesque harvest festival in early September, with a harvest queen, decorated floats, the solemn pressing and blessing of the first fruits, and a fountain flowing free wine.

A good base for visiting the PENEDES, the best of its many hotels are the four-star Calípolis and Terramar, both on the sea-front, and the three-star Antemare.

Tarragona

The Imperial Tarraco of the Romans, Tarragona is a city rich in historic remains, including massive walls built by the Romans on a much earlier foundation of monolithic blocks, an aqueduct and forum, and a fine Gothic cathedral. It is an important wine city specializing in the blending of wines, both from the surrounding region and other parts of Spain, and their bulk export. It is most reputed for the Tarragona *clásicos*, sweet dessert wines, both red and white, containing up to 23 percent alcohol – it was a cheap *clásico*, sold as 'Tarragona' and also known by the less complimentary

names of 'poor man's port' and 'red biddy', that was once
so popular in English pubs. Another important activity in
the town is the elaboration of vermouths and liqueurs.

Tarragona is a good base for visits to the outlying
regions, and the most comfortable hotels are the four-star
Imperial Tarraco and three-star Lauria.

Tarragona DO r w dr am ★→★★

Tarragona, with 23,812 hectares under vines and an average
annual output of 38 million litres, is divided into the
subregions of CAMP DE TARRAGONA, FALSET and RIBERA
D'EBRE. Its beverage wines, made mainly in cooperatives,
tend to be sturdy and high in alcohol, and thus very suitable
for blending, but lack the delicacy of those from the
PENEDES to its north.

Terra Alta DO r w dr ★→★★

The newly demarcated Terra Alta, with 10,100 hectares
under vines and an average annual output of 8·4 million
litres, lies in mountainous country in the extreme southwest
of Cataluña, bordering the province of Teruel. It makes
robust but characterful wines, white and red, the best from
the Cooperativa Agrícola GANDESA and Pedro ROVIRA. With
modern equipment, the wines are becoming lighter.

Torres, Miguel DO r p w dr s/sw sw g res ★★→★★★★ Red: 70,
71, 73, 74, 75, 76, 77, 78, 80, 81, 82, 84, 85, 87, 88
White: 74, 75, 76, 78, 79, 80, 81, 82, 83, 84, 85, 86, 87, 89
Vilafranca del Penedès (Barcelona). DO Penedès. The
Torres family has been making and selling wine in the
PENEDES since the 17th century. It is now the most reputed
firm in Cataluña to make still wines, exporting them all
over the world – exports to the USA alone top 1·8 million
bottles annually – and is still very much a family concern.

Miguel Torres Riera, with a French degree in oenology,
has been responsible for introducing a variety of foreign
vines to the Penedès, grown in addition to native vines, on
the firm's 800 hectares of vineyards, where the quality of
the fruit has been improved by clonal selection of the vines

and careful evaluation of the soils for the most suitable varieties. Like almost all Spanish *bodegas*, it also buys grapes from independent farmers. The foreign varieties include the white Chardonnay, Gewürztraminer, Riesling, Sauvignon Blanc; and the red Cabernet Sauvignon, Cabernet Franc, Petit Syrah and Pinot Noir; and vines accustomed to a cooler habitat are grown in the hills of the hinterland.

Torres has also been responsible for many technical innovations and was the first winery in Spain to introduce temperature-controlled fermentation in stainless steel. Typical of the cold-fermented whites are the dry, fresh and fruity Viña Sol and the oak-aged Gran Viña Sol Green Label, now named after Fransola where the grapes are grown; the Waltraud Riesling and luscious semi-dry Esmeralda, made with a blend of Gewürztraminer and Moscatel d'Alsace. MILMANDA, a Chardonnay of exceptional quality, is fermented and aged in traditional fashion in small French oak casks.

The red wines spend less time in oak casks – usually one to two years – and correspondingly more time in bottle than traditional Riojas, and are therefore less oaky in nose and flavour. Tres Torres and the fruity and full-bodied Gran Sangre de Toro are made with native grapes. Viña Magdala contains Pinot Noir, and the award-winning GRAN MAGDALA and Mas Borras are made with 100 percent Pinot Noir. A new introduction is a light and fruity Las Torres

Merlot for summer drinking, but the pride of the Torres
stable, velvety, smooth, intensely fruity and long in finish,
is the GRAN CORONAS BLACK LABEL MAS LA PLANA made with
selected Cabernet Sauvignon. It is now history that at the
Gault-Millau 'Olympiad' held in Paris in 1979, the 1970
vintage was judged by a short head to be better than the
less fully developed 1970 Château Latour.

Torres also makes a RANCIO, excellent brandies (*see* page
281) and an orange liqueur; has acquired vineyards and a
winery in Chile; and has begun to make wine in California.

Trobat, Bodegas DO r p g ★★
Garriguella (Girona). DO Ampurdán-Costa Brava. This
small firm makes the fresh and delicious rosé served by the
famous Hotel-Restaurant Ampurdán in Figueres and also
produces a good 100 percent Garnacha dessert wine.

Unió Agraria Cooperativa r p w dr sw res ★→★★
Reus (Tarragona). This vast combine, founded in 1962,
handles wines from all 180 cooperatives in the province. It
sells large quantities of wine to private firms for further
elaboration and bottling. More select growths, such as the
Priorat Seco Especial, Priorat Dulce and Priorat Centrum
from the Cooperativa de Gratallops, are matured in the
central cellars at Reus, and then bottled and sold under their
own label. Among its many other labels are the red and
white Tarragona Unión; red, white and rosé Yelmo; the
dry, semi-dry and rosé Collar Perla, Collar Zafiro and
Collar Rubí; and also *reservas*.

Vallformosa, Masia DO r p w dr g res ★★→★★★ 80, 84
Vilobí del Penedès (Barcelona). DO Penedès. Family firm
producing fresh white and rosé wines, and good red *reservas*
made both with native grapes and Cabernet Sauvignon. *See
also* Sparkling Wines, page 266.

Ventura, Jané DO w dr p ★★★ DYA
El Vendrell (Tarragona). DO Penedès. Small family firm
making a fresh, flowery and well-structured white wine

from Xarel-lo, Parellada and Macabeo, and equally distinguished rosé from Ull de Llebre, Cariñena and Monastrell. *See also* Sparkling Wines, page 266.

Vilafranca del Penedès

Vilafranca, a small town off the *autopista* between Barcelona and Tarragona, is the centre of the still-wine industry in the PENEDES and the home of many of its best-known *bodegas*. It also makes some sparkling wine by the champagne process and is the headquarters of the Spanish offshoots of Cinzano and Cointreau.

Apart from the *bodegas*, the great point of interest is the Wine Museum, installed in a 13th-century palace of the Kings of Aragón, and one of the best in the world. The exhibits begin with tableaux illustrating winemaking from ancient times onwards; and there are numerous examples of amphorae – Greek, Carthaginian and Roman. The main hall houses every type of agricultural implement, press and barrel, many of them originating from old *bodegas* in the region. There are also pictures and drawings, drinking glasses and PORRONES. The visit ends in a small bar, where local wines may be sampled. Closed Monday. The Museum is also the headquarters of the old-established Academía de Tastavins de Sant Humbert, a wine fraternity devoted to maintaining the traditions and quality of the Penedès wines.

Vilafranca possesses a number of pleasant restaurants (*see* Wine and Food, page 106), and two modern four-star hotels, the Domo and Alta.

Wine and Food

Cataluña has a long-established tradition of gastronomy, and the raw materials, especially the fish, shellfish and fresh vegetables, are first rate. There are five famous sauces: *ali-oli* (the *aïoli* of Provence), and the piquant *picada, chanfaina, sofrito* and *romesco*. Appetites are hearty, and in the smaller regional restaurants even the soups and starters are meals in themselves. The more sophisticated restaurants of places like Barcelona and the province of Girona have been much influenced by the *nouvelle cuisine*.

Anec amb figues Duck with figs.

Bolets Field mushrooms, often cooked on a charcoal grill with garlic and parsley. Torres Viña Sol, Balada Viña Toña or other dry white.

Botifarra catalana White sausage, resembling *boudin blanc*, eaten raw, cooked on its own or used in other dishes.

Brandada de bacalla Creamed salted cod.

Calçotada Made only in the spring, this is spring onions sliced in half and grilled over a wood fire. They are served with a sauce resembling *romesco*. Marqués de Monistrol Vin Natur Blanc de Blancs or other light dry white.

Conill con cargols Young rabbits stewed with snails, herbs, cinnamon, almonds and biscuit crumbs. One of the lighter reds from René Barbier, Hill, Conde de Caralt, Torres.

Costellas amb allioli Grilled ribs of lamb served with *ali-oli*. A medium-bodied red such as Raimat Tempranillo.

Crema catalana The local variation on cream caramel or 'flan', made with egg yolks, milk and cinnamon and topped with a brittle layer of caramel. Bach Extrísimo.

Eriços de mar gratinados al cava Sea urchins au gratin with *cava*.

Escudella i carn d'olla This most typical of Catalan dishes is served in two parts: first the *escudella*, a meaty soup with pasta; and then the *carn d'olla*, a rich stew containing veal, chicken, pork, blood sausage, egg, breadcrumbs and vegetables. A full-bodied red, such as Cartoixa Scala Dei or the less potent red Bach Viña Extrísima.

Espinacs a la catalana Boiled spinach with pine kernels and raisins. Try one of the lighter *rancios*.

Favas a la catalana Vegetable dish containing fresh broad beans, *botifarra negra* (Catalan black sausage) and belly of pork, together with spring onions, fresh mint, bay leaf and parsley. Marqués de Monistrol rosé or Trobat Rosado.

Llagosta a la catalana Stewed lobster with onions, carrots, garlic, herbs, parsley, saffron, pepper, sweet paprika, chocolate, nutmeg and brandy. This obviously calls for a wine of character such as the Torres Gran Viña Sol Green Label, with its body and hint of oak.

Mel y mató Fresh cream cheese with honey. Torres San Valentín or other sweet or semi-sweet wine.

Menja blanc A dessert made from ground almonds, cream, kirsch and lemon. Ideally, De Muller Moscatel Muy Viejo, Solera 1926.

Oca amb peres Roast goose with pears.

Pa amb tomàquet Catalan country-style bread rubbed with fresh tomatoes, oil and salt. It appears at the beginning of the meal and is sometimes served with slices of cured ham. Any full-bodied Mediterranean-type dry white.

Panellets A sweet made with almonds, sugar and eggs, or alternatively with pine kernels in the form of a marzipan.

Parrillada de peix amb salsa romesco Mixed grill of fish served with the typical Catalan *romesco* sauce and mayonnaise.

Perdiu a la catalana Partridge stewed with herbs and lemon. Marqués de Monistrol Gran Reserva or Raimat Cabernet Sauvignon.

Pollastre en chanfaina Chicken stewed with aubergines, green peppers, tomatoes, wine and herbs, and served with croûtons. Cavas Hill Castell Roc or other light red.

Postre de música Mixed plate of almonds, raisins, hazelnuts, walnuts, figs or other dried fruit.

Rap a la Costa Brava Anglerfish cooked with fresh peas, red pimientos, mussels, saffron, garlic, parsley and white wine, with a little lemon. Cavas del Ampurdán Pescador.

Salchichón de Vic A type of salami, for which the mountain town of Vic, in the Pyrenees near the French frontier, is famous.

Sarsuela de mariscs Literally a 'variety show', this most famous of Catalan dishes is a mixture of shellfish and firm white fish in a sauce made with saffron, garlic, white wine and parsley. With seafood such as this the Spaniards often drink red rather than white wine, and the choice is between a good medium-bodied red, such as a Conde de Caralt or René Barbier Tinto, or a dry white like the Jean León Chardonnay with sufficient character to stand up to the rich assortment of flavours.

Sopa de musclos catalana A soup made with mussels and flavoured with tomatoes, *aguardiente*, garlic, parsley and cinnamon. Torres Dry Solera, a dry sherry or Montilla, or a spicy white from Valencia, Jumilla or Alicante.

Sopa de pilotes Chicken broth containing small meatballs and flavoured with cinnamon, garlic and chervil. Dry sherry.

Suquet Catalan fish and potato soup.

Truita de botifarra i mongetes A hearty omelette containing Catalan sausage and served with haricot beans, first boiled and then fried. Alella Marfil Tinto, Perelada Tinto Cazador or other honest-to-goodness red.

Restaurants

Barcelona is full of good restaurants, and recommendations
include: *Eldorado Petit* (also in New York; Catalan food
cooked with elegance and sophistication); *Jaume de Provença*
(for connoisseurs of Catalan and *nouvelle cuisine* dishes);
Neichel (leading and sophisticated Barcelona exponent of
the *nouvelle cuisine*); *Agut d'Avignon* (near the cathedral,
fashionable, good value for what it is, Spanish and
international cooking); *Reno* (old-established and as good as
ever); *Florian* (small and inventive with attractively priced
young wines); *Casa Costa* (in the port area, fresh seafood,
Catalan style).

Cambrils (near Tarragona) *Can Gatell*; *Casa Gatell*; *Eugenia* (all
specializing in fish and seafood).

Figueres *Ampurdán* (in the Hotel Ampurdán outside Figueres;
highly sophisticated restaurant started by Josep Mércader,
founder of the new Catalan cuisine); *Hotel Durán* (good
Catalan food and long list of Ampurdán wines).

Lleida *Forn del Nastasi*.

Platja d'Aro *Big Rock* (first-rate restaurant in an old hilltop
mansion, run by one of Cataluña's leading chefs, Carles
Carmos).

S'Agaro *La Gavina* (sophisticated international cooking in this
most elegant and expensive of Costa Brava hotels).

Sant Feliú de Guixols *Eldorado Petit* (the original of the
restaurants later opened by Luís Cruanyas in Barcelona and
New York).

Sitges *Mare Nostrum* (fish, especially *sopa de pescadores*).

Tarragona *Mesón del Mar, Sol Ric*.

Vilafranca del Penedès *Airolo; Casa Juan*. Outside, on the road
to Sitges: *Celler de Penedès, Masia Segarulls* (both simple
restaurants with typical and substantial Catalan fare). Just to
the north, at San Martí Sarroca, *Ca L'Anna* (regional
cooking with sophistication).

Extremadura and the Southwest

The Extremadura lies between the two Castiles and Portugal in the southwest of Spain. It suffered from mass depopulation after the expulsion of the Moors in the 13th century, and again in the 16th, when the Extremeños joined in the conquest of the New World.

It remains an empty and sparsely populated area, and in its high *sierras*, clothed with cork-oak, beech and chestnut, sheep are more numerous than humans. Cultivation of vines is somewhat sporadic, the most densely planted area being the provisional DO of the Tierra de Barros in the province of Badajoz. Here, the summers are hot and the rainfall low, with an annual average of only 411 millimetres. The principal grape is the Cayetana Blanca with an astonishingly high yield, 36 hectolitres per hectare, of a neutral white wine of low acidity. Of the annual output of some 160 million litres, much goes to Jerez, Asturias and Galicia for blending, the remainder being consumed locally or distilled.

Two small areas in the Extremadura, Cañamero and Montán-chez, produce *flor*-growing wines of marked individuality; but to taste them you will have to visit the region, which is, although usually ignored by tourists, one of great scenic and historical interest, with its forgotten towns of Medellín and Trujillo, the birthplaces of Cortés and Pizarro, the splendid monastery of Guadalupe and, above all, Mérida, with its little-known and marvellous Roman monuments.

Outside Extremadura, the other vine-growing area in the far southwest is the demarcated region of Condado de Huelva, again with nostalgic historical associations, since it was from Palos, near the city of Huelva, that Columbus first sailed for the Americas. It is known for its decent white table wines, but more especially for *generosos* in the various styles of sherry, which would be more familiar if they had not for so long been sent to Jerez de la Frontera for blending.

It is difficult to list more than a handful of *bodegas* which actually bottle the wine, since so much of it, especially from the Extremadura, is made by small proprietors for consumption in local bars and restaurants, or sold in bulk by the cooperatives for blending outside the region.

Almendralejo

The main wine town of the provisionally demarcated
region of TIERRA DE BARROS in the province of Badajoz. Its
dusty main street is crowded with *bodegas* and distilleries.

Badajoz

Province of Extremadura flanking the Portuguese frontier
and lying between those of Cáceres to the north and
Huelva to the south. The principal vine-growing area is
that of TIERRA DE BARROS.

Bollullos del Condado

The most important of the wine towns in the DO
CONDADO DE HUELVA with numerous *bodegas* making white
table wine and sherry-like *generosos*. It is also a centre for
distilling the *holandas* used for making brandy (*see* Spirits,
Aromatic Wines and Liqueurs, page 276).

Cáceres r w dr

Province of Extremadura bordering Portugal and to the
north of Badajoz, whose most characterful wines are
CAÑAMERO and MONTANCHEZ. The other winemaking areas
are those of Miajados, west of GUADALUPE, and Jerte,
Hervás, Cilleros and Ceclavin, scattered around the historic
old towns of JARANDILLA and Plasencia in the north of the
province. In the main, their wines are *tintos* and *claretes*, but
Cilleros on the Portuguese border makes a sturdy white,
characteristically turbid and of 15 percent strength.

Cañamero w dr ★★

The small hill town of Cañamero, a few miles southwest of
GUADALUPE, is famous for a *flor*-growing white wine much
sought after by Spanish aficionados. The soils consist of
clays layered with slate and quartzite and the vineyards
extend to 1,000 hectares. Some 80 percent of the grapes are
made up of the white Alarije, Bomita, Airén and Marfil;
the red varieties are the Garnacha Tinta, Morisca, Palomino
Negro and Tinto Fino. The wines are made in the cement
vats of the small *bodegas* and develop a film of yeasts on the

surface in the manner of sherry. The wine is thereafter aged in oak casks and becomes turbid after some 14–18 months, but subsequently clears. The wines are yellow, becoming paler with age, round and smooth on the palate with a fragrant, sherry-like nose, and of some 15 percent strength.

CEVISUR w dr s/sw r ★
Almendralejo (Badajoz). An abbreviation for Compañía Exportadora de Vinos del Suroeste de España, this is a family firm and one of the few in the region to bottle representative wines: the dry white Torre de Almendralejo, the semi-sweet white Viña Almendra and a spicy red Palacio de Monsalud.

Condado, Cooperativa Vinícola del DO w dr g ★→★★
Bollullos del Condado (Huelva). DO Condado de Huelva. The best of the cooperatives in the DO CONDADO DE HUELVA, making white table wines and *generosos* in the style of sherry.

Condado de Huelva DO w dr g ★→★★
The province of Huelva lies in the southwest corner of Spain between the Portuguese frontier and the Atlantic. The demarcated region covers 10,500 hectares and in 1983 produced some 50 million litres of wine, which comprised white table wine, *generosos* of the sherry type and other wine used for distillation. The region has always been overshadowed by its more famous neighbours, Jerez and Montilla, and the best of its *generosos* were sent to Jerez for blending. However, when the region was demarcated in 1964 this practice was outlawed. The soils are chalky and of the same general type as those of Jerez, though they are darker in colour. In the past, 90 percent of the vineyards were planted with the white Zalema, but this is being replaced by Palomino, Mantúa, Garrido Fino, Pedro Luis and Pedro Ximénez.

The *solera*-made *generosos* are of the same general types as those of Jerez – *fino, amontillado, oloroso* – but lack the finesse of the best sherry. The white table wines, now being

cold-fermented, are acceptable enough for holiday
drinking, without any great distinction.

Condado de Niebla

Ancient domain of the Guzman Counts, who occupied it
after its reconquest from the Moors, and now the heart of
the vine-growing area of the province of Huelva.

Galán y Berrocal w dr r ★★

Montánchez (Cáceres). The only considerable *bodega* in this
village north of MERIDA to make the typical *flor*-growing
wines, ageing them in oak and distributing them outside
the area. Its labels are: the fruity young *2° año* Castillo de
Montánchez and the full-bodied, oak-aged *3° año* Trampal.

Guadalupe

High in the mountains northeast of Mérida, the little town
of Guadalupe clusters around a monastery founded by
Alfonso XI in 1340 in thanksgiving for his victory over the
Moors at Salado. It later became the shrine of the
conquistadores and was enriched by generations of princes
and grandees; among its many treasures is a magnificent
series of paintings by Zurbarán. The bars of Guadalupe are
the best place to sample the *flor*-growing CAÑAMERO; it is
also the house wine at the comfortable Parador Nacional
Zurbarán, facing the monastery and housed in a 15th-
century hospice for pilgrims.

Hijos de Francisco Vallejo DO g ★★

Bollullos del Condado (Huelva). DO Condado de Huelva.
Family firm making honest wines of the *generoso* type.

Huelva

See Condado de Huelva

Industrias Vinícolas del Oeste (INVIOSA) w dr r ★★ 84, 87

Almendralejo (Badajoz). Since its establishment in 1980 this
concern has made the best wine from the TIERRA DE BARROS,
but not from the native grapes. The cold-fermented white

Lar de Barros is made from Macabeo, and both the red Lar de Barros *reserva* and the full-bodied and spicy Lar de Lares *gran reserva* are made from a Riojan blend of Tempranillo, Garnacha and Graciano. INVIOSA is the only concern in the Extremadura to export its wines.

Jarandilla r ★

The *claretes* from Jarandilla, in the north of the province of Cáceres, were once rated among the best in Spain and were the prime favourites of the Emperor Charles V during his last years at the nearby monastery of Yuste.

Lar de Barros, Lar de Lares r w ★★

Names of the wines from INVIOSA, the best in the Extremadura.

Lepe

Small town west of Huelva near the Portuguese frontier, famous because its wines were the precursors of sherry and were mentioned by Chaucer.

Mérida

Once the tenth city of the Roman Empire, Mérida, in the north of the province of Badajoz, is the best placed and most interesting town from which to visit the winemaking areas of Extremadura. Its Roman remains, including a theatre, a circus, an amphitheatre and a triumphal arch, as well as bridges, aqueducts and tessellated pavements, are among the most impressive in Europe. Both of its hotels, the four-star Parador Nacional Vía de la Plata and three-star Emperatriz, are housed in historic buildings and offer regional wines and cooking.

Montánchez r w dr ★→★★

This small village, high in the hills above MERIDA, is remarkable for making a red wine which grows a *flor* in the manner of sherry. The wines, both red and white, are aged in earthenware *tinajas* (*see* Castilla-La Mancha, page 47) for about a year after vinification, when the yeasts appear on the surface. They emerge slightly turbid with a pronounced and aromatic sherry-like nose, and the 'red' is in fact more of an orange colour. Of around 13–14·5 percent strength, they are usually drunk as apéritifs and may be sampled in the bars of Mérida.

Pulido Romero, Bodegas José r p w dr ★→★★

Medellín (Badajoz). Sizable *bodega* in Medellín, the birthplace of Hernán Cortés, and maker of the better than average Castillo de Medellín in an area where most wine is either peasant-made for local consumption or produced in cooperatives for bulk shipment and blending.

Ruiz Torres, Bodegas w dr ★★

Cañamero (Cáceres). The only *bodega* of any size to make and bottle the individual *flor*-growing white wine of CAÑAMERO. It may be sampled at the *parador* or in the bars of nearby GUADALUPE.

Salas, Bodegas DO g ★★

Bollullos del Condado (Huelva). DO Condado de Huelva.

Wine estate near Bollulos del Condado

Family firm making some of the best of the sherry-like wines from the region.

SOVICOSA DO w dr p ★→★★ DYA

Bollullos del Condado (Huelva). DO Condado de Huelva. Belonging to the Sanlúcar firm of José Medina (*see* Sherry, page 225), the *bodega* makes fresh young Viña Saltes and Viñaodiel wines, among the best of their type.

Tierra de Barros DOP r w dr ★→★★

The Tierra de Barros, with 55,000 hectares under vines and centring on ALMENDRALEJO in the province of Badajoz, has the somewhat dubious distinction of making the cheapest wine in Spain, even exporting some of it to La Mancha! Some 75 percent of the grapes are Cayetana Blanca, producing dry white wines, neutral in character, without much acid and of 12–13·5 percent, whose main use, apart from current consumption, is for blending. The little village of Salvatierra de los Barros on the verges of Portugal does, however, make small amounts of an aromatic and intensely coloured red wine, prized by Spanish connoisseurs.

Wine and Food

When General Junot sacked the monastery of Alcántara in 1807 and ordered its medieval manuscripts to be used for making cartridges, one was salvaged and sent to the famous chef Escoffier, who commented that 'it was the only positive advantage which France reaped from the [Peninsular] War.' It contained the first directions for the use of truffles, still abundant in the region, and for making *pâté de foie gras*. Its pheasant Alcántara-style remains a classic recipe, but today the region is perhaps best known for its remarkable charcuterie – *chorizo* (pepper sausage), *jamón serrano* (cured ham) and the rest.

As regards the wines, the difficulty is to find the local growths in the better hotels and *paradors*, which offer the standard list of Riojas. Nevertheless, the house wine at the *parador* in Guadalupe is a thoroughly typical white Cañamero; at the Hotel Emperatriz in Mérida there is some choice of the better Extremaduran wines; and in hotels and restaurants generally, the carafe wine (when available) will probably be a sturdy red or white from Almendralejo.

Boquerones en adobo Fresh anchovies, marinated in olive oil, vinegar, garlic, parsley and seasoning and eaten raw.

Cochifrito Lamb cooked and served in an earthenware dish with onions, garlic, paprika, freshly ground pepper, parsley and lemon juice.

Coliflor al estilo de Badajoz Cauliflower, boiled and divided into florets, dredged in egg and breadcrumbs and then fried crisp in olive oil.

Frito típico extremeño Kid fried with garlic, parsley, black pepper and bay leaves.

Huevos a la extremeña A sauce is first made with olive oil, onions and fresh tomatoes, and to it are added boiled potatoes, *chorizo*, ham and seasoning. The eggs are broken on the top and the dish finished in the oven.

Huevos serranos Large tomatoes, halved, scooped out and stuffed with chopped ham, then topped with fried eggs, sprinkled with grated cheese and browned in the oven.

Riñonada A dish made with a mixture of lambs' kidneys and sweetbreads.

Solomillo de cordero Lamb marinated with salt, pepper, olive oil and red wine, and cooked slowly with the liquid in a casserole.

Restaurants

Badajoz *El Sotano* (best restaurant in the Extremadura; four-year-old wines from Almendralejo); *El Tronco* (regional food).

Guadalupe *Hospedería del Real Monasterio* (typical dishes at moderate prices).

Huelva *Los Gordos* (start with the Jabugo ham and continue with the mixed fried fish).

Jarandilla de la Vera *Parador Nacional Carlos V*.

Mérida *Hotel Emperatriz* (good range of regional wines); *Parador Nacional Vía de la Plata* (the Parador has won various gastronomic awards for its cooking).

Galicia

Galicia, in the far northwest of Spain, bounded to the south by Portugal and to the west and north by the Atlantic, comprises the provinces of La Coruña, Lugo, Pontevedra and Orense, of which only the two last produce significant amounts of wine. With its green hills, its chestnut forests, its unspoilt sandy coves and wide *rías* (deep salt-water inlets like fjords), it is a romantic part of Spain. Its wines, too, will appeal to wine romantics; but the visitor may well come back disappointed, because the best of them – the Albariños – are made in small but well-equipped private *bodegas* and tend to be expensive and difficult to come by.

The granitic soils and wet climate are very similar to those of northern Portugal; and traditional methods of viticulture, especially in the more westerly coastal districts, are strikingly alike, with high-climbing vines being trained away from the damp ground on chestnut stakes or grown in the form of a pergola along wires stretched from granite pillars. The wines often undergo a prolonged secondary or malolactic fermentation, which leaves them with a subdued and refreshing *pétillance*.

Many of the grape varieties are the same or akin to those of the Vinho Verde area of Portugal, such as the Albariño (Alvarinho), Dona Branca, Espadeiro, Loureira (Loreiro) and Treixadura (Trajadura), so that it is hardly surprising that there should be a strong family resemblance between the wines from both sides of the Miño (or Minho) river. Having said as much, it must be pointed out that the Portuguese, with their numerous well-organized cooperatives and sophisticated private *adegas* (wineries), have been more scientific in their methods than the Galicians, and their wines have consequently been a good deal more consistent.

There were until recently only six cooperatives in the whole of Galicia, and, in two of the winemaking areas, Valdeorras and Monterrey, there are few private firms which bottle the local wine. Much of it continues to be made in the simplest of *bodegas* by small proprietors, who sell them in the immediate vicinity. On balance, Galicia consumes more wine than it produces; and what has added to the natural difficulties of cultivating vines on the steep, terraced hill slopes is a persistent emigration from the region, especially to South America. In face of this, some of the larger private firms have taken to 'stretching' the local wine, often flowery and fruity in flavour but distinctly acidic, with neutral white wines from La Mancha.

In a definitive study of the wines, *Os Viños de Galicia*, Xosé Posada has listed and described no less than 136 grape varieties grown in the area. The more important of them are mentioned in the A–Z listing in connection with the different regions. Of these, three have been demarcated: Ribeiro and Valdeorras in the province of Orense to the southeast, and the new DO Rías Baixas, comprising three separate areas in the province of Pontevedra.

In Monterrey, the most easterly region, the vines are grown low, *a la castellana*, as in most other parts of Spain, and are pruned and trained by the method of *poda en vaso* ('goblet-shape'). Its wines, mostly red and of some 14 percent strength, more resemble those of León than those from the more westerly regions of Valdeorras and Ribeiro, where the vines are grown higher and the wines are lower in strength and often *pétillant*.

The best and most characterful wines are made with the white Albariño, sometimes with the addition of a smaller proportion of Treixadura or Loureira, from the zones of the Val do Salnés, O Rosal and the Condado de Tea. It is said that the Albariño was introduced to the region from the Rhine by the Benedictine monks from Cluny – though the taste of the wines sometimes seems to me to have more in common with Chardonnay from the monks' native Burgundy. Until some ten years ago very little was made, the famous originals, the Albariño de Fefiñanes and the Albariño del Palacio, being fermented and matured in oak. However, the producers have taken a leaf from the book of the Portuguese, where superb Alvarinho wines such as the Palácio da Brejoeira, having little in common with the run of *vinho verde*, have long been made by cold fermentation in stainless steel tanks. A new generation of small 'boutique' *bodegas*, equipped with the latest in hi-tech equipment, has sprung up, and their fat and fragrant wines now command some of the highest prices for white wine in Spain and are rivalling or surpassing those from the Rioja or the Penedès.

Cooperative-bottled wines like Pazo from the Ribeiro are easily enough obtainable. Probably the best way for the visitor to sample the others, which are not in such wide circulation, is in restaurants such as those listed later, where the proprietors obtain them direct from the growers.

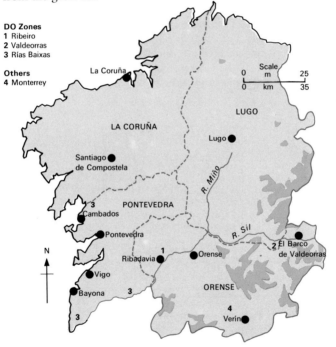

DO Zones
1 Ribeiro
2 Valdeorras
3 Rías Baixas

Others
4 Monterrey

Albariño

This most famous of Galician grapes is similar to the Portuguese Alvarinho. Such is the quality of its white wines, crisp and flowery with overtones of apple, pear or peach, that in the first place (in 1980) a *reglamento* was promulgated covering wines made from the grape, irrespective of their origin. This was replaced in August 1988 by the DO RIAS BAIXAS covering the three areas where the Albariño is most prevalent.

Albariño de Fefiñanes w dr ★★★
For decades before the present vogue for young, cold-fermented wines, this most famous of Albariños was made by the Marqués de Figueroa in a tiny *bodega* equipped with modern German presses and occupying a wing of the historic palace of Fefiñanes on the outskirts of CAMBADOS. Delicate, dry and fruity, it is not, however, *pétillant*, since all the wines are aged in oak casks for two years, and the *reservas* for six. It is therefore a deeper yellow, fuller in flavour and less acid than the typical wines from the area.

Albariño del Palacio w dr pt ★★→★★★ DYA
Despite its name, this wine, made by a brother of the Marqués de Figueroa, is not from the palace. Pale, flowery, extremely dry and somewhat acid, it is elegant and markedly *pétillant*.

Amandi r ★
According to tradition, the *claretes*, made exclusively from

the Mencía grape, produced by this small village in the
province of Lugo, were once favourites with Caesar
Augustus, who drank them with his spiced lamprey.

Cambados

Small seaside town northwest of Pontevedra and the only
place of any size in the VAL DO SALNES. The Parador del
Albariño, near the sea in a garden shaded by eucalypts, is
the pleasantest of places to stay and to sample the famous
Albariños with the local shellfish and regional dishes.

Cambados celebrates an annual *Fiesta del Albariño* on the
first Sunday of August, at which the wines are judged by
expert tasters and are also available to the public.

Cervera Hermanos, Fernández DO w dr ★★★ DYA

O Rosal (Pontevedra). DO Rías Baixas. A subsidiary of La
Rioja Alta (*see* page 194), this small firm makes a first-rate
100 percent ALBARIÑO, pale straw in colour, light,
refreshingly acidic and highly aromatic.

Chaves, Bodegas w dr pt ★★→★★★ DYA

Barrantes-Cambados (Pontevedra). Small family firm with
its own vineyards and a *bodega* equipped with modern
stainless steel fermentation and storage tanks and
refrigeration equipment for precipitating tartrates. Most of
its annual 30,000 bottles of good *pétillant* ALBARIÑO go to
local hotels and restaurants, but its Castel de Fornos was one
of the very first Albariño wines available in the UK.

Condes de Albarei DO w dr ★★★ DYA

Flowery 100 percent ALBARIÑO from the VAL DO SALNES,
made by Bodegas Salnesur, founded in 1988.

Cosecheros del Vino del Ribeiro DO r w dr ★

Ribadavia (Orense). DO Ribeiro. Bottlers of representative
RIBEIRO wines under the labels of Ouro and Agarimo.

Fillaboa, Granxa DO w dr ★★★ DYA

Salvatierra de Miño (Pontevedra). DO Rías Baixas. One of

the newer small Galician *bodegas* (established in 1986) with modern equipment and making one of the best of the ALBARIÑO wines.

Gallega, Bodegas r w dr ★

Los Peares (Lugo). Because of emigration and of the difficult terrain in the steep valleys of the Miño and Sil, wine production in this area of Lugo has greatly declined, and the Tres Rios from this *bodega*, once produced locally, is now a blend of wines from León and La Mancha.

Jesús Nazareno, Bodega Cooperativa DO r w dr ★→★★★

El Barco (Orense). DO Valdeorras. Apart from supplying wine in bulk, the cooperative bottles sizable amounts of very drinkable dry red and white wine. It is without *pétillance* and is sold as Valdeorras Tinto, Valdeorras Blanco and Moza Fresca. In addition it makes a superior Viña Abad Gran Vino Godello from vineyards replanted with the best of the traditional grapes.

Martín Codax w dr ★★★ 90, 91 DYA

One of the best of ALBARIÑOS from Bodegas de VILARIÑO–CAMBADOS.

Miño, Condado de

See Tea, Condado de

Miño, River

The Miño, rising in the centre of Lugo province, is the principal river of Galicia, flowing south through Orense and finally forming the northern border of Portugal, where it is known as the Minho.

Monterrey r p w dr ★

Small wine area and former DO in the south of the province of Orense, centring on the valley of the River Támega and bordered by Portugal. It is subdivided into the districts of VERIN, Monterrey, Castrelo and Oimbra. Sheltered by the Sierra de Larouco, the vines grow low *a la castellana* and produce the strongest of Galician wines, of up to 14 percent strength. About 70 percent of the wine is red and made from the Alicante Negro, Garnacha, Tintorera (Mencía), Tinta Fina, Tinta de Toro and Monstelo. The main white grapes are the Godello, Dona Branca and 'Xerez' (Palomino). The most important producer is the Cooperativa de MONTERREY.

Monterrey, Cooperativa de r p w dr ★

Verín (Orense). The cooperative, founded in 1963, is, astonishingly, the only concern in the region of Monterrey, in the south of Galicia near the Portuguese border, to bottle its wines. It makes fresh young red, rosé and white wines labelled simply as Monterrey, and also a two-year-old Castillo de Monterrey.

Morgadio-Agromiño DO w dr ★★★ DYA

Crecente (Pontevedra). DO Rías Baixas. The 100 percent Albariño Morgadio is clean, flowery and intense with a long finish.

Orense

Orense is the most southerly of the provinces of Galicia, bounded by Pontevedra to the west and Portugal to the south. It embraces the demarcated regions of RIBEIRO and VALDEORRAS as well as the undemarcated MONTERREY and some smaller areas. Orense itself is not the most attractive of Galician towns, and it is pleasanter to stay in VERÍN or on the coast.

Pazo (r p) w dr ★→★★ DYA

One of the biggest-selling and most frequently encountered branded Galician wines; it is made by Bodega Cooperativa del RIBEIRO.

Pazo de Señorans DO w dr ★★★ DYA

Vilanoviña (Pontevedra). DO Rías Baixas. New small *bodega* (founded in 1989) making a fresh and fruity estate-grown ALBARIÑO.

Pontevedra

Province in the southwest of Galicia, bordered by the River Miño and Portugal to the south and by the Atlantic to the west. Its green and hilly coastline is deeply penetrated by the picturesque *rías*, on one of which stands the port of Vigo. It is in this region that the famous ALBARIÑO grape and the high-climbing vines, trained on wires stretched between granite pillars, come into their own. All three subzones of the DO RIAS BAIXAS lie within this province.

There is a *parador*, housed in an old baronial house, in the historic old town of Pontevedra, and another at the frontier post of Tuy on the Portuguese border. The four-star Parador Nacional Conde de Gondomar at Bayona, on the coast south of Vigo, is one of the most luxurious in Spain. Situated in extensive grounds on a peninsula overlooking the Atlantic, its beaches, swimming pool, tennis courts and yachting basin make it an ideal place to combine a vacation with visits to the winemaking areas.

Queimada

See Spirits, Aromatic Wines and Liqueurs, page 280

Rías Baixas DO w dr (r) ★→★★★

Instituted in 1988, the DO replaces a provisional measure of 1980 applying to the ALBARIÑO grape rather than the area of production. It covers the three subzones of the VAL DO SALNES, centring on the town of CAMBADOS, and O ROSAL and the CONDADO DE TEA, lying back from the coast along the River Miño on the Portuguese frontier. Their combined area is 10,197 hectares, of which 1,200 are demarcated. Production in 1990 amounted to 45,000 hectolitres.

Ribeiro DO r p w dr pt ★→★★

The most productive vine-growing area in Galicia, situated in the west of the province of Orense in the basin of the River Avia. At a height of 100–300 metres and with 2,500 hectares under vines, it produced 22·5 million litres of wine in 1990. It is subdivided into three districts: Ribeiro de Avia, the oldest and most traditional area, making excellent white wines from Gomariz and reds from Beade, Regada and Costeira; Ribeiro del Miño, also producing good red and white wines; and Ribeiro de Arnoia, with its light and fragrant growths. The best of the white grapes are the Treixadura, Torrontés, Godello, Macabeo, Albilla and Loureiro, the Godello in particular giving the wines a fresh and fragrant nose. The best and most perfumed of the red wines are made from the Sonsón.

By far the largest producer in the region is the Bodega Cooperativa del RIBEIRO.

Some dozen other concerns bottle their wines, of which the newest and most spectacular is Bodegas Lapatena, opened in 1990, on whose wines it is as yet too early to make any comment.

Ribeiro, Bodega Cooperativa del DO r p w pt $\boxed{\star \rightarrow \star\star}$
Ribadavia (Orense). DO Ribeiro. Situated in Ribadavia at the confluence of the Miño and Sil rivers, this is by far the largest cooperative in Galicia, with some 1,600 members. It is equipped with modern equipment for vinifying, refrigerating and bottling the wine, and produces some seven million litres annually with storage capacity for another four million.

The best of its wines, made with selected grapes, are sold under the label of PAZO (meaning a baronial house). The white is flowery, dry and not too acid, without much sparkle, and has won prizes in international exhibitions. The red is definitely *pétillant*, dry and astringent to a degree, and resembles the red *vinhos verdes* from over the border. The cooperative also bottles cheaper and less delicate wines under the labels of Xeito and LAR and also a very select Bradomin made with ungrafted Treixadura and Torrontés in classical style.

Rodrigón
A post, usually made of chestnut, used for training the vines clear of the damp ground, especially in the more westerly districts of Galicia.

Rosal, O DO (r) w dr pt ★→★★★ DYA

Small subzone of the DO RIAS BAIXAS to the extreme southwest of the province of Pontevedra near the mouth of the River Miño. The main grapes are the Albariño, Treixadura and Loureira Blanca. In the past the wines, made unscientifically by a host of small proprietors, have been variable in quality. New regulations require DO wines to be made from at least 70 percent Albariño or 70 percent Loureira (or a blend of both), and a new generation of small modern *bodegas* is producing fresh, soft wines, often with a peachy flavour.

Salvatierra, Condado de

An alternative name for the Condado de TEA.

Santa María de los Remedios, Cooperativa DO r w dr ★

Larouco (Orense). DO Valdeorras. The cooperative bottles limited amounts of dry red and white VALDEORRAS, without *pétillance*, under the label Silviño.

Santiago de Compostela

Santiago lies to the northeast of the VAL DO SALNES, less than an hour's drive from CAMBADOS. It is the only city in Galicia with direct flights from Madrid, Barcelona and abroad; it possesses an old university, but most importantly it is the shrine of Saint James the Apostle, the patron saint of Spain, whose remains are buried there, and from the 11th century onwards it has been the object of pilgrims from all over Europe. Its cathedral is one of the most impressive in Spain, and the Parador de los Reyes Católicos, installed in a 16th-century palace in the magnificent cathedral square, is among the most famous in the country.

Santiago Ruiz DO w dr ★★★

San Miguel de Tabagón (Pontevedra). DO Rías Baixas. This is one of the best *bodegas* in O ROSAL, and Don Santiago makes and bottles a first-rate Albariño along the lines of the Alvarinhos from Monção just the other side of the border with Portugal.

Socalco

Name given to the steep hillside terraces in Galicia, sometimes so difficult of access that the peasants set up simple presses to vinify the wine *in situ*.

Tea, Condado de DO w dr r ★→★★★ DYA

Also known as the Condado de Salvatierra, this small subzone of the DO RIAS BAIXAS lies in the south of the province of Pontevedra, flanking the River Miño. Principal grape varieties are the black Caiño, Brancellao, Espadeiro and Alicante; and the white Treixadura and Albariño. The predominant wines are traditionally red and claret-like, but the new hi-tech *bodegas* make fresh and characterful Condado de Tea white from at least 70 percent Albariño or 70 percent Treixadura (or a blend of both).

Tutor

Another name for the RODRIGON, a wooden post for supporting high-growing vines.

Val do Salnés DO w dr ★★→★★★

Now a subzone of the DO RIAS BAIXAS, the Val do Salnés, lying along the coast and *rías* north of Pontevedra, has always been the heartland of the famous Albariño grape. According to the new regulations, its DO wines must contain at least 75 percent Albariño and are frequently made with 100 percent. At their best they are marvellously fresh and crisp with long finish. When in CAMBADOS, it is instructive to visit the *bodega* of the Marqués de Figueroa in the palace of Fefiñanes (if you find it open) to see how the oak-aged Albariño from the old master compares with the modern style.

Valdeorras DO r w dr ★→★★

The most easterly of the winemaking areas of ORENSE, Valdeorras lies in the mountainous valley of the River Sil and comprises three subregions, those of Rúa-Petín, Larouco and El Barco de Valdeorras, each possessing its own cooperative. About 90 percent of the white wine is made from the 'Xerez' (a variety of the Palomino) and 80 percent of the red from the Garnacha de Alicante. The white wine is of 11–12 percent alcohol, clean and a little drier than that from RIBEIRO; the red is cherry-coloured, fragrant and of 11–12 percent.

By far the largest producer of bottled wine is the Bodega Cooperativa JESUS NAZARENO.

Verín

Wine town in the southeast of the province of Orense. The comfortable Parador Nacional de Monterrey, on a hill above the town and facing the castle of Monterrey, offers local wines and food.

Vilariño–Cambados, Bodegas de DO w dr ★★★ DYA

Cambados (Pontevedra). DO Rías Baixas. New 'boutique' *bodega* with stainless steel and the latest equipment, founded in 1986. Its MARTIN CODAX is an excellent example of the new generation of clean, fruity and flowery Albariños.

Viña Guirian DO w dr ★★

Worthwhile 100 percent Godello white from Bodegas Senen Guirian Velasco in VALDEORRAS.

Vino de aguja

Term used to describe wines, like many of those from Galicia, with a slight *pétillance* resulting from a secondary malolactic fermentation. They are also known in Spain as *vinos verdes* – to the annoyance of the Portuguese, who have registered the description *vinho verde* or 'green wine' with the OIV (Office International du Vin).

Virgen de las Viñas, Bodega Cooperativa DO r w dr ★

Rúa (Orense). DO Valdeorras. The cooperative sells most of its output in bulk, but bottles smaller quantities of red and white wine under the labels of Rúa, Pingadelo, Amavia and Brisel-Godello.

Wine and Food

Galicia is famous for its *mariscos* or shellfish, which include mussels, lobsters, scallops, prawns, scampi in all shapes and sizes, clams, cockles, oysters, *percebes* (an edible barnacle) and *nécoras* (a species of spider crab). In seaside places you will often find *marisquerías* which serve nothing else, pricing the portions by weight. There are strong affinities with the cooking of northern Portugal, especially in the soups, rich fish stews and highly spiced tripe, hearty fare appropriate to the long wet winters.

As regards wine to go with this rich and nourishing assortment of dishes, the Galicians by preference drink a white Albariño with shellfish, which is perfectly matched by the acidity of the wine. The astringency of the red wines is a good counter to the richness and full flavour of the more substantial dishes.

Caldeirada gallega Akin to the French *bouillabaisse*, this is served in two parts: first the broth with slices of toast, and then the fish.

Caldo gallego A nourishing thick soup made with shank or hock of ham and haricot beans.

Callos a la gallega Tripe with chickpeas, pigs' trotters, paprika, *chorizo* and hot seasoning.

Centollo relleno/Changurro relleno The meat from a spider crab is removed and boiled, then added to a mixture of cooked hake, onion, parsley, garlic and lemon juice. This is filled back into the shell, topped with breadcrumbs and grated cheese and browned in the oven.

Empanada gallega Savoury tart containing a variety of meat or fish with tomatoes, onions and *chorizo*. *Xouba*, for example, is filled with small sardine-like fish; and *Raxo* with loin of pork.

Filloas Thick, fluffy pancakes, usually rolled and filled with jam.

Lacón con grelos Smoked shank of ham cooked with *chorizo* and sprouting turnip tops.

Lamprea a la gallega Lamprey prepared with shallots, garlic, olive oil, vinegar, sweet paprika, cinnamon and white wine.

Merluza al hinojo Hake cooked with fennel.

Pato al estilo de Ribadeo Duck cooked with turnips, orange segments, carrots, boiled chestnuts, pork, white wine, *anís* and a bouquet garni.

Pulpo a feira Stewed octopus with a sauce of olive oil, garlic and sweet red peppers.

Rape al queso Anglerfish baked with grated cheese.

Salsa zalpiscada Sauce made with hard-boiled eggs, onion, garlic, vinegar, olive oil and seasoning. It is served with fish and shellfish.

Santiaguiños Large crayfish appropriately marked with the cross of Santiago (Saint James).

Tarta de almendras Almond tart.

Tarta de Puentedeume A tart made with almonds, sugar and egg yolks.

Vieiras al Albariño Scallops marinated in Albariño wine, then seasoned with parsley, garlic and nutmeg, and sprinkled with breadcrumbs before being browned in the oven or under the grill.

Restaurants

Cambados *O'Arco* (near the palace of Fefiñanes; shellfish, regional dishes and Albariño wines).

La Coruña *Casa Pardo* (seafood, lobster salad).

Orense *Sanmiguel* (regional food, Ribeiro and Condado de Tea wines).

Pontevedra *Casa Solla* (seafood and Albariño wines).

Santiago de Compostela *Anexo Vilas* (regional cooking and wines); *Chita* (well-prepared regional food, Ribeiro and Albariño house wines).

Vigo *Puesto Piloto Alcabre* (beach restaurant, fish and regional dishes, Albariño and Condado de Tea house wines); *Sibaris* (salads of red peppers, marinated sea bass; liver sautéed with apples); *El Mosquito* (especially for fish and shellfish).

Villagarcía de Argosa (near Pontevedra) *Chocolate* (best restaurant in Galicia, with splendid wine list); *Loliña* (Galician shellfish at its fresh and splendid best).

Málaga

Sweet wines from Málaga were already famous in Roman times, and reached the zenith of their popularity during the 19th century, when the largest exports were to North America. In common with other sweet dessert wines, their popularity has declined, and the explosive development of the tourist industry along the Costa del Sol has taken its toll of vineyards and *bodegas*. In 1829 production amounted to some 17·5 million litres, whereas in 1988 only 3·7 million litres qualified for *denominación de origen*. Nevertheless, Málaga at its best remains a glorious wine; and not all of it is sweet.

The grapes are grown in two areas of the surrounding hills, one to the north of the city and neighbouring the DO Montilla-Moriles, and the other to the east. Because of the mountainous terrain, especially in the eastern area of Axarquia, where access to the small vineyards is often only by way of rough tracks, most of the wine is vinified on the spot; but it must be matured in one of the large *bodegas* of Málaga itself to qualify for DO.

In the sheltered south of the area, the climate is mild, warm and predictable; in the north there are sharp frosts in winter and the summers are short and very hot. Most of the rainfall is in winter, and is usually torrential while it lasts – conditions ideal for vines and for 'sunning' grapes destined for dessert wines.

In days past, there was a profusion of vine varieties, including the Moscatel, Pedro Ximénez, Airén, Moscatel Morisco, Romé, Jaén Blanco, Jaén Tinto and Jaén Doradillo. However, in 1876 Málaga was one of the first areas in Spain to suffer from phylloxera – probably introduced direct from America – and many of the old varieties have disappeared. Today, the Consejo Regulador authorizes only the Pedro Ximénez and Moscatel for new plantations.

The must is usually fermented in cement containers resembling the earthenware *tinajas* of Montilla or Valdepeñas (*see* Castilla-La Mancha, page 47, and Montilla-Moriles, page 148), but larger, cylindrical in shape and reinforced with steel rods. On its arrival by road tanker in Málaga it is blended according to type, refrigerated to precipitate tartrates and then matured in *soleras* like those of Jerez (*see* Sherry, page 233), the older wine being 'refreshed' with the younger. Although some of the grapes are so sweet as to leave residual sugar in the must after fermentation is complete, an *arrope*, or syrup, made by boiling down unfermented must, is often added.

There are many different styles of Málaga, separately described in the A–Z listing. The most common is the *dulce color*, dark amber in colour, full-bodied and sweet (sometimes cloyingly so) right through to the end; but there are others, more resembling tawny port, with a bitter-sweet flavour and dryish finish.

A number of the leading *bodegas* and their wines are separately described; the full list of firms which export wines with *denominación de origen* is:

Barceló, Luis	Montealegre, Bodegas
García Gomara	Pérez Texeira
Garijo Ruiz, José	Sánchez Ajofrin, José L
Larios	Sánchez y Sánchez y Cía, Juan
López García, Salvador	Scholtz Hermanos
López Hermanos	Suárez Villalba, Hijos de José
López Madrid, Antonio	

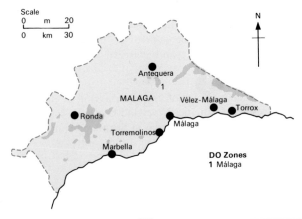

Antequera

The old town of Antequera lies north of Málaga on the winding uphill road to Córdoba and Sevilla and on the southern fringe of one of the two main vineyard areas of the DO MALAGA. This northern area, at a height of some 500 metres, is a limestone region, and the predominant grape is the Pedro Ximénez.

The *parador* is a pleasant place to spend a night in the area, and the cooking in its restaurant using local ingredients is inventive.

Arrope

A syrup used in certain Málagas which is made by evaporating down unfermented must in a copper pan, and adding alcohol to prevent subsequent fermentation. A dark treacle colour, *arrope* tastes of caramel.

Axarquia

The second and larger of the vineyard areas of the DO Málaga, to the east of the city and stretching back from Vélez-Málaga and Torrox near the coast into the mountains, which rise sharply to a height of some 2,000 metres. The soils are a mixture of decomposed slate and a limestone clay, and its vineyards are planted with 90 percent Moscatel. There are three bands: some near the coast, used mainly for growing dessert grapes; an intermediate zone producing raisins; and a higher and more northerly strip where most of the grapes are vinified. There is some overlap in the usage of the fruit, and about ten percent of the total crop is converted into wine.

Barceló, Luis

Málaga. DO Málaga. A firm specializing in *vinos quinados* (*see* Spirits, Aromatic Wines and Liqueurs, page 282), tonic or medicated wines popular in Spain and containing quinine extract.

Baumé scale

As Málagas are sweet wines, one needs to refer to degrees

Baumé, a measurement of the sugar content of wines. As a guide, 2° Baumé corresponds to 20·3 grams per litre of sugar; 4° to 54·6 grams per litre; 6° to 91·4 grams per litre; 8° to 144·6 grams per litre; and 10° to 169·8 grams per litre.

Blanco seco

The least known of the styles of Málaga, this is made by fermenting out Pedro Ximénez musts to completion. Yellow or pale gold in colour according to age, it resembles certain Montillas and is dry and aromatic with the nutty flavour of a good *amontillado* sherry, with an alcohol content of 15–22 percent.

Borge

One of the main vineyard areas of the AXARQUIA to the northeast of Málaga.

Cono

A large wooden vat, so called because of its truncated conical shape, in which the wine is first stored when it is brought down to Málaga.

Dulce color

The most familiar style of Málaga, sweetened with ARROPE, to which it owes its dark amber colour, the hint of treacle in the nose and high 8–12° Baumé. The alcohol content ranges from 14–23 percent.

Lágrima

The word means a 'tear' and is used to describe the choicest and most luscious of the wines, made with the juice which emerges from the grapes without the use of mechanical means and simply as a result of the pressure from the grapes at the top of the load. It therefore comes from the pulp nearest the skins of the ripest grapes, and is vinified separately from the *yema* (or 'yolk') obtained by further light pressing. The wine is old gold in colour, very fully bodied, with an aromatic *oloroso* nose and long sweet finish. It has 6–10° Baumé and 14–23 percent alcohol.

Lágrima Cristi

Sweeter variant of LAGRIMA, of 8–12° Baumé and 15–18 percent strength.

Larios

Málaga. DO Málaga. Known for its gin, Larios also makes good Málagas, especially the aromatic, fruity and honey-like Colmenares Moscatel. *See also* Spirits, Aromatic Wines and Liqueurs, page 276.

López Hermanos

Málaga. DO Málaga. Founded in 1885 and run by the third generation of the López family, the *bodega* makes some of the most popular of Málagas in Spain, including the dry Trajinero and the sweet dessert Málaga Virgen, both made from Pedro Ximénez, and the luscious Moscatel Gloria.

Málaga

The city of Málaga lies on the coast at some distance from the vineyards in the hills behind it, but to qualify for DO the musts have either to be vinified in one of its *bodegas* or, as is more usual, brought there for blending and maturation. Its historic buildings are not of great interest, and at first sight it seems that little remains of the romantic city sung of by Lorca only 50 years ago. The inexorable pressure of tourism has ringed it with high-rise apartments and squeezed out the old *bodegas* into a peripheral no-man's land. But the port remains, and, behind the port, a network of narrow streets clustering around the market, some with restaurant tables on the pavement and cavernous bars where one may settle down to serious tasting of Málagas in all their variety. Most of its hotels are geared to the package holiday industry, and since the demise of the splendid Miramar the quietest place to stay is at the Parador Nacional de Gibralfaro, set on a hill above the centre.

Mollina

The most important of the vineyards in the northern zone, beyond ANTEQUERA.

Moscatel

As the name implies, a style of Málaga made solely with Moscatel grapes, from the AXARQUIA. The colour varies according to age from golden yellow to light golden brown, and the wine is soft and sweet, with a deep and fruity Moscatel nose. It varies from 6–13° Baumé with an alcohol content of 15–20 percent.

'Mountain Wine'

Soubriquet for Málaga in its Victorian heyday. You can occasionally find silver wine labels with this name in antique shops.

Pajarete

A dry or semi-dry style of Málaga, amber or dark amber in colour with a reddish cast. It contains 15–20 percent of alcohol, and 2–6° Baumé.

Pedro Ximénez

A style of Málaga made solely with Pedro Ximénez grapes from the northern zone. When fully mature it is a dark treacly colour with yellow rim and intense *oloroso* nose, and is full-bodied and very soft with a bitter-sweet finish. It varies from 6–13° Baumé with an alcohol content of 16–20 percent.

Pérez Texeira

Málaga. DO Málaga. The most outstanding wine from this *bodega* is the Lágrima Viejo, made with musts obtained without mechanical pressing of the grapes.

Romé

These wines, made from the Romé grape, may be either red or gold in colour with 2–8° Baumé and 15–20 percent of alcohol.

Semi-dulce

As the name indicates, one of the drier styles of Málaga, either golden yellow or ruby in colour. The wines are bitter-sweet, with a full dry finish and deep *oloroso* nose. They range from 2–4° Baumé and the alcoholic strength is 16–23 percent.

Scholtz Hermanos

Málaga. DO Málaga. One of the best and most famous of the *bodegas*, the firm was founded in 1807, but changed its name in 1885 when it passed into German control, reverting to Spanish ownership after World War II. The vinification plant is at MOLLINA, but the wine is brought to the *bodega* itself to be matured. This was formerly in the centre of the city, but now occupies modern premises on the outskirts with capacity for making two million litres of wine annually, of which half is exported. Among its 18 or so styles of wine are the dry Seco Añejo ten-year-old, Moscatel Palido, Málaga Dulce Negro and Lágrima ten-year-old, but the best known is the Solera 1885. The date is of no particular significance, and it is in fact made with ten percent of a near-black Solera 1787 Pedro Ximénez Lágrima Bisabuelo, ten percent Montilla Añejo, and 80 percent Amontillado Viejo. Old gold in colour, with overtones of good tawny port and *oloroso*, it is a complex and intensely fruity wine, with a bitter-sweet taste and long dry finish, and of 18 percent strength.

Tintillo
    A red Málaga of 6–10° Baumé containing 15–18 percent of
    alcohol.

Vélez-Málaga
    Principal town in the vine-growing area of AXARQUIA, east
    of Málaga and just back from the coast towards the hills.
    The pleasantest place to stay is at the *parador* in Nerja,
    beautifully situated above the shore.

Wine and Food

On gastronomic maps of Spain, Andalucía is often labelled the *zona de los fritos* or 'region of fried food', and high on the list of such dishes must come the fries of mixed fish, equally good around Málaga or in Cádiz and the sherry region. The shellfish is varied and abundant; another great speciality is the *gazpachos* or cold soups, always containing garlic and a little olive oil and vinegar, but made with a variety of vegetables, chopped or puréed.

    Málaga is not for drinking with a meal, but afterwards; the *blanco seco* is an unusual variant on *amontillado* as an apéritif.

Ajo blanco con uvas de Málaga A cold soup made with
    almonds, garlic, vinegar and olive oil, together with white
    grapes, skinned and without pips.

Chanquetes A minute fish (*Aphia minuta*) fried crisp like
    whitebait.

Dulce malagueño A sweet made with semolina, egg yolks,
    sugar, raisins and *membrillo*, a quince paste.

Frito de pescados a la andaluza A mixed fry of small fish,
    sometimes dipped in seasoned flour or maybe dredged in
    egg and breadcrumbs, and fried in hot olive oil. Fish such as
    chanquetes, *boquerones* (fresh anchovies), or squid cut into
    rings are also fried and served by themselves.

Moraga de sardinas Motril Fresh sardines marinated with salt, olive oil, white wine, lemon juice, parsley and garlic.

Raya en pimentón Skate cooked with sweet paprika.

Salsa andaluza Sauce made with pumpkins, tomatoes, pepper and garlic.

Sopa al cuarto de hora A soup so called because of the cooking time of 15 minutes, and containing chopped ham, clams, hard-boiled eggs, onion, parsley, garlic and bread.

Sopa de almendras de Ronda A sweet soup containing pounded almonds, sugar, a stick of cinnamon and grated lemon peel, with thin slices of bread.

Tarta helada Sweet made with layers of sponge cake and ice cream.

Tortilla al Sacramonte Omelette originating from the gypsy quarter of Granada and containing lambs' brains, sweetbreads, fresh peppers, potatoes and toasted breadcrumbs.

Restaurants

Antequera *Parador Nacional* (inventive Andalucian food).
Málaga *Escorpio* (near the *parador*, sophisticated French-style cuisine with local ingredients); *Antonio Martín* (with terrace overlooking the sea; fish and seafood); *Casa Pedro* (on the shore and vastly popular; mixed fried fish and first-rate shellfish).

There are also scores of good restaurants, some outstanding, in places like Marbella and Torremolinos, in the Costa del Sol resorts.

Montilla-Moriles

Montilla-Moriles, one of the hottest and sunniest parts of Spain, lies in hilly country south of Córdoba. It makes wines of the sherry type matured in *solera*, and until it was demarcated in 1945 much of its wine was in fact shipped to Jerez for blending. Quantities of sweet Pedro Ximénez wine are still, by special dispensation, supplied to the sherry *bodegas* for making sweet *olorosos* and cream sherries.

The best of its soils is the chalky white *albero* resembling the *albariza* of Jerez; but by far the most predominant grape is not the Palomino, but the Pedro Ximénez, picked here when fully ripe, but while still waxy white, and fermented to completion without sunning. Other grapes are the white Airén, Baladí and Moscatel. The yield from the low-pruned vines is small: with 14,500 hectares under cultivation, 75 percent of the area of vines of Jerez, the region produces only 50 percent of the volume of the sherry area.

The main difference between the making of sherry and Montilla is that in Montilla-Moriles the must was traditionally fermented in the pear-shaped earthenware *tinajas*, also typical of Málaga and La Mancha (*see* Castilla-La Mancha, page 47), but as elsewhere these are now being replaced by temperature-controlled stainless steel tanks. When the wine 'falls bright', some months after completion of its secondary fermentation, it is transferred to a *solera*, operated in almost exactly the same fashion as those in Jerez, except that the musts are so rich in sugar that they produce wines a little higher in alcohol and are not fortified.

As in Jerez, the musts are classified by the cellar master and emerge as one or other of the styles familiar in Jerez: *fino, amontillado, palo cortado, oloroso* (*see* A–Z listing for details). The style for which the region is best known is the light, aromatic and very dry *fino*, which is made from the first pressing of the grapes and develops a vigorous *flor*. The *olorosos* are made from a must obtained by a second and firmer pressing.

It should be mentioned that some years ago the sherry shippers brought a legal action in England, contesting the use of the terms *fino* and *amontillado* as descriptions of Montilla – ironically, as it happens, since, in the first place, the Jerezanos borrowed the name 'amontillado' from Montilla. For this reason, Montilla on sale in the UK is often labelled 'fine dry', 'medium' and 'cream'; it contains between 13 and 15 percent alcohol.

Until 1980 exports of Montilla were slow and some firms struggled to survive, but thanks to excellent quality and competitive prices, there was a marked revival, especially in Britain. The largest of the firms, Alvear, exports some 25 percent of its production, and Compañía Vinícola del Sur some 50 percent. The most important foreign markets are Britain and the Netherlands. More recently, Montilla, in common with fortified wines, has suffered a decline in sales. To combat this, some of the producers have turned to making *joven afrutado* (young and fruity) beverage wines. Whether these can compete with the white wines from the regions of the north remains to be seen.

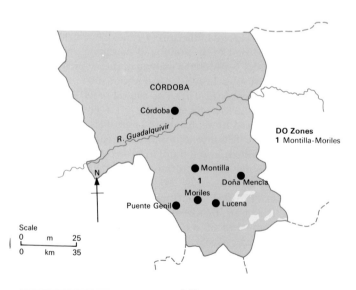

Albero

The best of the soils, containing 30–60 percent chalk. It is most widespread in the *sierras* of Montilla and Alto Moriles, where most of the large *bodegas* have vineyard holdings. Production is higher in the lower-lying areas, but the wines are not of the same alcoholic degree or quality.

Alvear

Montilla (Córdoba). DO Montilla-Moriles. The firm, the largest in the region, was founded by the Alvear family, which first settled in Montilla in 1729, planting vineyards and establishing the original *bodega*. It was much expanded by Don Francisco de Alvear y Gómez de la Cortina, Conde de la Cortina, during the early years of the present century and now possesses 17,000 American oak casks in its SOLERAS and has a storage capacity of five million litres. It makes Montilla in some dozen styles, including two excellent dry *finos*, the soft and delicate Fino Festival and Fino CB, named after a former head cellarman, Carlos Billanueva; Amontillado Carlos VII, fruity, fragrant and bone dry, more resembling a *fino* than an *amontillado* from Jerez: Oloroso Pelayo Seco, lighter-bodied than its Jerez counterpart; the bitter-sweet Oloroso Asman Abocado; a sweet Cream; and a smooth, full-bodied Pedro Ximénez 1830 with a flavour of figs. Alvear also produces large amounts of brandy made from *holandas* (*see* Spirits, Aromatic Wines and Liqueurs, page 270).

Amontillado

This was the original style of Montilla, first made by a Conde de la Cortina in the 18th century, but without maturation in SOLERA. The Jerezanos later produced a wine with somewhat similar characteristics, but aged it in *solera*; and the *bodegueros* from Montilla subsequently followed suit. *Amontillados* from Montilla are of 16–22 percent strength, amber-coloured, full on the palate and with a pungent, nutty nose.

Aragón y Cía

Lucena (Córdoba). DO Montilla-Moriles. Well-known firm whose wines include the Moriles 47, Pacorrito, Boabdil, Moriles Palo Cortado and Araceli Pedro Ximénez.

Benavides

Its vineyards are among the best in the MORILES area.

Compañía Vinícola del Sur

Montilla (Córdoba). DO Montilla-Moriles. Large company, formerly within the RUMASA group (*see* pages 230–231), whose Monte Cristo wines are well known in Britain, and their Dry, Medium, Pale Cream and Cream are also exported to the USA.

Conde de la Cortina

Montilla (Córdoba). DO Montilla-Moriles. The company is controlled by ALVEAR, with which it shares premises. Its best-known brands are the well-made Cortina Pale Dry, Medium, Cream and Pale Cream.

Córdoba

A little to the north of the DO Montilla-Moriles, Córdoba is the headquarters of a number of firms which maintain *bodegas* and *soleras* in the city for maturing their wines.

For 300 years, until the Caliphate disintegrated in 1031, Córdoba was the capital of Moorish Spain; and the Great Mosque, now the cathedral, resembling nothing so much as a cool grove of palm trees with its myriad arches and columns, was the most important in western Islam and second only in size to that of Mecca. Other Moorish survivals are the 14th-century Alcázar or fortified palace, with its mosaics and gardens, and the Judería or ancient Jewish quarter, a maze of narrow alleys, crisscrossing at random and providing shelter from the sun.

About half-an-hour's drive from Montilla, Córdoba, with its historic interest and restaurants, is the obvious base for a visit to the region. It possesses a number of good hotels, including the five-star Adarve and Meliá Córdoba, the four-star Gran Capitán and the three-star Maimónides opposite the Mosque; but perhaps the quietest and most relaxing resting place is the spacious and comfortable modern Parador Nacional de la Aruzafa, looking down on the city from the north.

Doña Mencía

Village to the southeast of Montilla with three concerns making DO wines:

Crismona, Bodegas   Lama, Bodegas (Miguel
Luque, Bodegas   Fernández Gan)

El Bombo

One of the best vineyard areas near MORILES.

El Naranjo

Another favoured vineyard area near MORILES.

Fino

Pale and dry with a greenish tint, slightly bitter, and light and fragrant on the palate, the unfortified *fino*, containing 14–17·5 percent alcohol, is the best known of the various styles of Montilla.

Gálves

Village in the Sierra de Montilla renowned for its vineyards.

Gracia Hermanos

Montilla (Córdoba). DO Montilla-Moriles. Family firm making traditional and good quality Montillas. Among their labels are Corredera *fino*, Montearruit *amontillado*, Cream *oloroso* and PX Dulce Viejo.

Lucena

Pleasant little town southeast of Montilla and halfway between Córdoba and Antequera (*see* Málaga, page 134). Apart from wine, it produces olive oil and is known for its decorative metalwork.

Montilla

Together with the nearby village of MORILES, this quiet hill town, the Munda Betica of the ancients and birthplace of Gonzalo de Córdoba, the Gran Capitán, numbers among its attractions the charming early 18th-century house of the ALVEAR family, with its splendid arcaded patio. Montilla is the wine centre of the region, and possesses a number of *bodegas* making DO wines. There is a two-star hotel, the Don Gonzalez, just outside Montilla on the road to Antequera.

Montulia, Bodegas

Montilla (Córdoba). DO Montilla-Moriles. Long-established and well-known maker of some dozen styles of Montilla, including JR *fino*, *amontillado*, Fabiola, Pedro Ximénez and an excellent *palo cortado*. The firm also makes brandy and *anís*.

Moriles

Although famous for its wines, and lying at the centre of some of the best vineyards in the area, Moriles remains only a tiny village on a by-road some 20 kilometres south of MONTILLA.

Navarro, Bodegas

Montilla (Córdoba). DO Montilla-Moriles. Sizable exporter among whose wines are Andalucía, Montilla and La Aurora *finos*; NR *oloroso*; and a sweet Pedro Ximénez.

Oloroso

Style of wine resembling its counterpart from Jerez (*see* page 226), with 16–18 percent of alcohol, rising to 20 percent when very old, mahogany-coloured, full-bodied, soft and highly aromatic; it can be either dry or with a hint of sweetness.

Palo cortado

With 16–18 percent alcohol, this is a style combining the nutty bouquet of *amontillado* with the flavour of *oloroso*.

Pedro Ximénez

A sweet wine with high alcoholic degree, which takes its
name from the vine. It is made in part with sunned grapes,
is a dark ruby colour and contains a massive 272 grams per
litre of sugar at least.

Pérez Barquero

Montilla (Córdoba). DO Montilla-Moriles. Another
company that was formerly part of the RUMASA group
(*see* pages 230–231). Among its labels are Diogenes and
Viña Amalia light white wines and Gran Barquero *fino,
amontillado* and *oloroso*, all three of outstanding quality.

Puente Genil

Small town southwest of Montilla. As well as its wines, it
also enjoys fame as the chief producer of *membrillo*, the
quince paste so popular in Spain. It is the headquarters of:

Cooperativa Vitivinícola de
la Purísima
Delgado Hermanos

Melero Muñoz, Damaso
Varo Campos, Antonio

Raya

A style of Montilla similar to OLOROSO, but with less
flavour and bouquet.

Ruedo

This is not a Montilla proper, but a dry, pale and light
white wine containing about 14 percent alcohol and made
without maturation in SOLERA.

Ruedos de Montilla, Los

Its grapes are among the best from the Sierra de Montilla.

Solera

An assembly of 500-litre butts used for maturing the wine.
As in Jerez (*see* page 233), the butts are loosely stoppered
and arranged in 'scales' containing progressively older wine,
and when wine is drawn off for shipment or bottling, the

final 'scale' is 'refreshed' with younger wine. A Montilla *solera* usually contains five 'scales' for the *finos* and four for the *olorosos*. The *soleras* are operated almost exactly like those in Jerez, except that the musts are brandied only in occasional years when they are low in alcohol.

Tercia, La
Well-known vineyard area near MORILES.

Tinajas
These are the large, pear-shaped earthenware vessels traditionally used for fermenting the wine. The tops are left open during the first stages of fermentation and later covered with wooden lids. Once the wine clears after completion of the secondary fermentation, it is racked and transferred to a SOLERA for maturation. In the larger, more modern *bodegas*, *tinajas* are being replaced with stainless steel tanks. *See also* Castilla-La Mancha, page 47.

Tomás García
Montilla (Córdoba). DO Montilla-Moriles. The firm belongs to the same group as Carbonell, one of the largest producers of olive oil in Spain and until recently makers of Montilla which it matured in its cellars in Córdoba. Tomás García makes a fresh Verbenera *fino*, a fragrant, intense Flor de Montilla *amontillado*, a complex, well-structured Nectar TG *oloroso* and a sweet 100 percent Pedro Ximénez TG.

Zona del Albero
Name given to the area around MORILES, whose soils are particularly rich in the chalky ALBERO.

Wine and Food

With local variations, the food from the Córdoban area and Montilla-Moriles is that of Andalucía as a whole, and many of the typical dishes are described under Sherry (Jerez), pages 236–239, and Málaga, pages 139–140. Although Córdoba is not near the coast like the other two regions, the restaurants serve a variety of shellfish, and mixed fries of fish are also popular. It is usual to begin with a glass of chilled *fino* Montilla, often served with *aceitunas aliñadas* or king-sized olives, and to continue drinking it throughout the meal.

Brazo de gitano Popular sweet made with eggs, flour and jam, and resembling a Swiss roll.

Callos a la andaluza Tripe stewed with calves' feet and chickpeas.

Caracoles a la andaluza Snails cooked with garlic, toasted almonds, sweet paprika, tomatoes, onions, white pepper and lemon.

Huevos a la flamenca Eggs cooked in an earthenware dish with onions, ham and fresh tomatoes, and decorated with prawns, slices of *chorizo*, asparagus tips and red pepper.

Membrillo A sweet quince paste, served on its own as a sweet or with cheese.

Perdices a la torera 'Bullfighters' partridge', garnished with ham, anchovies, green peppers and tomatoes.

Polvorones A dry, powdery sweetmeat, a speciality of Estepa, just west of Montilla-Moriles, made with flour, pork fat, sugar and cinnamon; often served with sherry or Montilla.

Rabo de toro Popular Córdoban stew of oxtail with vegetables.

Revuelto de aspárragos trigueros Scrambled eggs with young asparagus.

Salmorejo A thick Córdoban variation of *gazpacho*, made with garlic, olive oil and breadcrumbs, but without peppers or tomatoes.

Salsa de patatas A sauce from the Sierra Morena, north of Córdoba, made with fried puréed potatoes, peppers, bay leaf, cumin, olive oil and seasoning, and served with fish.

Ternera con alcachofas a la cordobesa Veal served with artichokes and cooked with Montilla and seasoning.

Tocino de cielo A sweet popular throughout Andalucía and made with egg yolks and sugar flavoured with vanilla.

Restaurants

Córdoba *El Caballo Rojo* (facing the Mosque, sophisticated Andalucian cooking); *Almudaina* (Córdoban cooking, which hardly rises to the charming surroundings); *Pepe 'El de la Judería'* (small bullfighters' haunt in the old Jewish quarter with delicious and reasonably priced *tapas*).

Montilla *Las Carmachas* (formerly owned by the Cobos family and known for its regional cooking). *See also* Antequera, page 140.

Navarra and the Basque Country

Navarra, to the west of Cataluña and extending from the Pyrenees to the Ebro basin, was a kingdom in its own right until it fell to Ferdinand the Catholic in 1512. At one time it extended over the Pyrenees, hence the alternative spelling of 'Navarre' for the portion now lying in France.

It is an autonomy with wide variations in climate between the subhumid conditions of the mountainous north and the dry, Mediterranean-like climate of central and southern Spain which is felt in the Ebro in southern Navarra. The soils are in general chalky, with deposits of silt and gravel along the river valleys, and are well suited to viticulture.

The vine-growing districts extend south from the provincial capital, Pamplona, and were demarcated in 1967. The DO Navarra is further subdivided into the *comarcas* of Baja Montaña, Valdizarbe, Tierra de Estella, Ribera Alta and Ribera Baja, with a combined area of 23,500 hectares under vines and an output in 1989 of 34·5 million litres of wine. The small area of the Rioja Baja spilling into the province of Navarra and including the town of San Adrián is separately described (*see* Rioja, pages 195–196). To the west of Navarra, the Basque country (País Vasco) and autonomy of Cantabria drink considerably more wine than they produce.

The predominant grape – until recently to the extent of some 80 percent – is the red Garnacha Tinta, but the producers are being encouraged by the government research station EVENA to plant Tempranillo in the interests of making longer-lived red wines more suited to oak-ageing. Some 1,000 hectares have been planted; there are smaller plantations of the red Graciano and Mazuelo, and of the white Viura, Malvasía and Garnacha Blanca. Cabernet Sauvignon, Merlot and Chardonnay are also now being grown here on an experimental scale.

In the past Navarra has been a prolific producer of sturdy red wines and fresh rosés, and they are said to have been a favourite of Catherine the Great of Russia in the early 18th century. In more recent times it has been the rosés – among the best in Spain – for which the region has been known and for which the Garnacha is well suited, but the present thrust is towards quality red wines. Bodegas Ochoa have produced an entirely delicious 100 percent Tempranillo, but in general EVENA is thinking along the lines of red wines made with some 50 percent Tempranillo, 30 percent Garnacha and 20 percent Cabernet Sauvignon. The Garnacha is also ideal for making fresh young wines (*vinos jovenes*) in the style of Beaujolais Nouveau by carbonic maceration.

Thanks to the innovative ideas of EVENA and the re-equipment of the cooperatives, Navarra is making great strides and is a region to watch. Like Aragón, the district may be visited en route to the Rioja from Barcelona via the A2 and A68 *autopistas*; and the A15 to Pamplona, branching off the road to Logroño beyond Tudela, will take you through the heart of the vine-growing areas.

Vintages

1976	*good*	1984	*red, good; white and rosé, very good*
1977	*fair*		
1978	*very good*	1985	*red, excellent; white, very good*
1979	*fair*		
1980	*fair*	1986	*good*
1981	*excellent*	1987	*good*
1982	*excellent*	1988	*very good*
1983	*very good*	1989	*very good*

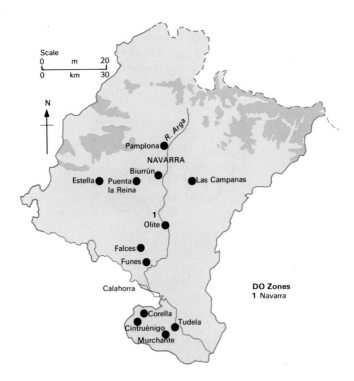

Agramont DO r p w dr ★★
One of the labels used by Bodegas CENALSA for its well-made wines.

Baja Montaña DO p ★→★★
Subdivision of the DO Navarra lying to the east of the province on the borders of Aragón. It is the highest and wettest of the vine-growing areas and produces some of the best rosés, of 12–15 percent strength.

Las Campanas
Village to the south of Pamplona and headquarters of one of the best-known wine concerns, VINICOLA NAVARRA, which uses the name for some of its wines.

Cantabria

Autonomy in the north of Spain, bounded by the Bay of Biscay and to the south by the Cantabrian Mountains. One of the wettest parts of Spain, it produces no wine except for the *pétillant* and astringent CHACOLI.

Carricas, Bodegas DO r p w dr ★★ 76, 83, 86

Olite (Navarra). DO Navarra. Old–established firm with *bodegas* picturesquely located in the subterranean passages of the 15th-century castle of OLITE. The innovative Carricas brothers label their wines as Mont–Plané: they include a 100 percent Garnacha rosé and reds made from 100 percent Garnacha, 100 percent Tempranillo or a blend of both.

Cenalsa, Bodegas DO r p w dr sw ★★

Murchante (Navarra). DO Navarra. This large firm, founded in 1982, has done much to improve the standards of winemaking in Navarra. It makes its wines either by blending and maturing musts bought from the cooperatives or by buying in grapes and vinifying them. Its labels include Agramont, Príncipe de Viana and Viña Rubican. The 1989 Príncipe de Viana, made with 100 percent Cabernet Sauvignon, was outstanding.

Chacolí (Txacoli) DO (r) w ★ DYA
A 'green', *pétillant* wine from the Basque country (País Vasco), containing only some 9–11·5 percent of alcohol. Although the vineyard area runs to only 47 hectares, it was, surprisingly, given DO status in 1990. The best of the wines are from around Guérnica, and especially from Guetaria and Zarauz on the coast near San Sebastián. There are two types, the red *txacoliñ zuri* and white *txacoliñ gorri*, made from the white Ondarrubi Zuria grape (akin to the Courbut Blanc) and the red Ondarrubi Beltza. Both are thin, astringent and rather acid, though the nose is fragrant enough; and the best thing is to drink them, as do the Vizcaínos, in mouthfuls with the excellent local shellfish.

Chivite, Bodegas Julián DO r p w dr res ★★→★★★ 81, 82, 83, 87
Cintruénigo (Navarra). DO Navarra. Founded in 1860, this family firm is the largest private wine concern in Navarra, with a total capacity of 18·75 million litres and vineyards and *bodegas* in other districts of Navarra and in the provinces of Logroño and Aragón. Its well-made wines range from fresh and fruity young whites and rosés to the attractive young red Viña Marcos, soft and plummy GRAN FEUDO *crianza* and the rich and oaky 125 Aniversario *reserva*.

Cintruénigo
Wine town just to the south of the Ebro in the RIBERA BAJA.

Corella w sw ★→★★
The village of Corella makes small amounts of a luscious Moscatel near CINTRUENIGO.

Ebro, River
After crossing the Rioja, the Ebro skirts the far south of Navarra, flowing through the RIBERA BAJA. The other more northerly wine districts lie in the basins of its tributaries, the Ega, Arga, Cidacos and Aragón.

EVENA

This is the government-funded 'Estación de Viticultura y Enología de Navarra'. Founded in 1981 and headed by Don Javier Ochoa, it is one of the most forward-looking and up-to-date oenological research establishments in Spain. Apart from field studies it maintains elaborately equipped laboratories at OLITE and its advice is available not only to the cooperatives and large concerns, but also to the humblest smallholder.

Ezcaba, Chacolí tinto de r dr pt ★

One of the few wines to be made in the mountainous north of Navarra, astringent and *pétillant*, like the better-known *chacolís* from CANTABRIA.

Falces r p ★→★★

Vine-growing area in the south of the RIBERA ALTA making good red and rosé wines and of interest for possessing one of the few monasterial *bodegas* to survive in Europe, that of Nuestra Señora de la Oliva.

Funes

This village between FALCES and Calahorra is the site of a well-preserved Roman winery dating from the first century AD. With cement paving and chambers for making and storing the wine, its capacity was of the order of some 75,000 litres.

Gran Feudo DO r p w dr ★★

Well-made and inexpensive range of wines from Bodegas Julián CHIVITE.

Irache, Bodegas DO r p w dr res ★★ 73, 78, 82, 85, 87

Estella (Navarra). DO Navarra. Well-known and old-established firm, whose *bodega* is picturesquely situated next to the beautiful monastery of Irache near Estella. A plum-coloured and full-bodied young Irache has been shipped to the UK. More mature wines, matured in its 2,000 American oak *barricas*, include red *crianza* Gran Irache, *reserva* Castillo Irache and *gran reserva* Real Irache, all made with a sizable proportion of Tempranillo.

Magaña, Bodegas r res ★★★ 81, 82, 83

Barillas (Navarra). Small *bodega* making distinguished red wines from 100 percent Merlot or a blend of Merlot and Cabernet Sauvignon from grapes grown on its own 72 hectares of vineyards.

Malumbres, Bodegas Vicente DO r p w dr ★★ 86, 88, 89

Corella (Navarra). DO Navarra. Sizable concern with 128 hectares of vineyards. The wines are labelled as Malumbres, Don Carvi and Viña Arances. Best are the Viña Arances rosé and red, made respectively from 100 percent Garnacha and from a blend of Tempranillo, Garnacha and Mazuelo.

Nuestra Señora del Romero, Cooperativa DO r p w dr ★★ 78, 81, 82

Cascante (Navarra). DO Navarra. This is one of the largest cooperatives in Spain and although situated in an area best known for its robust Garnacha wine, by modern methods it has succeeded in making wines such as the magnificently light, fresh and fruity Malón de Echaide rosé, an attractive young Nuevo Vino in the style of Beaujolais Nouveau, and good Señor de Cascante *gran reservas* which include 60 percent Tempranillo.

Ochoa, Bodegas DO r p w dr ★★→★★★ 75, 78, 80, 82, 85, 86, 88

Olite (Navarra). DO Navarra. This small firm, with 12 hectares of vineyards near OLITE, has been in family hands since 1845, and its oenologist, Don Javier Ochoa, is one of the most expert in the region. All of its wines are well made by modern methods and among the best from Navarra. They include a 100 percent Viura white, a 100 percent Garnacha rosé, and intensely fruity red *crianzas* and *reservas* made from 100 percent Tempranillo, 100 percent Cabernet Sauvignon or a blend of both.

Olite

Olite, south of Pamplona in one of the best of the winemaking areas of the RIBERA ALTA, is the site of a fortified palace, once the favourite residence of the Kings of Navarra. Begun by Charles III ('The Noble') in 1403, in its finished form it was the largest in Spain. Much remains, and it has entered a new lease of life as the Parador Nacional Príncipe de Viana. Lying more or less centrally in the wine area, this is an ideal base for visiting vineyards and *bodegas*, and its restaurant offers a good selection of regional dishes and local wines.

Pamplona

Pamplona, too, capital of Navarra, dear to Hemingway and famous for the bull-running through its streets during the Festival of San Fermín in early July, is a good centre for visiting the more northerly wine areas. An elegant city with a fine cathedral and a spacious central square, it possesses numerous good restaurants and an extremely comfortable five-star hotel, Los Tres Reyes.

Puente la Reina

A small town southwest of Pamplona and only a few kilometres from one of the most famous of Navarra's *bodegas*, that of the Señorío de SARRIA, Puente la Reina was one of the staging posts on the medieval pilgrim route from France to Santiago de Compostela, its medieval bridge the joining place of the two main roads over the Pyrenees. Well worth a visit are its great stone bridge across the River Arga, and honey-coloured churches, especially those of the Crucifix (Crucifijo) and Saint James (Santiago), decorated with the scallop shells of the pilgrims.

Ribera Alta DO r p (w dr) ★→★★★

Lying centrally between VALDIZARBE and BAJA MONTAÑA to the north and RIBERA BAJA to the south, this is the largest of the subregions, with 30 percent of the province's vineyards. The best of its wines are the soft, fruity reds and rosés from around OLITE, containing some 11·5–15 percent of alcohol.

Ribera Baja DO r (w dr) ★→★★

The Ribera Baja centres on the Ebro basin in the extreme south of the province. The climate is hotter and much drier than in the more northerly *comarcas* and the soils contain large amounts of alluvial silt, conditions producing large quantities of sugar in the grapes. Cascante and CINTRUENIGO are prolific producers of sturdy, full-bodied wines of up to 16 percent strength.

Sanguesa (r w) p

Area in the hilly BAJA MONTAÑA centring on the basin of the River Aragón. Its soils are a mixture of gravels and chalk, and the best of its wines are the fresh and drinkable rosés.

Sarría, Bodegas de DO r (p w dr) res ★★→★★★ 64, 70, 73, 75, 78, 81, 82, 84, 85

Puente la Reina (Navarra). DO Navarra. The Señorío de Sarría has been making wines since medieval times, and they have always been among the best from Navarra. The vineyards and winery, now the property of a local bank, were the brainchild of a Señor Huarte, of the large Spanish construction company, who bought the abandoned estate in 1952. Its 1,200 hectares embrace a large French-style château, orchards, farms, 60 kilometres of cypress-lined private roads and 100 hectares of vineyards, planted with Tempranillo (60 percent), Garnacha (20 percent), Mazuelo (10 percent) and Graciano (10 percent), together with extra growths in small amounts of Cabernet Sauvignon for red wines, Malvasía, Viura and Garnacha Blanca for whites.

Sadly, with the departure of the Huarte family, the model village is deserted, but the winery is still active. Made in Rioja style, the wines are matured in the *bodega*'s 6,000 *barricas*, 70 percent of Armagnac oak and the rest of American or Yugoslavian. They include a white Blanco Seco; a fresh young rosé; the sound three-year-old red Viña Ecoyen; a more mature and very smooth and fruity Viña del Perdón of some 13 percent strength; and the excellent old Gran Vino del Señorío de Sarría red *reservas*, which continue to improve for a decade or more in good vintages.

Tierra de Estella DO r p ★★→★★

Subdivision of the DO Navarra, lying to the northeast of the Rioja Alavesa and centred on the old town of Estella, a place of Romanesque churches and balconied houses overhanging the River Ega, and once the court of the Kings of Navarra. Its wines are very similar in character to those of VALDIZARBE further east, some full-bodied and robust reds and finer *reservas*.

The medieval bridge at Puente la Reina

Valdizarbe DO r p ★→★★★

A subdivision of the DO Navarra, immediately south of PAMPLONA in the basin of the River Arga. Because of its chalky soils and more temperate climate, produces perhaps the best wines of the region as a whole, including those of the Señorío de SARRIA and the VINICOLA NAVARRA.

Vinícola Navarra DO r (p w dr) res ★★ 78, 84

Las Campanas (Navarra). DO Navarra. Now controlled by Bodegas y Bebidas (formerly Savin, *see* page 174), this thoroughly traditional *bodega*, founded in 1880, is built against the wall of an old abbey on the pilgrim route. It still begins maturation of some of the wines (or did until recently) in large oak vats inherited from an earlier French concern. The dry white Las Campanas, made from 80 percent Viura and 20 percent Malvasía, is an admirable wine, clean and appley with refreshing acidity. The best of the reds is the Castillo de Tiebas *reserva*, full and fruity, the very embodiment of good traditional winemaking.

Wine and Food

The cooking of Navarra has similarities both with that of Aragón to the east, and the Basque country to the north. The mountain region in the north is famous for its lamb, served as *espárragos montañeses* ('mountain asparagus' – in fact, lambs' tails stewed in sauce), *cochifrito*, a fricassée (*see* Extremadura, page 115), or in a spicy *chilindrón* sauce (*see* Aragón, page 29). Another speciality is the trout, sometimes served with ham.

The local wines are varied enough to accompany these dishes without looking further afield. The vegetable dishes and fish call for a white wine; try a rosé with the snails and choose a good red with the lamb.

Alcachofas con almejas Artichokes with clams.

Caracoles a la corellana Snails cooked with garlic, parsley, cloves, bay leaves, thyme and lemon juice.

Caracolillas de Navarra Small snails cooked in earthenware dishes with olive oil, tomatoes, green peppers, chillis, breadcrumbs and seasoning.

Cardo a la Navarra Boiled cardoon (a vegetable resembling celery) with a white sauce with ham.

Ensalada de pimientos piquillo Fish salad with langoustines, monkfish, fennel, garlic, olive oil and sherry vinegar.

Huevos revueltos con ajos tiernos Eggs scrambled with young garlic shoots.

Menestra de habas de Tudela Fresh broad beans cooked with garlic, mint, saffron, almonds, artichoke hearts, boiled eggs, white wine, thyme and seasoning.

Remojón Orange and cod salad.

Ternasco asado Roast leg of lamb basted with lemon juice and white wine.

Tortilla de Tudela Omelette made with the excellent local asparagus.

Truchas a la Navarra The trout is first marinated and then cooked in an earthenware dish with onions, red wine, pepper, mint, thyme and bay leaves.

Truchas con jamón Fried trout served on top of or stuffed with slices of fried ham.

Restaurants

Olite *Parador Príncipe de Viana* (regional dishes and good list of local wines).

Pamplona *Sarasate* (salad of tiny squid; artichokes with clams); *Hartza* (hake with scallop sauce; *menestra*); *Josetxo* (particularly recommended for its game and *foie gras* with grapes; good wine list); *Rodero* (sophisticated French and local cuisine); *Shanti* (thoroughly traditional restaurant serving regional dishes).

Puente la Reina *Mesón del Peregrino* (pleasant country style).

Tafalla *Tubal* (crêpes with borage and clam sauce; pheasant breasts with onion).

Tudela *El Choko* (good local dishes, pleasant red house wine); *Mesón Julián*.

Rioja

Apart from sherry, Rioja is the best known of Spanish wines, and thanks to good quality and reasonable prices, foreign sales have leapfrogged in recent years: in Britain alone, they have increased from 180,000 litres in 1970 to the current figure of some 3·6 million litres, with corresponding huge increases in Denmark, Germany, Switzerland and the USA. The bulk of its wines are red and have traditionally been characterized by the long periods which they spend in cask and their oaky nose and flavour, but in recent years the Rioja has also been making a new style of white wine, light, fresh and fruity, without age in wood.

Rioja was the first of the Spanish regions to be demarcated, when a Consejo Regulador was set up in 1926 to control production and quality. It now comprises some 47,000 hectares of vineyards lying within the provinces of La Rioja (formerly known as Logroño), Alava and Navarra, with an average production over the last six years of 150 million litres of wine. The vineyards extend for some 120 kilometres on both sides of the River Ebro, which flows from the rocky Conchas de Haro in the hilly west of the region to Alfaro in the east. The valley is bounded by mountains on either side and is of a maximum width of 40 kilometres. The soils are a mixture of calcareous clay, ferruginous clay and alluvial silt, with a predominance of calcareous clay in the Rioja Alavesa (one of the three subregions) to the north of the river.

In the west of the area the climate is temperate and fairly predictable, with mild, wet springs, short, hot summers, long, warm autumns and a little snow and frost in winter. The hotter and more Mediterranean-like Rioja Baja in the east is classified as semi-arid.

The DO Rioja is divided into the three subregions of Rioja Alta, Rioja Alavesa and Rioja Baja, of which the first two produce the more delicate wines. In this chapter the subregion, not the province or DO zone, is given in brackets.

Wine was being made in the Rioja long before the Roman occupation of the area; and the traditional method, still practised in the *bodegas* of smallholders, was to tip the bunches of grapes, stalks and all, into open stone troughs or *lagos*. Fermentation then proceeded in stages, with progressively firmer crushing of the

grapes. Production of Rioja in its present style began after the double disasters of oidium and phylloxera in France in the late 1800s, when French *négociants* moved into the district and introduced the methods employed in Bordeaux, notably the destalking of the grapes and the ageing of the wines in 225-litre oak casks. Long after the French reduced the period in wood, the Riojans continued to age the wines, both red and white, for long years in oak – hence the characteristically vanilla-like bouquet and flavour – and it is only recently that more attention has been given to bottle-age. With the widespread production of cold-fermented white wines without maturation in cask, matters have recently turned full circle, and wine critics are now beginning to lament the passing of the old-style white Riojas with a character all their own!

The first great Rioja boom took place during the latter decades of the 19th century; and the *bodegas* constructed at that period – Riscal, Murrieta, López de Heredia, CVNE, La Rioja Alta and the rest – are still among those producing the best wines. There was another phase of expansion, financed by banks, sherry firms, Spanish industrialists and foreign wine concerns, during the 1970s. These *bodegas* are characterized by their size and the modernity of their equipment, but all of them, in conformity with the regulations of

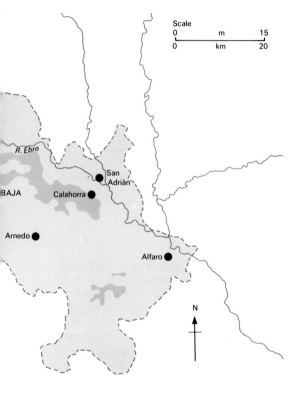

the Consejo Regulador, mature their better red wines in the traditional 225-litre oak *barricas*. More recently, a new generation of small *bodegas* has sprung up, often based on old houses or castles, relying entirely on grapes grown in their own vineyards.

Although most of the large *bodegas* own sizable vineyards of their own, and some of the newer ones, such as Domecq, have embarked on extensive new plantations, traditional patterns of agriculture persist, with most of the grapes being grown by smallholders on plots interspersed by wheat, potatoes and other vegetables. All the large concerns buy substantial amounts of fruit from the independent farmers, and some also make use of wine made in the cooperatives, of which there are some 30 in the area. In contrast to Bordeaux, the vines are normally grown low, without supporting stakes and wires, and pruned *en vaso* ('goblet-shaped'), with three *brazos* or main stems, each of which bears two *sarmientos* or grafted shoots, bearing two bunches of grapes, so there are 12 in all.

Grape Varieties

Of the many vine varieties formerly grown in the Rioja, the Consejo Regulador now approves only seven:

Black

Tempranillo Also known in other parts of Spain as the Ull de Llebre, Cencibel, Tinto Fino or Tinto del País, this is the Rioja grape *par excellence*, making up 50 percent or more of the red wines from the Rioja Alta and some 80 percent or more of those from the Rioja Alavesa. Thick-skinned and intensely black, its grapes produce wines of 10·5–13 percent alcohol, with good acid balance and very suitable for ageing, but tending on their own to be short-lived.

Graciano Small, round and black, the grapes make fresh and aromatic wines, but are too scarce and produce wines too low in alcohol (10–12 percent) to be used on their own.

Mazuelo Large and of pointed shape, the grapes yield musts rich in colour, extract and tannin, valuable in making wines which are aged for a long time in wood.

Garnacha/Garnacho Medium-sized, thin-skinned and resistant to oidium, this is the typical grape of the Rioja Baja and is widely grown in many other parts of Spain and also, under the name of Grenache, in the Rhône Valley in France. Its musts contain up to 15–16 percent alcohol and are blended with others to contribute alcoholic degree and body. On their own, however, Garnacha wines oxidize very easily and it is difficult to judge their age from the colour, since they soon turn a brick red.

In addition to these native varieties, plantings of **Cabernet Sauvignon** are permitted on an experimental scale.

White

Viura Also known as the Macabeo in other parts of Spain, the Viura yields musts with about 11 percent alcohol and plenty of tartaric acid. Being resistant to oxidation, they are particularly suitable for making light and fruity white wines by cold fermentation.

Malvasía Vigorous and large-leaved, these vines are somewhat prone to attack by mildew. The grapes, white tinted with red when fully mature, produce fresh wines of about 11 percent, often made in admixture with Viura.

Garnacha Blanca Not so much used in the Rioja as the other two varieties, the grapes produce pleasant white wines, but higher in alcohol and with less acid than the others.

There is a popular superstition that red Riojas are made in *solera* (*see* Sherry, page 233). This is entirely untrue, but they *are* made by blending wines from different grape varieties, often grown in separate areas of the region, and there is sometimes a limited admixture of wines of different vintage, but the bottle must contain not less than 85 percent of the vintage stated on the label. It was usual in the past – and the custom lingers in other parts of Spain – to label them with a description such as *3° año* or *5° año*, meaning that the wine had been bottled during the third or fifth calendar year after the harvest. Without knowing how long the wine had been in bottle, it was impossible to say how old it was or in what year it had been made; all exported wines are now labelled with a vintage.

Vintages

Because of the more predictable climate and the former practice of blending a proportion of better wine with the poorer growths, in the past vintage years were not as variable as in Bordeaux, but are important, and increasingly so as the Consejo Regulador tightens the regulations. Outstanding among earlier years were:

1915	1931	1949	1968
1920	1934	1952	1970
1922	1942	1955	1973
1924	1947	1958	
1925	1948	1964	

Ratings for more recent years follow, though it must be said that in some generally disastrous years, when the crop, because of hailstorms or excessive rain, was affected by mildew or oidium, the only two pests in the Rioja, individual *bodegas* still made good wines – such as the 1971 red Riscal or 1977 Cune.

Year	Yield (millions of litres)	Rating
1974	131	*average*
1975	84	*fair*
1976	93	*good*
1977	65	*very bad*
1978	81	*excellent*
1979	140	*average*

1980	125	*good*
1981	130	*very good*
1982	113	*excellent*
1983	106	*good*
1984	130	*average*
1985	176	*good*
1986	120	*good*
1987	133	*very good*
1988	132	*good*
1989	160	*very good*
1990	166	*very good*

As when visiting most wine areas, it is a great advantage to have a car, though, once in Logroño, there is a charming local train which wends its leisurely way by Fuenmayor, Cenicero and Briones to Haro, depositing you on the doorstep of many of the *bodegas* and affording better views of the Ebro and the vineyards than those from the main road.

The quickest approach to the region is to fly to Bilbao, hire a car and drive to Haro or Logroño, one and a half to two hours away off the A68 *autopista*. An alternative is to take the car ferry to Santander and join the A68 at Bilbao, or, again, drive from Barcelona by way of Zaragoza and the A2. This route will take you through the heart of the Rioja Baja. It is easy enough to make a leisurely circuit of the Rioja Alta and Rioja Alavesa in a day by driving from Logroño to Haro on the N232 by way of Fuenmayor, Cenicero and Briones, and returning by the road north of the Ebro, also labelled the N232, through Labastida, Abalos and Laguardia. It is especially worthwhile to visit Briones and Laguardia, just off the road, two of the most picturesque hilltop towns of the Rioja.

Stay either in Logroño, Haro or Santo Domingo de la Calzada for the Rioja Alta and Rioja Alavesa, or in Calahorra for the Rioja Baja (*see* A–Z listing for hotels). There are numerous restaurants serving good regional food and wines in towns and villages up and down the region (*see* Wine and Food, page 203).

Abalos

This picturesque village east of Haro is set in a small enclave of the RIOJA ALTA to the north of the Ebro. Dominated by the mountains of the Sierra Cantábrica and surrounded by vineyards, it possesses an old palace and impressive 15th-century church, and is the headquarters of Bodegas REAL DIVISA.

AGE, Bodegas Unidas DO r (p) w dr res ★→★★ 73, 74, 78, 80, 81, 82, 83, 84, 85, 87

Fuenmayor (Rioja Alta). This large *bodega* was formed in 1964 by the union of three much older concerns, Azpilicueta, Cruz García and Entrena, and is now jointly owned by the American firm of Schenley and the Banco Español de Crédito. Its wines are vinified in Navarrete and bottled in the main *bodega* in Fuenmayor. The best of them are the red Marqués de Romeral and Siglo *reservas*, the latter presented in a distinctive sack. Older vintages of Romeral were very fine. The *bodega* also makes dry white Romeral and Siglo and a semi-sweet Blanco Parral.

Ageing

Riojas, both red and white, have traditionally been aged in cask for much longer than Bordeaux or Burgundy wines, and have sometimes been criticized for a pronounced oaky nose and flavour (*see* Oak). The present trend is to cut down on the period in cask and to give the better red wines at least a year or two in bottle. *See also* Crianza.

Alambrado

A fine wire mesh often used around bottles of *reservas*, now decorative but originally designed to prevent the fraudulent replacement of the contents.

Alavesas, Bodegas DO r (p) w dr res ★★→★★★ 68, 70, 73, 74, 75, 76, 78, 80, 82, 83, 84, 85, 86, 87

Laguardia (Rioja Alavesa). A fairly new concern with 200 hectares of vineyards, and a modern *bodega* with a capacity of 18 million litres and 8,000 oak BARRICAS, which has rapidly made a name for the quality of its wines. Made entirely from grapes grown in the near vicinity, its red wines (containing 100 percent Tempranillo) are light in

colour and body, fragrant, soft, quick to mature and thoroughly typical of the RIOJA ALAVESA. The whites are pleasantly acidic and refreshing. Both reds and whites are labelled as Solar de Samaniego (after a local poet).

Alfaro
Town at the eastern extreme of the RIOJA BAJA. The home of two *bodegas*, it takes its name from El Faro ('the lighthouse'), the furthest point on the Ebro reached by the Phoenicians in their shallow-draught boats. It is an attractive little place with some fine baronial houses and a beautiful 17th-century church.

Amezola de la Mora, Bodegas DO r 86, 87
Torremontalbo (Rioja Alta) Winemaking at Torremontalbo, a historic castle between Logroño and Haro, was revived in 1986, when the 130-year-old cellars were completely re-equipped. The estate-grown wines show great promise.

Arnedo
Picturesquely situated in the gorge of the River Cidacos with its red sandstone cliffs, Arnedo is one of the pleasantest

of the towns of the RIOJA BAJA and possesses two hotels, the three-star Victoria and two-star Virrey, and a most individual restaurant, Sopitas (*see* page 203).

Artadi DO r ★★→★★★ 89
Label used by COSECHEROS ALAVESES for its well-made young wines.

Banda Azul DO r ★★
Made by Federico PATERNINA, this is one of the biggest-selling of red *crianza* Riojas. It went through a bad period after the transfer to the large modern *bodega* in Haro, but thanks to a massive investment in new oak casks, it is now a pleasant and reliable young wine.

Barón de Ley, Bodegas DO r ★★★ 85
Mendavia (Rioja Alta). A new single-estate wine from a concern with close ties to Bodegas EL COTO. The elegant and well-balanced 1985 is the first vintage to be released.

Barrica
The 225-litre oak cask in which all the CRIANZA wines must statutorily be matured is a legacy of the *vignerons* from Bordeaux who settled in the Rioja during the phylloxera epidemic of the late 19th century.

Berberana, Bodegas DO r (w dr) res ★→★★★ 70, 73, 75, 76, 78, 80, 82, 83, 85
Cenicero (Rioja Alta). The company, now one of the largest in the Rioja, was founded in 1877 by the Berberana family in Ollauri, where it still maintains cellars for ageing the wines in bottle. It underwent a major expansion in 1972 and belonged for a period to RUMASA after which it was temporarily nationalized and then sold to various shareholders in 1985. The vinification plant in Cenicero incorporates modern stainless steel fermentation tanks and a huge ageing floor accommodating 40,000 oak BARRICAS. Berberana embarked on ambitious new plantations of some 900 hectares at Monte Yerga near Aldeanueva del Ebro in

the RIOJA BAJA, growing a high proportion of Tempranillo and Viura in addition to the Garnacha typical of the area, but these are now controlled by a separate company. The red CARTA DE PLATA is one of the biggest-selling *crianza* wines; it also makes an inexpensive *sin crianza* Preferido; and full-bodied and velvety older wines, including CARTA DE ORO, together with a Berberana Reserva and Berberana Gran Reserva, of which the 1973 was outstanding.

Berceo, Bodegas DO r w dr p res ★★→★★★ 82, 83, 85
Haro (Rioja Alta). Sister ship of Bodegas GURPEGUI, making worthwhile red wines.

Beronia, Bodegas DO r w dr res ★★→★★★ 75, 78, 80, 83, 85
Ollauri (Rioja Alta). The firm, with ten hectares of vineyards in one of the best areas of the RIOJA ALTA, began operations in 1970, working from a small *bodega* in the village of Ollauri. Later it moved to an elegant new winery in the midst of the vineyards, and the intention of Don Javier Bilbao Iturbe was to make wines by traditional methods on a limited scale, but also to take advantage of modern technology. Such was the success among the cognoscenti of the dry, fruity and well-balanced red Beron and the Beronia *reservas* made with a high percentage of Tempranillo that in 1982 the *bodega* was taken over by the sherry firm of González Byass, which has since more than tripled production.

Bilbainas, Bodegas DO r (p) w dr sw sp res ★★ →★★★ 70, 73, 74, 75, 76, 78, 83, 85
Haro (Rioja Alta). Bilbainas, founded in 1901, was one of the first firms to build a *bodega* adjacent to the newly opened railhead from Bilbao, and its wines have long been known in the UK, where at one time it maintained its own cellars and sales office. It owns 275 hectares of vineyards, mostly around Haro, with a smaller holding at Leza in the RIOJA ALAVESA. Its wines include the dry white and red Viña Paceta and sweeter Cepa de Oro; a light and first-rate Viña Zaco; the more fully bodied red VIÑA POMAL, made

basically with grapes from Leza; and good Vendimia Especial *reservas*. The firm also makes wines by the champagne method (*see* Sparkling Wines, page 255).

Bodegas y Bebidas

Formerly called Savin, this is one of the largest Spanish wine companies, specializing in inexpensive branded wine made to good standards. It also possesses wineries up and down Spain; in the Rioja it operates a *bodega* at Aldeanueva del Ebro in the RIOJA BAJA and also controls CAMPO VIEJO in Logroño and the MARQUES DEL PUERTO in Fuenmayor.

Bordelesa

Alternative name, reflecting its Bordeaux origins, for the 225-litre oak BARRICA.

Briones

A little east of Haro, the small hilltop town of Briones, with its stone-built baronial houses, statuesque church and long views over the Ebro, is one of the most attractive in the RIOJA ALTA.

Calahorra

The largest town in the RIOJA BAJA, the birthplace of Quintilian and famous for its protracted siege by Pompey in the first century BC, Calahorra is a convenient stopping place en route to Logroño from Zaragoza and as a base for visiting the subregion. There is a comfortable Parador, the Marco Fabio Quintiliano.

Campeador DO r res ★★★ 80, 81

Label used by MARTINEZ LACUESTA for its oaky old *reservas* and *gran reservas*.

Campo Viejo, Bodegas DO r (p w dr) res ★→★★★ 70, 71, 73, 78, 80, 81, 82, 84, 85

Logroño (Rioja Alta). Owned by the ubiquitous firm of BODEGAS Y BEBIDAS and situated in Logroño itself, Campo Viejo is one of the largest firms in the Rioja with a total

capacity of 50 million litres. Its widely advertised San
Asensio is among the biggest selling of young *sin crianza*
Riojas, and the *bodega* also produces some big red *reservas*,
including the first-rate Marqués de Villamagna.

Carlos Serres, Bodegas DO r (p w sw) res ★→★★★ 70, 73, 75,
79, 80, 83, 85
Haro (Rioja Alta). Well-known Haro firm, whose younger
wines are labelled as Carlos Serres. Its best wines are the red
Carlos Serres and Onomástica *reservas* and *gran reservas*.

Carta de Oro DO r ★★
Fruity *crianza* wine from BERBERANA.

Carta de Plata DO r ★
A young *crianza* red from BERBERANA. It has been criticized
in Spain for lack of consistency, but the quality of the wine
shipped abroad is always reliable.

Casa del Vino
See Laguardia

Castillo de Cuzcurrita DO r res dr ★★→★★★ 75, 85
Rio Tirón (Rioja Alta). The old 14th-century castle houses
its own small *bodega* which makes good but somewhat
astringent red wines from grapes grown in its own
vineyards. The wines are labelled as Señorio de Cuzcurrita,
Castillo Cuzcurrita and Reserva Conde de Alacha.

Castillo Ygay res ★★★★ 17, 25, 34, 42, 62, 68
Gran reserva from the MARQUES DE MURRIETA, made only in
exceptional years. The 1934 was one of the most complete
and beautiful Riojas I have ever tasted.

Cenicero
Town on the Ebro west of Logroño in the RIOJA ALTA, and
the headquarters of five important *bodegas*. It was the burial
place of the Roman legions stationed in the area, hence the
name, which in Spanish means 'ashtray'. Cenicero stages an

interesting wine festival in September, held in its large, covered *pelota* court.

Compañía Vinícola del Norte de España (CVNE) DO r (p) w dr sw res ★★→★★★★ 70, 73, 74, 75, 76, 78, 82, 83, 85, 87
Haro (Rioja Alta). CVNE was founded in 1879 in the full flush of the 19th-century Rioja boom, and has been making excellent wines ever since – at one time they included sparkling wine made by the champagne method and a brandy. The *crianza* Cune is one of the most reliable of young red Riojas; and the Imperial and VIÑA REAL *reservas*, the latter a full-bodied and aromatic Alavesa made in Elciego, are outstanding. CVNE is now making a new-style white Rioja without maturation in wood, but its Monopole, so popular in Spain itself with its restrained hint of oak, remains one of the best of traditional white Riojas. Its superior single-vineyard red wine, CONTINO, is grown in 40 hectares of vineyards at La Serna, in the Rioja Alavesa west of Oyón. These big, mellow, full-bodied wines with blackberry flavour and long finish are among the best from the Rioja.

Conde de los Andes DO res ★★★★ 64, 70, 73
Gran reserva from Federico PATERNINA, named after the Madrid gastronome, and of appropriate quality.

Conde de Valdemar DO res ★★★ 73, 75, 82, 83, 85
Excellent red *reservas* from MARTINEZ BUJANDA.

Contino DO res ★★★★ 75, 85
Very superior single-vineyard red *reserva* made in the RIOJA ALAVESA by the Sociedad Vinícola Laserna, owned by COMPAÑIA VINICOLA DEL NORTE DE ESPAÑA.

Corral, Bodegas DO r (p w dr) ★★→★★★ 71, 73, 75, 76, 78, 80, 81, 85
Navarrete (Rioja Alta). One of the newer *bodegas* located in Navarrete. Best of its wines is the Don Jacobo red *reserva*.

Cosecheros Alaveses, Sociedad Cooperativa DO r w dr
★★→★★★ 87, 88, 89
Laguardia (Rioja Alavesa). Innovative cooperative best
known for its unoaked red Artadi, well-balanced and fruity.

Crianza
Literally 'nursing'; in terms of wines the word refers to
their maturation in oak cask. The regulations of the
Consejo Regulador are strict; and to be labelled '*con
crianza*', a Rioja, red or white, must be matured for two
years with a minimum of one in a 225-litre oak BARRICA
and not released before the third year. For *reservas* and *gran
reservas*, *see* Glossary, pages 19–20. Riojas need not,
however, be aged in oak to qualify for *denominación de
origen*. There are no rules as regards the ageing of wines *sin
crianza* ('without ageing'), which may nevertheless spend a
few months in cask.

Cumbrero DO r w dr ★★
Label used by Bodegas MONTECILLO for its excellent young
red and white Riojas.

CVNE
Abbreviation of COMPAÑIA VINICOLA DEL NORTE DE ESPAÑA,
whose wines are known colloquially in Spain as 'Cune'.

Domecq, Bodegas DO r (p) w dr ★★→★★★ 73, 76, 78, 81, 82,
83, 85
Elciego (Rioja Alavesa). The origins of the company date
from the early 1970s, when the sherry concern of Pedro
Domecq and the Canadian firm of Seagram joined forces to
take over Bodegas PALACIO. The partners later parted ways,
and Pedro Domecq constructed its own *bodega* with
modern stainless steel fermentation tanks and a capacity of
some 22,000 oak BARRICAS for maturing the wines. It has
also planted 571 hectares of new vineyards in one of the
best parts of the RIOJA ALAVESA, a venture notable among
other aspects for training the vines in Bordeaux style, rather
than pruning them low in the traditional Riojan fashion.

Apart from a pleasant and inexpensive young Viña Eguia, the best known of its wines are the dry white and red DOMECQ DOMAIN (launched in Spain as Privilegio del Rey Sancho). After a promising start with the red 1973, the 1976 was a first-rate Alavesa wine, well-balanced, deep and fruity. The MARQUES DE ARIENZO *reservas* are excellent wines, fruity, complex and with long finish.

Domecq Domain DO r w dr ⟦★★→★★★⟧ 75, 76, 78
Label used abroad for the well-made wines sold in Spain as Privilegio del Rey Sancho.

Ebro, River
The Ebro flows through the Rioja from west to east, entering it through the rocky gorge of the Conchas de Haro and leaving it near Alfaro in the Rioja Baja. The vineyards extend upwards from both sides of the river or are located in the valleys of its seven tributaries, the Tirón, Oja, Najerilla, Iregua, Leza, Cidacos and Alama.

El Coto, Bodegas DO r w dr ★★→★★★ 73, 76, 78, 79, 80, 82
Oyón (Rioja Alavesa). Large *bodega* founded in 1973. Later acquired by Alexis Lichine, it has recently been bought by the BARON DE LEY and has a capacity of 6·5 million litres and 8,000 oak BARRICAS. Its red wines, made with 100 percent Tempranillo from the RIOJA ALAVESA, the best labelled as Coto de Imaz, are light and very soft with a fragrant nose. Among the best were the well-balanced 1978 and 1982, with deep raspberry flavour.

Elciego
Hill village in the RIOJA ALAVESA over the Ebro from Cenicero, a place of steep, narrow streets, with a church at the top dominating the surrounding vineyards, and famous as the home of the *bodegas* of the MARQUES DE RISCAL.

Estación de Viticultura y Enología
Government laboratory in HARO, working in conjunction with the Consejo Regulador. Its main work is the analysis

of wines to ensure that they conform to the standards of the *Reglamento*, but it also conducts research into the production of Rioja wines. It possesses an excellent wine museum.

Faustino Martínez, Bodegas DO r (p) w dr res $\boxed{\star\star}\mapsto\star\star\star$ 64, 68, 70, 73, 74, 75, 76, 78, 81, 82, 86

Oyón (Rioja Alavesa). The Martínez family has been making good wines in Oyón, just north of Haro, since before 1860, and began bottling them in 1931. It is still a family firm, and owns 400 hectares of vineyards in one of the best areas of the RIOJA ALAVESA. There are some 23,000 BARRICAS in its cellars; but the *bodega* does not believe in ageing its wines overlong in oak, and its *gran reserva*, the Faustino I, outstanding in the 1964, 1968 and 1970 vintages, spends only two years there, followed by more in bottle. The other red wines are the Faustino V and Faustino VII; and the *bodega* was one of the first in the field with a new-style white Rioja, Faustino VII, not aged in oak, light and fresh with an intriguing lemony finish. The *bodega* markets a *vino joven* (young) red, made in traditional fashion by fermenting whole grapes in a *lago*: it is a dark plum colour, with yeasty nose and good blackberry flavour reminiscent of Beaujolais Nouveau.

Franco–Españolas, Bodegas DO r (p) w dr sw res $\star\to\star\star\star$ 64, 68, 74, 76, 78, 82, 85

Logroño (Rioja Alta). Large and old-established firm with *bodegas* in the heart of Logroño just across the bridge over the Ebro, taken over by RUMASA in 1973 and since resold. The semi-sweet white Diamante has long been a favourite in Spain and goes well with desserts. The *bodega* also makes dry white Viña Soledad. Its Rioja Bordón is a full-bodied red, but perhaps the most stylish of the wines are the lighter Royal *reservas* and Royal Tête de Cuvée *gran reservas*.

Fuenmayor

On the main road from LOGROÑO to HARO and close to the Ebro, Fuenmayor, together with CENICERO, is next in importance to Haro among the Riojan wine towns.

Gomez Cruzado, Bodegas

Haro (Rioja Alta). One of the old *bodegas* in Haro, at one time belonging to Carbonell, the well-known producers of olive oil, the company now belongs to Bodegas Campo Burgo in the Rioja Baja.

Gran Condal DO r w dr p res ★★→★★★

Label used by Bodegas RIOJA SANTIAGO. The reds especially are of good quality.

Granja de Nuestra Señora de Remelluri DO r res ★★★ 76, 83, 85, 86, 88

Ribas (Rioja Alavesa). This small, family-owned *bodega* was founded by Don Jaime Rodriguez in 1970. With 40 hectares of vineyards planted high up on the slopes of the Sierra Cantábrica, it is one of the few in the Rioja to make wine entirely from its own grapes. Much appreciated by connoisseurs, they are soft and fruity with long finish.

Gurpegui, Bodegas DO r p w dr ★★→★★★ 88, 89

San Adrián (Rioja Baja). Large family firm, founded in 1921 and owning 250 hectares of vineyards in the vicinity of San Adrián. A large supplier of bulk wine, its inexpensive bottled wine is sold under the label of Viñadrian. The rosé has always been particularly fresh and good. *See also* Berceo.

Haro

Near the western tip of the region, Haro, a busy little town with a population of some 9,000, is the wine capital of the RIOJA ALTA and the home of no less than a dozen *bodegas*. Built uphill and downhill above the Ebro, it is a place of narrow streets and stylish old houses, with a wide central square, one of whose points of interest is the wine shop of Juan Gonzalez Muga specializing in old and rare vintages and special offers on Riojas from the local *bodegas*. Haro is the headquarters of a government wine laboratory, the ESTACION DE VITICULTURA Y ENOLOGIA. It now boasts a good hotel, Los Agustinos, housed in an old convent, and there are a couple of good restaurants (*see* page 203). At Briñas, on the road north to Vitoria facing the rocky Conchas de Haro, there is a wine museum displaying bottles from most of the *bodegas* in the Rioja.

Hormilleja

Village near Nájera in the centre of vineyards producing most of the Garnacha grown in the RIOJA ALTA.

Labastida

Village in the RIOJA ALAVESA northeast of Haro, and home of one of the best cooperatives in the region.

Labastida, Unión de Cosecheros de DO r (p) w dr res

★ → ★★★

Labastida (Rioja Alavesa). The cooperative, founded in 1956 and enlarged in 1965, has some 160 *socios* (members) growing grapes in three of the best areas of the region (Labastida, Samaniego and Villalba). With a total capacity of three million litres, it is one of the few cooperatives in the Rioja to possess oak BARRICAS and to bottle its wines.

The quality of the fruit is reflected in that of its wines. The fresh young white, unaged in oak and made almost entirely from Viura with a small amount of Blanquirroja, is the best of its type in the Rioja. A pale straw colour, round and intensely fruity, it is made not by cold fermentation but by leaving the grapes overnight in a cement *depósito*, running off the must which separates under the weight of the load and transferring it to a vat for fermentation. The reds, too, are first-rate – higher in strength than most Alavesas, and containing up to 13·5–14 percent alcohol, they include a pleasant young Manuel Quintano; a well-balanced Montebuena; and excellent Castrijo and Castillo Labastida *reservas* and *gran reservas* with a fruity Tempranillo nose, raspberry flavour and long finish.

Laguardia

Old walled town crowning a hill in the heart of the RIOJA ALAVESA, and a landmark for miles around. Its narrow streets and old, dark houses are honeycombed with small peasant *bodegas*, now mostly disused, and there are three large modern wineries on the outskirts. Quiet enough on weekdays, at weekends and on holidays it is a target for visitors from Bilbao and San Sebastián, who come to picnic and to fill their carafes with local wine.

The old baronial house of the Fabulista Samaniego, the 18th-century author of some rather pointless fables, formerly housed a pleasant hotel, but has recently been converted into a centre for the study of Alavesa wines, the Casa del Vino. Apart from its interesting exhibits on local history as well as viticulture and oenology, it possesses modern laboratories and advises the smaller producers or *cosecheros* of the region.

Lagunilla, Bodegas DO r (p) w dr res ★★→★★★ 70, 73, 75, 78, 80, 81, 82, 85

Fuenmayor (Rioja Alta). Founded in 1885, the firm was one of the pioneers in introducing American grafts after the phylloxera epidemic of the early 1900s. It now occupies a large modern *bodega* outside Fuenmayor, and was bought by Croft, part of the IDV (International Distillers and Vintners) group. The best of its wines are the red Viña Herminia *reservas*.

Lan, Bodegas DO r (p) w dr res ★★→★★★ 70, 73, 75, 78, 81, 83, 86

Fuenmayor (Rioja Alta). Large modern *bodega* founded in 1969, taken over by RUMASA and now one of those controlled by Don Marcos Eguizábal. Equipped with the most modern and sophisticated plant, it possesses 14,000 BARRICAS for ageing its wines, which include a fresh white Lan not matured in oak; a fruity red Lan *crianza* wine; and Lander and Viña Lanciano *reservas*, often outstanding.

Libano, Señorío de DO r res ★★★ 83, 85

Small *bodega* making sophisticated Castillo de Sajazarra *reservas* from grapes grown on its 25 hectares of vineyards.

Logroño

Capital of the province of La Rioja, Logroño, with a population of 111,000, is the only large town in the Rioja and the commercial centre of the wine industry. It is a handsome city by the Ebro, with a spacious tree-lined square, the Espolón, the focus of the Fiesta de SAN MATEO, held from September 21 to mark the beginning of the grape-picking season. It is the headquarters of the Consejo Regulador and of the Grupo de Exportadores and also of three of the largest Rioja *bodegas*, FRANCO-ESPAÑOLAS, CAMPO VIEJO and OLARRA. It possesses numerous good restaurants (*see* page 203), and its hotels are the four-star Bracos and Carlton Rioja, and three-star Gran Hotel; but a favourite with the wine community is the three-star Murrieta, which has the advantage of a good cafeteria and restaurant.

López Agos, Bodegas

See Marqués del Puerto, Bodegas

López de Heredia, Viña Tondonia, R DO r (p) w dr sw res
★★→★★★★ 68, 70, 73, 75, 76, 78, 81, 82, 84, 85

Haro (Rioja Alta). López de Heredia was founded in 1877 at the height of the phylloxera epidemic in France, and is one of the most traditional of the *bodegas*; all its buildings are of quarried stone, the vessels for making and maturing the wine are of American oak, and the cellars, like the famous El Calado, are tunnelled out of the sandstone 17 metres below ground, so that the temperature remains an even 12°C with a relative humidity of 80 percent all the year round. The wines, made with no concessions to modernity, start rather tannic, but age gloriously after long periods in oak. They include a beautiful white 1971 Tondonia with a subtle blend of oak and fruit, and the legendary 1953, a revelation to people who think that white wines of this age must necessarily be flat and oxidized. The youngest of the reds is the stylish young Cubillo; older reds include Tondonia and Bosconia *reservas*, the Bosconia being rather softer and fuller-bodied. Some of the *reservas*, such as the 1942 Bosconia, can only be described as classics.

Marqués de Arienzo DO r res ★★★ 76, 78, 81, 82, 85
Label used by Bodegas DOMECQ for its excellent red *reservas* and *gran reservas*.

Marqués de Cáceres, Bodegas DO r (p) w dr res ★★→★★★
70, 73, 75, 78, 81, 85, 86, 87
Cenicero (Rioja Alta). The *bodega* was founded in 1970 by Don Enrique Forner, who, with his brother, owns châteaux in the Haut-Médoc; its methods are more similar to those of Bordeaux than most of the concerns in the Rioja, since it was planned with advice from Professor Peynaud of Bordeaux University. It describes itself as a 'Unión Vitivinícola', grapes being supplied by a group of substantial local producers.

The inexpensive Rivarey reds are being phased out and most of the wines are sold under the Marqués de Cáceres label. The *reservas* are fruity, well balanced and less oaky than the typical red Riojas, with a blackberry flavour and long finish. The firm was the first to introduce a new-style white Rioja made by cold fermentation and unaged in cask. Exceptionally light, fresh and fruity, it is still perhaps the best wine of its type. The *bodega* has now added a CRIANZA white, of which the 1987, with an attractive lemon and vanilla taste, is the first vintage.

Marqués de Murrieta, Bodegas DO r (p) w dr ★★★→★★★★
60, 68, 70, 76, 78, 80, 81, 82, 83, 84, 85

Ygay (Rioja Alta). Second only in seniority to the MARQUES
DE RISCAL, the *bodega* was founded by the Marqués de
Murrieta in Ygay, a village just east of Logroño, in 1872. It
remained in the family until a few years ago, when it was
bought by Vicente Cebrián, Conde de Creixel. With Riscal,
it has been regarded as the aristocrat of Riojas, and the
tradition has been to age the red wines for very long
periods in oak; and until new regulations came into force
they were kept in BARRICA and bottled only immediately
prior to shipment. Its new owner has lovingly restored the
old buildings, and has constructed a new fermentation plant
and made plans for extending the *bodega*'s vineyards so as to
supply not just 40 percent of the grapes, as in the past, but
the whole requirement – thus making Murrieta a single-
estate wine.

The youngest of the reds is the soft and fruity Etiqueta
Blanca, and there is also a very round and fruity oak-aged
white wine. Pride of the *reservas* is the superb CASTILLO
YGAY, one of the most sought-after and expensive of
Spanish wines. It is made only at very rare intervals, the
next in line after the glorious 1934 being the 1942, 1962 and
1968. For connoisseurs of old and rare wines, the *bodega*
rates the best vintages of earlier years as 1920, 1925, 1931,
1934, 1935, 1942, 1948 and 1949.

Marqués de Riscal, Herederos del DO r (p) res ★★→★★★★
64, 65, 68, 70, 71, 73, 76, 78, 80, 81, 82, 83, 86
Elciego (Rioja Alavesa). Founded in 1860 by Don Camilo,
Hurtado de Amézaga, Marqués de Riscal, the *bodega* was
designed by a *vigneron* from Bordeaux and was the first in
the Rioja to use French methods for making its wines.
Then, as now, a proportion of Cabernet Sauvignon was
used, though as elsewhere in the RIOJA ALAVESA the
preponderant grape is the Tempranillo.

Riscal now has 20 hectares of vineyards under Cabernet,
half of the vines old and the rest young, and uses some five
percent in all its red wines. These have always been light,
stylish and elegant, and more in the style of claret than most
Riojas. At times they have tended to be a little hard when
young; recent vintages have been uneven but are now back
on form and given time in bottle they age graciously,
gaining both in fragrance and intensity of flavour. Even in
years like 1971 and the notorious 1972, when Riscal rejected
some 40 percent of the crop, the *bodega* has made good
wines; and it is difficult to describe vintages such as 1952
and 1938 as anything but perfect. The remarkable 1922,
deep in colour, gloriously fragrant and fruity and long in
finish, reminds one of nothing so much as one of the best
old *crus* from St-Emilion.

As at MARQUES DE MURRIETA, none of the wine is sold
younger than in its fourth year. Riscal has just introduced
the first (1986) vintage of an exclusive and very expensive
Barón de Chirél, made with 50 percent Cabernet
Sauvignon. The *bodega* posesses a library of all the vintages
from its inception. The best of the older vintages of the
present century were: 1910, 1920, 1922, 1925, 1938, 1942,
1943, 1947, 1950, 1964, 1965 and 1968.

Riscal makes a little rosé in the Rioja, but its white wine
is from Rueda, near Valladolid (*see* Castilla-León, page 68).

Marqués del Puerto, Bodegas DO r (p w dr) res ★★→★★★
73, 76, 78, 82, 85, 86, 87
Fuenmayor (Rioja Alta). Founded in 1972 as Bodegas López
Agos, this is a small concern which makes its wines with

some care. The name was changed to Bodegas Marqués del Puerto in 1983 and the firm now belongs to BODEGAS Y BEBIDAS. The red *reservas*, labelled as Marqués del Puerto or Señorío de Agos, have been much praised in Spain.

Martínez Bujanda, Bodegas DO r p w dr res ★★→★★★ 73, 75, 78, 80, 83, 84, 85, 86, 89

Oyón (Rioja Alavesa). A family concern founded in 1890, Martínez Bujanda owns 200 hectares of vineyards and moved into one of the most modern and best-equipped wineries of the region in 1984. One of its most successful wines is a very fruity young (or *joven*) red made in the manner of Beaujolais Nouveau without time in oak. It also makes a fresh, cold-fermented white containing 80 percent Viura and 20 percent Malvasía, and rounded red CONDE DE VALDEMAR *reservas*.

Martínez Lacuesta, Bodegas DO r (p) w dr sw ★→★★★ 70, 71, 73, 76, 81, 82, 83, 85, 87

Haro (Rioja Alta). This old-established *bodega* in the centre of Haro was founded in 1895 and remains in the family. The *bodega* has a sizable capacity of some four million litres with 7,000 oak BARRICAS for maturing the wines. At one time it owned vineyards and made its wine, but this is now bought from local cooperatives for maturation and bottling. Its red wines, familiar to travellers on Iberia Airlines, are of two types. The full-bodied CAMPEADOR, in Burgundy-type bottles, contains a high proportion of Garnacha, while the lighter Martínez Lacuesta is made with some 75 percent of Tempranillo. The *reservas* and *gran reservas* of both types are often excellent wines.

Monte Real DO r ★★★

Among the best of the red wines made by Bodegas RIOJANAS, this is made with a high proportion of Tempranillo, both from CENICERO in the Rioja Alta and from the RIOJA ALAVESA.

Montecillo, Bodegas DO r (p) w dr ★★→★★★ 70, 73, 75, 76, 78, 80, 81, 84, 86
Navarrete (Rioja Alta). Founded in 1874, the company now belongs to the sherry firm of Osborne (*see* page 226). It owns 77 hectares of vineyards and a modern vinification plant near NAVARRETE, and *bodegas* for maturing its wines in CENICERO. Its young white CUMBRERO and red *crianza* Montecillo are excellent wines and first-rate value; and the firm also produces good red Viña Monty *reservas*, of which some of the best were the 1970, 1973, 1978, 1984 and 1986.

Monteleiva, Bodegas DO r w dr ★★→★★★ 85, 86
Fuenmayor (Rioja Alta). A new *bodega*, brainchild of oenologist Victor Leiva, formerly of CVNE and LAN. The white is a delightful wine in traditional oaky style, light and with fresh pineapple fruit.

Muerza, Bodegas DO r (w dr) ★★ 78, 80, 84, 86, 87
San Adrián (Rioja Baja). Maker of sound and modestly priced RIOJA BAJA reds.

Muga, Bodegas DO r w dr res ★★→★★★★ 70, 73, 75, 76, 78, 80, 81, 82, 85, 86
Haro (Rioja Alta). This small family firm was founded in 1926, but moved to a new *bodega* near the station in Haro in 1971. It is entirely unlike the great new *bodegas* constructed during the Rioja boom of the 1970s in that it started with only 500 BARRICAS – the minimum entitling it to export its wines – but such has been its subsequent success that the number has grown to 7,500. Everything is done in traditional style by a tiny and dedicated workforce, headed by the Muga brothers themselves. Its wines reflect the care that goes into their making and are currently among the best from the Rioja. Those labelled as Muga, made with grapes grown in the firm's own vineyards and others bought from farmers in Abalos, are exceptionally light and fragrant, while the Prado Enea is a deeper-coloured, velvety and more fully bodied wine, sold in bottles with wax capsules. The 1970 and 1981 were exceptional. The firm

also produces small quantities of a dry white wine and of a pleasant and very light sparkling wine made by the champagne method (*see* Sparkling Wines, page 263).

Murua, Bodegas DO r res ★★ 75, 78, 85, 86
Elciego (Rioja Alavesa). Small *bodega* making light Alavesa-type red wines, which tend to rapid ageing.

Nájera
On the hilly southern fringes of the RIOJA ALTA, west of Logroño, this picturesque little township is the site of a former residence of the Kings of Navarra; and the 11th-century monastery of Santa María contains the tombs of many of the kings and queens of Navarra, Castile and León.

Navajas, Bodegas DO w dr r res ★★→★★★ 82, 83, 85, 87
Navarrete (Rioja Alta). Best known for its full and fruity red wines with vanilla oak.

Navarrete
Hill town and winemaking centre southwest of Logroño. It was the site of the battle in 1367 in which the Black Prince and Peter the Cruel defeated Henry of Trastamara, and possesses a fine 16th-century church and baronial houses.

Oak

The pioneer of the oak barrel for maturing wines, now the 'trademark' of the Rioja, was Manuel Quintano, who in 1787 encouraged a group of producers in LABASTIDA to make their wines along French lines. The experiments were short-sightedly discontinued; and it was not until the phylloxera epidemic of the late 19th century and an influx of *négociants* from Bordeaux that ageing in oak became standard practice. Between them the *bodegas* of Rioja now deploy no less than 600,000 barrels.

Because of its dense and even texture, permitting slow transpiration of oxygen, the favourite type of oak is American, though French oak from Nevers and Alliers is increasingly being used. Maturation is much faster in new barrels, and although the casks are systematically scoured, washed and disinfected after each racking of the wines (decantation from the lees), the pores of the wood gradually become clogged. This is a factor which is not sufficiently recognized when visitors to the *bodegas* exclaim at the time their *reservas* spend in wood. Owing to the high cost of replacing them, some of the barrels in the older *bodegas* are over 50 years old.

It is perhaps because the casks in the newer *bodegas* are so much richer in essential oils and resins, conferring an excessively oaky bouquet on the wines, that the *canard* about oak essence arose. Such artificial extracts exist, but no self-respecting *bodega* uses them – and would in fact be heavily penalized if caught *in flagrante delicto*, and the fact that the new concerns have invested millions of pounds in oak BARRICAS hardly supports stories of its widespread employment.

Although maturation in oak, in combination with adequate bottle age, is essential in making good red wines, its use in making white Riojas has declined, since the producers found that it is a great deal less expensive to make the fresh young white wines, now so popular abroad, without maturing them in oak. Fortunately, there has been something of a return to oak-aged whites.

Oja, River

Tributary of the EBRO, flowing into it at Haro, which has given its name to the region.

Olarra, Bodegas DO r (p) w dr sw res ★★→★★★ 70, 73, 75, 76, 78, 80, 81, 83, 85

Logroño (Rioja Alta). The firm was founded in 1972 by a group of Spanish industrialists, and its *bodegas*, on the outskirts of Logroño, in the shape of a three-pointed star symbolizing the three subregions, are among the largest in the region, equipped with stainless steel fermentation tanks and highly sophisticated computerized systems for controlling the flow of the must and other operations. Maturation is, however, carried out by traditional methods in its 25,000 oak BARRICAS. Its wines are well made and of high standard, and include a dry, refreshing new-style white Reciente; the well-balanced Blanco Seco Olarra which is given a little time in oak; and excellent red Añares and Cerro Añon *reservas*, typically full and fruity.

Ollauri

Small village in the RIOJA ALTA just south of Haro and the birthplace of Bodegas PATERNINA and BERBERANA, both of which still maintain their original cellars there for ageing their wines in bottle.

Oyón

Industrial town in the RIOJA ALAVESA, just across the river from Logroño and the home of the Bodegas EL COTO and FAUSTINO MARTINEZ.

Palacio, Bodegas DO r (p) w dr sw ★→★★ 78, 81, 82, 85, 87

Laguardia (Rioja Alavesa). The old *bodegas*, on the road to Elciego, produced a most enjoyable red Glorioso, round, full and fruity. After the firm was bought by Seagram in 1973 and moved to a modern *bodega* just outside LAGUARDIA, there was a drastic decline in quality – probably because wine was bought in from cooperatives. Since 1980, when the firm began making the wine, standards have steadily improved, and the Glorioso *crianza, reserva* and *gran reserva* are excellent wines. The young red *vino del año* ('wine of the year') is fresh and attractive and the Cosme Palacio y Hermanos 1987 was a first-rate wine.

Palacios Remondo, Bodegas DO r w dr (p) res ★★→★★★
78, 81, 86
Mendavia (Rioja Alta). At their best the red Herencia Remondo *reservas* are elegant and complex.

Paternina, Federico r (p) w dr res ★→★★★ 64, 70, 73, 76, 80, 82, 86
Haro (Rioja Alta). Founded in 1896 by Don Federico Paternina Josué, Paternina was already one of the largest and most successful of the firms in the Rioja before its purchase by the RUMASA group and subsequent sale to Don Marcos Eguizábal. Since its inception it has moved successively from the original cellars in OLLAURI to a larger *bodega* bought from a Haro cooperative and to the present great modern plant with its 53,000 BARRICAS capable of maturing 12 million litres of wine. BANDA AZUL, with a brief lapse from popularity during teething troubles at the new plant, has always been a household word among the younger red Riojas; and the more mature Viña Vial is a big, fruity, well-balanced wine. There is a CONDE DE LOS ANDES *gran reserva*, outstanding in its 1964, 1970 and 1973 vintages. The dry white Banda Dorada and Rinsol are cold-fermented and the style is light and fruity.

The crowning glory of Paternina is the rare old vintages kept in the deep cellars of the old *bodega* at Ollauri. No system of stars could do justice to such beautiful old wines as the 1902, 1910, 1920, 1935, 1947 and 1959.

Ramón Bilbao DO r res ★★ 80, 82, 85
Haro (Rioja Alta). Maker of red wines including a Viña Turzaballa *gran reserva*.

Real Divisa, Bodegas DO r (p) w dr ★★★ 80, 85, 86, 87
Abalos (Rioja Alta). *Bodegas* of some note in a small enclave

of the RIOJA ALTA to the north of the Ebro, producing worthwhile red wines made mainly from the Tempranillo and sold as Marqués de Legarda.

Remelluri
See Granja de Nuestra Señora de Remelluri

Rioja Alavesa DO r (w dr) ★★→★★★★

The smallest of the three subregions of the DO Rioja with an area of 7,000 hectares under vines, the Rioja Alavesa is located in the province of Alava and extends north of the River Ebro from near the Conchas de Haro to a line a little east of Logroño. Because of the temperate climate, the southerly exposure of the vineyards and the composition of the soil, which is almost entirely calcareous clay, the Rioja Alavesa produces some of the best wines from the whole region – in the opinion of many experts, *the* best. Another factor is the very high proportion of Tempranillo used in making the red wines.

There are some dozen large *bodegas*, and also smaller ones, which export their wines, and others own vineyards in the area, blending the musts with those from the RIOJA ALTA. The main production centres are at LABASTIDA in the west, and ELCIEGO, LAGUARDIA and OYON towards the east.

In general, the red Alavesa wines are big, fruity and soft (though one or two are very light) with a pronounced and characteristic Tempranillo nose, somewhat resembling that of Cabernet Sauvignon, but mature more rapidly than those from the Rioja Alta and do not last as long. In poor years the Consejo Regulador authorizes the addition of a little Garnacha Tinta from the RIOJA BAJA, so as to obtain the necessary body and alcoholic degree, of which the minimum requirement is 11–11·5 percent.

The Rioja Alavesa subregion also produces smaller amounts of white wine with good acid balance, mainly made from the Viura and Malvasía.

Rioja Alta DO r (p) w dr sw ★★→★★★★

Together with the RIOJA ALAVESA, the subregion of the

Rioja Alta produces the best Rioja wines. It lies within the province of La Rioja, extending (apart from a small northern enclave around ABALOS) south of the Ebro from the Conchas de Haro in the west to just beyond Logroño in the east. The soils are more mixed than those of the Rioja Alavesa, comprising calcareous clay, ferruginous clay and alluvial silt. On the basis of this and of the microclimate, oenologists have subdivided the area, from west to east, into the zones of Cuzcurrita, Haro, San Asensio and Cenicero-Fuenmayor. The wines from the wetter and hillier area of the west tend to be more acidic and lower in alcohol than those from Cenicero, where there is a transition in climate from humid to semi-arid and a change to predominantly calcareous soils, particularly suitable for growing the Tempranillo grape.

There are some 30 large *bodegas* and numerous smaller ones in the Rioja Alta; and the main production centres are HARO in the west, CENICERO and FUENMAYOR in the centre, and LOGROÑO and NAVARRETE in the east.

Although the Tempranillo is the basic grape of the Rioja Alta, as of the Rioja Alavesa, its red wines contain a higher proportion of Mazuelo, Graciano and Garnacha, and tend to be brisker and fresher in nose, a little more acidic and longer lasting. As in the Rioja Alavesa, the whites are made mainly from the Viura and Malvasía, with some Garnacha Blanca. It is difficult to be more specific, since the large *bodegas* sometimes use a blend of wines made from grapes grown both in the Rioja Alta and Rioja Alavesa.

La Rioja Alta, Bodegas DO r (p) w dr res ★★→★★★★ 64, 68, 70, 73, 76, 78, 80, 81, 82, 83, 85, 86

Haro (Rioja Alta). A medium-sized family concern founded in 1890 and one of the first to build a *bodega* in the hallowed area near the railway station in HARO, La Rioja Alta has consistently maintained the quality and prestige of its wines. It owns some 250 hectares of vineyards, both in the RIOJA ALTA and RIOJA BAJA, and possesses some 25,000 BARRICAS for ageing its wines, made by strictly traditional methods. These include a characterful *crianza* Viña Alberdi (actually aged in oak for as long as many *bodegas' reservas*); the fruity, full-bodied and velvety red VIÑA ARDANZA (named after one of the five families that founded the *bodega*); a lighter and very stylish Viña Arana; and the excellent 904 and 890 *reservas*. It also makes a traditional white Rioja which is aged in cask, the Viña Ardanza Blanco Reserva, creamy and vanilla flavoured.

Gently rolling hills characterize the Rioja Alta

Rioja Baja DO r (w dr) ★→★★

The largest of the subregions of the DO Rioja, the Rioja Baja extends from just east of Logroño along the Ebro to Alfaro in the southeast. The larger part of the area lies in the province of La Rioja, south of the river, but there is also a narrow strip in Navarra to the north. The soils of the Rioja Baja are almost entirely composed of alluvial silt and ferruginous clay; the climate is semi-arid, of the Mediterranean type, and the predominant grape is the red Garnacha Tinta, which yields musts high in alcohol and extract, but quick to oxidize. For these reasons the typical wines are coarser than those of the cooler and hillier RIOJA ALAVESA and RIOJA ALTA, and are often used for blending to confer alcoholic degree and body. Nevertheless, the bold departure of Bodegas BERBERANA in planting the Tempranillo and Viura in calcareous soils in the higher part of the area, at Monte Yerga near Aldeanueva del Ebro, has proved very successful.

There are six major *bodegas* in the Rioja Baja, and the main centres of production are San Adrián, ALFARO, ARNEDO and Aldeanueva del Ebro, a sunbaked town which produces better asparagus and peppers than wine and is curiously named, because it is not, as the name implies, either a hamlet, new, or near the Ebro.

The typical wines are full-bodied reds, high in alcohol and more akin to those of the Ribera Baja (*see* Navarra, page 159) than the delicate growths of the Rioja Alta or Rioja Alavesa.

Rioja Santiago, Bodegas r p w res ★→★★★ 81, 84, 85, 86, 88
Haro (Rioja Alta). Old-established firm with *bodegas* in Haro, just across the bridge over the Ebro. The firm developed a large market in the USA for its bottled *sangría*, labelled as Monsieur Henri, and was eventually taken over by its American distributor, Pepsi Cola. It continues to make a range of normal Riojas, though the name Yago (now used for the *sangría*) and the characteristic tall, square bottles have been discontinued. Its best wines are the red GRAN CONDAL and Vizconde de Ayala *reservas* and the Gran Fino Enológica, only made in limited amounts in exceptional years.

Riojanas, Bodegas DO r (p) w dr s/sw res ★★→★★★ 64, 66, 68, 70, 73, 74, 75, 76, 78, 81, 82, 84, 85
Cenicero (Rioja Alta). This large and old-established *bodega*, founded in 1890, was built in flamboyant style with a castellated keep and with advice from Bordeaux; and there were French technicians working there until the early years of World War II. It is of interest in that part of the wine is still made in the old-fashioned Riojan style by fermenting

the grapes in open stone *lagos*. The *bodega* draws its grapes from both the RIOJA ALTA and the RIOJA ALAVESA from some 200 hectares of vineyards owned either by the company or its shareholders and also from private farmers. Small amounts of selected Garnacha grapes from the RIOJA BAJA are also used.

Its wines include a dry white Canchales, a semi-sweet white Albina, and an inexpensive red *sin crianza* Canchales. It also makes good Viña Albina *reservas*; but perhaps the most interesting wines are the red MONTE REAL *reservas* made with a sizable proportion (some 75 percent) of Tempranillo from the Rioja Alavesa.

Among the best of the older vintages were 1890, 1915, 1922, 1934, 1942, 1950, 1956, 1964, 1966, 1968 and 1970.

RUMASA

At its peak this great Spanish conglomerate, with extensive interests in banking, hotels and property as well as wines of all types, had taken over the important Rioja firms of PATERNINA, FRANCO-ESPAÑOLAS, LAN and BERBERANA. After its expropriation in 1983, the firms were first run by the government and finally sold to private interests, the first three to a Spanish businessman, Marcos Eguizábal, whose family is from the region. *See also* Sherry, pages 230–231.

Salceda, Viña DO r res ★★→★★★ 70, 73, 75, 76, 78

Elciego (Rioja Alavesa). The *bodega*, just beyond the bridge over the Ebro on the road from Cenicero to Elciego, is of modern construction, dating from 1974, and is equipped with stainless steel fermentation tanks together with the traditional oak BARRICAS for ageing the wines. Of medium size, it makes only red wine with a high proportion of Tempranillo: a Viña Salceda *crianza* and Conde de la Salceda *reservas* and *gran reservas* of excellent quality.

San Mateo, Festival of

One of many such festivals in the wine-growing districts, the Fiesta de San Mateo begins in LOGROÑO on September 21, rather before the official start of grape-picking on

October 10, and lasts for a week, with a uniformed band parading the streets, bullfights and firework displays in the Plaza del Espolón at midnight.

San Vicente de la Sonsierra

Picturesque village near LABASTIDA dominated by a ruined castle with magnificent views over the River Ebro and across the Rioja.

Santa Daría, Cooperativa Vinícola de DO r w dr p ★★

Cenicero (Rioja Alta). Well-equipped cooperative, one of the best in the Rioja, bottling and selling its wines under the label Santa Daría.

Santo Domingo de la Calzada

Just outside the demarcated region of the Rioja, Santo Domingo, south of Haro, is on the old pilgrim route from France to Santiago de Compostela and is one of the pleasantest places to stay when visiting the Rioja. Its 12th-century cathedral incorporates an unusual feature, a live cock and hen housed behind a grille high on one wall in commemoration of a miracle wrought by Saint Dominic, patron saint of the pilgrims. The *parador*, facing the church and built in medieval times as a hospice for the pilgrims, offers comfortable accommodation and regional cooking and wines.

Sierra Cantabria, Bodegas DO r res w dr p ★★★ 73, 78, 81, 82, 85, 88

San Vicente de la Sonsierra (Rioja Alta). Small *bodega* known for its excellent young red Murmurón, made by carbonic maceration, and fruity and well-balanced red Sierra Cantabria.

SMS, Bodegas DO r res ★★ 71, 73, 81, 85, 86

Villabuena (Rioja Alavesa). SMS are the initials of three families: Samaniego, Milans del Bosch and Solano. Founded before 1900 and originally called the Marqués de la Solana, the *bodega* is now owned by six brothers of the Simon

Milans del Bosch family and has a capacity of some 300,000 litres and 600 oak BARRICAS. The wines, all red, are made entirely with grapes grown in vineyards belonging to the family. They are fermented in wooden *tinos* before spending a year in cement vats and being further matured in cask and in bottle. Until 1981 the grapes were not destalked, so that the older wines are dark in colour, and mature more slowly than most from the RIOJA ALAVESA. Those currently available have a hint of cedar in the nose, and are fragrant, full-bodied, with a lot of fruit and a long, somewhat tannic finish.

Unión Vitivinícola
See Marqués de Cáceres

Velázquez, Bodegas DO r res ★→★★ 75, 78, 80, 84, 85, 87
Cenicero (Rioja Alta). One of the smaller *bodegas*, labelling its wines (all red) as Monte Velaz, La Rendición, La Tunica and Las Hilanderas.

Viña Albina DO r ★★★
Well-known red wine from Bodegas RIOJANAS.

Viña Ardanza DO r ★★★
Consistently satisfying red Riojas, smooth, fruity and full-bodied, from Bodegas LA RIOJA ALTA.

Viña Bosconia DO r ★★★
Excellent Rioja from LOPEZ DE HEREDIA, using grapes grown in its Bosconia vineyards on the south bank of the Ebro.

Viña Pomal DO r ★★→★★★
Full-bodied red Rioja from Bodegas BILBAINAS made with grapes from its vineyards in Leza in the RIOJA ALAVESA.

Viña Real DO r ★★★
Excellent red RIOJA ALAVESA *reserva* from the COMPAÑIA VINICOLA DEL NORTE DE ESPAÑA, made in an outlying *bodega* in Elciego.

Viña Tondonia DO r w dr ★★★→★★★★

First-rate and long-lasting red and white Riojas from
Bodegas LOPEZ DE HEREDIA.

Ygay

Hamlet in the Rioja Alta a little east of Logroño with the
bodegas of the MARQUES DE MURRIETA on its outskirts.

Wine and Food

It is perhaps a little pretentious to talk of the cuisine of the Rioja.
What the area offers is a range of genuinely regional dishes based on
the excellent lamb, pork, kid and spicy *chorizo* sausage, and fresh
vegetables in season. When André Simon first wrote about the
Rioja, he was, in fact, more enthusiastic about the vegetables than
the wines, and it is still an experience to visit the great open market
in Logroño.

The meals served to guests in the *bodegas* themselves, often in a
great cellar lined with casks, are simple and well designed to show
off the wines, and usually begin with fresh local asparagus or a
menestra of vegetables, followed by small lamb chops cooked over
glowing vine shoots and ending with the ubiquitous *flan* (cream
caramel) or the luscious peaches preserved in syrup. Such simple
delights are not to be despised; and when Paul Bocuse was engaged
by the Compañía Vinícola del Norte de España to cook its
centenary banquet, the story goes that, having sampled the *patatas
riojanas* prepared by the *bodega*'s regular cook, he asked why he had
been sent for.

Alubias con chorizo A rib-warming stew made with haricot
or butter beans, chopped onions, garlic, olive oil and highly
cured *chorizo* sausage, further seasoned with sweet paprika
powder and parsley. This calls for a full-bodied two- or
three-year-old red, or a *jarra* of the local house wine.

Bacalao a la riojana Dried cod cooked with olive oil, onions,
garlic, strips of canned red pepper and sweet paprika

powder. Drink one of the traditional oaky white Riojas with sufficient character to stand up to the rich assortment of flavours, for example a white Tondonia from López de Heredia, or the rather less oaky but complex Monopole from CVNE.

Cabrito asado Roast kid Rioja style. This is a good chance to show off the qualities of one of the many red *reservas*.

Callos a la riojana Highly spiced tripe, Riojan style.

Cardo Cardoon, a celery-like vegetable, served braised as a first course. Choose from among the numerous white Riojas, perhaps one with a hint of oak, such as Olarra, or the white Samaniego from Bodegas Alavesas.

Chorizo a la brasa *Chorizo*, the spicy cured pepper sausage, often home made, and roasted whole. Since this is extremely hot, a chilled glass of one of the young white Riojas, such as the Marqués de Cáceres or Faustino V, is a refreshing accompaniment.

Chuletas de cordero al sarmiento Small lamb chops grilled over glowing vine shoots and served in the *bodegas* to set off the better reds and *reservas*.

Cordero lechal asado Milk-fed baby lamb roasted in a baker's oven. Choose the best red *reserva* you can run to, for example a 1982 from Riscal, La Rioja Alta, López de Heredia, Muga, Riojanas, CVNE.

Espárragos The Rioja Baja grows some of the best Spanish asparagus, which is served as a starter either with vinaigrette or mayonnaise. Take your choice of the dry white wines.

Malvices Tiny birds (red-wings) fried crisp and eaten whole. A light red Alavesa wine, such as Coto de Imaz from El Coto.

Melocotones en almíbar Particularly large and luscious local peaches preserved in syrup. Try a sweet or semi-sweet wine, such as the Diamante from Franco-Españolas.

Menestra de verduras a la riojana A mixed vegetable dish made from whatever happens to be in season, such as broad beans and peas, together with chopped onions, tomatoes, bacon or ham, seasoning and sometimes hard-boiled eggs. It is cooked in olive oil and light red wine. Try the Viñadrian *rosado* from Bodegas Gurpegui.

Morcilla dulce *Morcilla* is a blood sausage akin to black pudding, usually made with onions and savoury rice, but in this version it is prepared with cinnamon, other sweet spices and a little sugar. Although it is usually eaten as a first course, anything but a sweet or semi-sweet white wine would seem tart.

Patatas a la riojana Potatoes in a clear orange-coloured sauce with *chorizo* sausage.

Picadillo A variant on *chorizo a la brasa*, the filling of the sausage being ground, cooked and served hot. This definitely calls for a chilled and cooling dry white wine. As an alternative to those already mentioned, try Rinsol from Paternina or the dry Lan.

Pimientos de piquillo rellenos a la riojana Regional variant on stuffed peppers, filled with a mixture of ground pork, beaten egg, nutmeg, garlic, parsley and a little pepper and salt, fried in hot olive oil and served in a piquant sauce. Order a full-bodied and robust red.

Pochas riojanas Substantial stew made from a local variety of haricot bean, allowed to fatten in the pod but not dried, and taking its dark red colour from the *chorizo* with which it is cooked. Best eaten with a *jarra* of the local red house wine or a robust bottle of Rioja Baja.

Quesos (cheeses). The best local cheeses are the soft Camerano made from goats' milk and the delicious Idiazábal from the Basque country, semi-hard and made from unpasteurized ewes' milk.

Revuelto de ajos tiernos Eggs scrambled with tender young garlic shoots. The traditional white Riojas, oaky or slightly oaky, balance this very well.

Sopa de ajo con huevos Traditional Castilian garlic soup, seasoned with sweet paprika powder and thickened with bread and beaten egg. Better to leave the table wine for later and ask for a glass of *fino* sherry.

Tapas Typical local *tapas* are *embuchados* (pork sausages), *lecherillas* (sweetbreads) and *champiñones a la plancha* (grilled mushrooms).

Restaurants

Arnedo *Sopitas* (tunnelled into the cliff with individual dining alcoves; try the excellent *revuelto de ajos*).

Ezcaray *El Echaurren* (vegetable soup, hake fillets in sauce).

Fuenmayor *Asador la Alameda; Mesón Chuchi.*

Haro *Beethoven II* (good regional cooking); *Terete* (the classical Haro restaurant, simple surroundings, marvellous roast baby lamb and long list of *reservas*).

Logroño *Mesón de la Merced* (installed in an old palace with elegant decor and sophisticated cooking); *Machado* (regional cooking and Rioja wines); *Mesón Lorenzo; Asador la Chata; Casa Emilio; El Cachetero* (small, popular, good selection of wines); *Robinson's English Pub* (for dancing and a late nightcap).

Oyón *Mesón de la Cueva* (good regional food in atmospheric surroundings).

Santo Domingo de la Calzada *El Rincón de Emilio* (vastly popular; its speciality is *callos a la riojana*).

Sherry (Jerez)

Sherry is, of course, the classical Spanish wine and one with particularly close associations with Britain, since the great sherry boom took place with the active participation of British merchants, many of whom settled in Jerez. Further than this, the UK consumes more sherry than Spain and, followed by the Netherlands, is still the largest foreign market. Sherry, in common with most other fortified wines and spirits, has recently suffered something of a set-back; but this is not the first in its long history. A glass of chilled *fino* remains the most satisfactory preliminary to a meal and the least likely to interfere with what follows, and, for a wine of such character and one so expensive to make, sherry of all types remains most reasonably priced.

The wines were well known even in Roman times, but it was Sir Francis Drake's raid on Cádiz in 1587 and seizure of some 2,900 pipes (110-gallon barrels) which firmly established them in England. The British presence had begun to be felt after the expulsion of the Jews from Spain by the Catholic monarchs in 1492; and during the late 18th and early 19th centuries English, Scottish and Irish merchants arrived in force. Their names survive in those of such famous sherry houses as Duff Gordon, Osborne, Garvey, Terry, Sandeman and Williams & Humbert.

The sherry district occupies a triangle with its apex near Cádiz, bounded by the Guadalquivir and Guadalete rivers and embracing the main centres of Jerez de la Frontera, Puerto de Santa María and Sanlúcar de Barrameda. The whole area is in the province of Cádiz. The best vineyards lie within a 32-kilometre radius north and west of Jerez, and the soils are of three classes. The most highly rated is the dazzlingly white *albariza*, containing some 40 percent of chalk, together with sand and clay, which enables it to retain moisture throughout the year in a region where average rainfall amounts to only 550 millimetres and temperatures rise to 40°C during the long, cloudless summers. Other types are the darker *barro* and a sandy *arena*, used mainly for Moscatel grapes.

The sherry grape *par excellence* is the white Palomino, which grows best in the chalky *albariza* and is used for all the different types of sherry and almost exclusively for the *finos*. Next in importance is the Pedro Ximénez, which can, as in Montilla (*see* page 141), produce excellent dry wines, but is principally used in Jerez for sweet dessert wines. Smaller amounts of Moscatel are also grown for blending with sweet sherries.

Sherry owes its entirely individual character to the method used in making it. Unlike table wines, it is matured with free access to the atmosphere, in a loosely stoppered cask with an air space above the liquid. This would ordinarily result in fairly rapid oxidation, were it not that the new wine spontaneously grows a *flor* (or 'flower') on the surface of the liquid. This layer of yeasts both regulates the access of air to the must and eliminates harmful vinegar-producing bacteria. The growth varies according to the type of wine and is thickest with *finos* (and even more so with the *manzanillas* from Sanlúcar de Barrameda) and less vigorous with the fuller-bodied *olorosos*, which are soon fortified to kill it and to protect the wine during physico-chemical maturation.

The other difference between the making of table wines and sherry is that it is aged by the *solera* system, providing for the progressive blending of older and younger wines. The *solera* consists of long rows of oak butts arranged in the *bodega* in tiers. Each row of butts or 'scale' contains wine of the same type but of different age. When wine is required for shipment or bottling, it is drawn off from the butts at the bottom containing the oldest wine. The contents are then made good from the 'scale' immediately preceding it in age, and so on through the system. In this fashion there is regular 'refreshment' of older wine with younger, and as Richard Ford said in 1846, 'houses are enabled to supply for any number of years exactly that particular colour, flavour, body, etc., which particular customers demand.' There are therefore no vintages in sherry, and a description such as 'Solera 1847' refers to the year in which the *solera* was first laid down.

The basic styles of sherry are the dry and light *finos*, such as Tio Pepe or La Ina, drunk chilled as an apéritif; the rather fuller *amontillados*, either dry or semi-dry; and the dark, fully bodied *olorosos*, the most maderized and fragrant of the wines. In their natural state, *olorosos*, such as Rio Viejo, are completely dry and are best drunk before a meal; but they are often blended with sweet wine to make a dessert sherry or cream, of which one of the best known is Bristol Cream. This does not exhaust the possibilities, however, and other varieties such as *manzanilla, palo cortado* and pale cream are described in the A–Z listing.

In the past it was very much a question of making the wine and then waiting to see how it would develop. Modern methods have enabled the *bodegas* to make these decisions at a much earlier stage; and in the latest of the continuous vinification plants, wine destined as a *fino* is drawn off after the lightest crushing of the grapes, which are then more firmly pressed to obtain the must for the *olorosos*.

In all essentials, sherry continues to be made along strictly traditional lines, but there have been many other innovations in recent years. González Byass has instituted a programme for eliminating plant diseases by the cloning (vegetative reproduction) of virus-free vines; the bacchanalian rite of treading the grapes with nail-studded boots has given way to modern horizontal or continuous presses. The wine is increasingly (but not always) fermented in temperature-controlled stainless steel tanks rather than in butts, and the bulk of the wine is no longer shipped in cask, but bottled in the *bodega*, although some large *bodegas* have found that their big-selling sherries reach the customer fresher if they are shipped in containers topped up with inert gas and bottled abroad.

Apart from visits to the *bodegas*, the sherry region is a delightful one in which to spend a holiday. There are the Atlantic beaches of places like Puerto de Santa María, Rota and Chipiona; the great nature reserve of the Coto Doñana across the Guadalquivir; the rugged mountains and hunting of the Sierra de Cádiz; the historic buildings of Cádiz and Sevilla; and by no means least the superb seafood from the Bay of Cádiz. Jerez is at its best in the late spring, or in the early autumn at harvest time.

The quickest way to reach the area is to fly to Madrid and then on to Jerez by an internal flight or by the fast and luxurious TALGO train; alternatively, one may fly to Sevilla, 84 kilometres to the

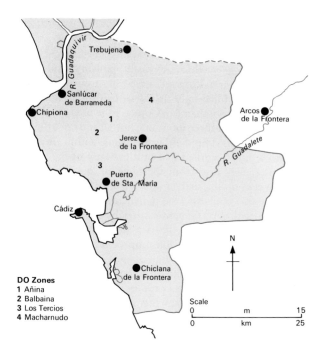

DO Zones
1 Añina
2 Balbaina
3 Los Tercios
4 Macharnudo

north by the A4 *autopista*, and hire a car. Once there, a car is not a necessity, as there is a local electric train to Puerto de Santa María and bus services to other places.

The larger *bodegas*, such as Pedro Domecq, González Byass and Williams & Humbert, are well organized for visits, which end with a generous tasting. Visiting hours are normally 9·30–13·00, but it is always advisable to check by letter or telephone beforehand. A letter of introduction from a wine merchant or shipper smooths the way in the case of smaller establishments.

As to the vineyards, you can get good views of the famous areas of Macharnudo and Carrascal to the north of Jerez by branching off the A4 from Sevilla at Las Cabezas and following the hilly by-road, through this almost lunar landscape of whitish sunbaked clay, by way of Lebrija and Trebujena and into Jerez.

Serving Sherry

Sherry is often ruined by improper serving and storage, especially fresh and delicate *finos* which are easily spoilt by oxidation. *All* sherries should be served in a glass tapering towards the top and large enough to be filled only a third or half full to allow for the development of the bouquet (*see* Copita, page 214). *Fino* begins to deteriorate after about three months in bottle; and once the bottle is opened, the contents should either be drunk within three days or poured into a tightly corked half-bottle. Many of the complaints about popular *finos* arise from the habit of keeping half-empty bottles for weeks on the shelves of a warm bar.

Much the same applies to the lighter *amontillados*, though they deteriorate more slowly. *Olorosos*, especially the sweeter styles, last much longer in bottle, and the rich dessert sherries sometimes improve because of the slow consumption of sugar, which gives them a dryish finish.

Fino and light *amontillado* should be served chilled, but not iced. The best thing is to leave the bottle in the refrigerator for a few hours before serving it; and the wine will also keep longer if stored in the refrigerator. Rather than suffer a lukewarm *fino* in a bar, it is better to ask for it to be poured into a larger glass and drink it 'on the rocks' – though chilling is preferable. *Olorosos*, the fuller-bodied *amontillados* and creams should be drunk at room temperature.

Albariza

The best of the soils, white in colour and containing some 40 percent of chalk, the residue consisting of sand and clay.

Almacenistas

Small concerns which mature wine from their own vineyards or bought from individual growers. They do not sell direct to the public, but only to the large shippers for improving their commercial sherries. Fine quality *almacenista* sherries are now much in demand, especially in the USA, and the firm that has specialized in bottling and shipping them for retail sale is Emilio LUSTAU.

Amontillado

Style of sherry, amber yellow in colour, with a dry, nutty flavour and of about 16–18 percent strength. It takes its name from wines formerly prepared in Montilla (*see* page 143), and the genuine article is made by allowing a *fino* to age for a further period after the FLOR has died or been eliminated by addition of alcohol.

Amoroso

Traditional name, in Spanish 'loving', not now much used, for a smooth, sweet *oloroso* made by adding Pedro Ximénez wine and VINO DE COLOR.

Añada

A young vintage wine as yet unblended in a CRIADERA.

Añina

District between Jerez de la Frontera and Sanlúcar de Barrameda, rated fourth of those with ALBARIZA soil.

Arcos de la Frontera

Picturesque town east of Jerez, perched on a rocky crag above the River Guadalete. With its narrow alleys and white houses, it is one of the pleasantest places to stay in the region. There is a comfortable *parador* housed in the old Casa del Corregidor, with splendid views over the gorge.

Arena

Reddish, sandy soil, containing some ten percent of chalk and the least favoured, except for the Moscatel vine.

Argüeso, Herederos de

Sanlúcar de Barrameda. Founded in 1822 and now belonging to A R VALDESPINO, this small firm makes excellent San León and Viruta *manzanillas*, and a good *amontillado* and Moscatel.

Arrope

A non-alcoholic syrup, prepared by evaporating down

must to 20 percent of its original volume and used in making the VINO DE COLOR for sweet sherries.

Balbaina

District to the west of Jerez, rated third in order of merit of those with ALBARIZA soil.

Barbadillo, Antonio

Sanlúcar de Barrameda. Founded in 1821, Barbadillo is the largest of the firms in Sanlúcar, with offices in the former bishop's palace and a complex of *bodegas* facing the church of Santa María de la O in the centre of the town; even its *bodega nueva* ('new cellar') dates from 1850. It possesses vineyards in the areas of BALBAINA, CARRASCAL, Campiz and San Julián, and has gone into partnership with John HARVEY & Sons in the development of 1,000 hectares of new vineyards and the most modern of vinification plants in Gibalbin, east of the A4 to Sevilla. Although Harvey's has a ten percent holding in the company, it remains a family concern. The late Don Manuel Barbadillo was the doyen of *manzanilla* wines and wrote the most authoritative book on the subject.

Barbadillo makes a superb range of *manzanillas*, including a fresh and aromatic Solear *fina*; the Eva *manzanilla pasada*, resembling a *fino amontillado* from Jerez; an entirely beautiful Cuco dry *oloroso*; and an exceptionally round and satisfying Eva Cream. It is also producing a fresh and fragrant young table wine from Palomino grapes, labelled as Castillo de San Diego.

Barro

A mud clay containing up to ten percent of chalk, dark in colour because of the presence of iron oxide, and second in quality of the soils.

Bertola

Jerez de la Frontera. The firm was founded in 1911 in partnership with the old-established port concern of C N Kopke & Co, as Kopke Bertola y Cía. It was subsequently taken over by Diez Hermanos and became part of RUMASA. It is now part of Bodegas INTERNACIONALES. Best known of its sherries is the Bertola Cream.

Bienteveo

These rough shelters, made of poles thatched with esparto grass, are still occasionally to be seen in the vineyards and were formerly manned by armed guards to prevent the depredations of thieves helping themselves to the ripe grapes. The literal translation is 'I see you well'.

Blázquez, Hijos de Agustín

Jerez de la Frontera. Old-established firm now owned by PEDRO DOMECQ, known particularly for its first-rate Carta Blanca *fino*; it also markets *finos, amontillados* and cream sherries under the labels of Don Paco, Carta Oro and Balfour, and makes the reliable and inexpensive Felipe II brandy. *See also* page 271.

Bobadilla

Founded in 1879 and now owned by OSBORNE, the firm is best known in Spain for its big-selling '103' brandy, but also makes worthwhile sherries, including a Victoria *fino*, Alcazar *amontillado*, Capitán *oloroso* and La Merced cream. *See also* page 271.

Bristol Cream

A proprietary name belonging to John HARVEY & Sons of Bristol, who decided during the 19th century to produce an even richer dessert sherry than the popular Bristol Milk by blending it with older *olorosos*. It is now the biggest-selling sherry in the world, with very large sales in the USA.

Bristol Milk

Bristol has for centuries been one of the most important ports in the UK for the shipping of wines, and has imported dessert sherries under the name of Bristol Milk since the 17th century. The best-known labels are those of HARVEY's and Avery's of Bristol.

Brown sherry

English name for a dark dessert sherry, usually only of very moderate quality.

Burdon, John William

John William Burdon, who began by working for DUFF GORDON, became one of the most successful of 19th-century sherry shippers. The firm was eventually taken over in 1932 by Luis CABALLERO, which still markets a well-known range of sherries under the Burdon label. They include a crisp and fresh Dry Fino; a Medium Amontillado; a Pale Cream; and a raisiny Rich Cream.

Butt (bota)

The standard butt used for maturing sherry in the SOLERA is of 500 litres capacity, and is made of American oak. There are also larger butts, less pointed in shape, such as the *bocoy* of 600 litres. Butts have become increasingly expensive and represent an appreciable proportion of the cost of a wine which is more expensive than most to produce. Since sherry butts are used for maturing Scotch whisky, some of the firms have arranged for them to be bought by the distilleries in Scotland and to pass them on after a couple of years' use in the *bodega*.

Caballero, Luis

Puerto de Santa María. The Caballero family was making wines in CHIPIONA as long ago as 1795 and shipping them from 1830. In 1932, by way of another takeover, the firm became the successors to John William BURDON, whose firm was one of the most successful of the English enterprises in Jerez during the 19th century. Apart from the Burdon sherries and its own well-known Pavón *fino*; the nutty Tío Benito *amontillado*; and the Benito range of Pale Dry Amontillado, Pale Cream and Cream, it also makes one of the most popular *ponches* (*see* page 279).

Cádiz

Capital of the province embracing the sherry region, Cádiz,

south of Jerez de la Frontera on a peninsula connected by a stone causeway, is one of the most stylish of Spanish cities. The only city uncaptured by Napoleon during the Peninsular War, it is a place of white houses, narrow streets and handsome squares, bounded by shaded gardens and a wide promenade with views out to the Atlantic. Its large port is now the main centre for shipping sherry.

Cádiz also has claims to being the gastronomic capital of Andalucía; the waters of its bay and the surrounding coast supply fish and shellfish in great variety, and its *freidurías*, where you may buy them freshly fried to take away, were the forerunners to the British fish-and-chip shop.

The quietest and most pleasantly situated hotel is the Atlántico, in a garden at the far tip of the peninsula overlooking the ocean. It belongs to the Parador chain and is thus very reasonably priced, its disadvantage being that it is a long walk through the narrow streets to the centre – and it would be an adventurous driver who took his car.

Camera

A wooden box containing a candle for judging the clarity of the wine.

Canoa

A wedge-shaped funnel traditionally used for transferring wine from one BUTT to another.

Capataz

The cellarman at a *bodega*, all-important in operating the SOLERA.

Carrascal

District to the immediate north of Jerez, whose ALBARIZA soils are rated second in order of merit.

CAYD

Sanlúcar de Barrameda. Founded some 100 years ago by the Bozzano family, of Italian descent, the *bodega* was sold in 1969 to the local Cooperativa de Campo Virgen de la

Caridad, which was by then supplying most of its wine. This embraces some 1,000 members with vineyards in the locality; and the combined capacity of the cooperative and the original *bodega* is some 30,000 butts. The musts are fermented in cement *tinajas* (*see* Montilla-Moriles, page 148), the first of which were in fact constructed by craftsmen from Montilla; some of the musts develop as typical *manzanillas* and others as Jerez-type wines. The *manzanillas* include Bajo de Guia and Sanluqueña *finas*, and others the Cayd *fino, amontillado,* medium and cream.

Chiclana

Village on the border of the sherry district south of Cádiz, producing wine in large quantity, but not of the highest quality. Its *finos* are sometimes blended with the less expensive sherries.

Chipiona

Seaside town on the coast road from Sanlúcar de Barrameda to Puerto de Santa María. Its ARENA vineyards are noted for their Moscatel, used in some of the sweet dessert wines.

Copita

The tall glass, narrowing towards the top, used for tasting sherry. It should be filled only a third to a half full, so that the full aroma of the wine may be appreciated. The small Elgin glasses habitually used in bars, pubs and restaurants, and filled to the brim, are entirely unsuitable for sherry, since the wine needs space and air for the nose and flavour to develop properly. When travelling in the sherry area, it is well worth bringing back a set of *copitas* or the larger *catavinos*. If you are served sherry in an Elgin or small thistle glass, ask for it to be poured into a tulip-shaped brandy or wine glass.

Cream sherries

These sweet dessert wines are of two types. The dark, full-bodied mahogany-coloured variety is made by sweetening an *oloroso* with a sugary must prepared from Pedro Ximénez and other grapes left to dry in the sun. The base wine for pale creams is a *fino* or pale *amontillado*, which is blended with a sweet, concentrated must.

See also Amoroso, Bristol Cream and Bristol Milk.

Criadera

The literal meaning of the word is 'nursery', and it is used to describe the series of butts from which wine is drawn off to 'refresh' or replenish a SOLERA.

Croft Jerez

Jerez de la Frontera. Croft is one of the oldest names in the port trade, but has been associated with sherry only since 1970, when IDV (International Distillers and Vintners), which had fallen heir to the company by way of W A Gilbey, decided to set up Croft Jerez to supply its large requirements of sherry. Starting from scratch, the company planted more than 370 hectares of vineyards, and in 1975 opened the Rancho Croft on the outskirts of Jerez, whose handsome, traditionally styled buildings with a capacity of some 50,000 butts house one of the most modern of sherry establishments. Thanks to a new vinification plant and well-organized handling procedures, the firm operates efficiently with only 60 workers, and at a time when other firms are finding themselves in financial difficulties, is one of the most flourishing in Jerez.

Its largest-selling sherry is the sweet Croft Original pale cream; Croft Particular is along similar lines but medium to dry; other labels are a light, dry and elegant Delicado *fino* and a first-rate and moderately priced *palo cortado*.

Crushing

See Zapatos de pisar

Delgado Zuleta

Prestigious Sanlúcar firm, founded in 1719 and most celebrated for its fragrant and magnificent La Goya *manzanilla pasada*, with which King Alfonso XIII is known to have toasted the crew of one of his submarines while it was submerged in the Bay of Santander.

Diestro, Jaime F
Jerez de la Frontera. A firm once part of the RUMASA group and now controlled by Bodegas INTERNACIONALES, particularly known for its *ponche* (*see* page 279).

Diez-Merito
Jerez de la Frontera. Diez Hermanos, a company of French origin, was founded in 1876 and has always specialized in selling wines for sale as 'own brands'. It absorbed the old-established firm of the Marqués de Merito before itself being taken over by the RUMASA group and is now controlled by Bodegas INTERNACIONALES. Best known of its sherries are the magnificent Fino Imperial (in fact almost an *amontillado*) and superb Victoria Regina *oloroso*.

Don Fino
Popular *amontillado* from SANDEMAN.

Don Zoilo
Superior range of sherries formerly made by Zoilo RUIZ MATEOS, the flagship of the expropriated RUMASA group in Jerez, and now marketed by DIEZ-MERITO. The best known is the round and aromatic *fino*, one of the best in its class.

Double Century
The best known of PEDRO DOMECQ's cream dessert sherries.

Dry Fly
Proprietary name belonging to the English shippers Findlater, Mackie, Todd. It was first used before World War II to describe its superior Findlater's Fino, which could not be protected by registration. More recently Findlater's has been marketing a very popular but somewhat sweeter apéritif sherry under the same name.

Dry Sack
A medium *amontillado*, the most popular of the wines from WILLIAMS & HUMBERT, sold in a distinctive sack, though the name, of course, is derived from the old-fashioned English name for sherry (*see* Sack).

Duff Gordon
Puerto de Santa María. The company was founded in 1768 by a Scot, Sir James Duff, who was British Consul in Cádiz at the time. The firm flourished, and in 1833 his son, Cosmo Duff Gordon, entered into partnership with Thomas Osborne of the sherry firm of the same name. OSBORNE finally bought out the interest of the Duff Gordon family in 1872, but, in addition to its own sherries, has continued to market the Duff Gordon wines under that name, though they are sold only abroad and are not found in Spain itself.

Made in the original *bodegas*, they embrace a wide range, including the Fino Feria, the popular El Cid medium-dry *amontillado* and Santa María Cream. The firm also makes a brandy and a Special Spanish Brandy.

Duke of Wellington
A good *fino* made by Bodegas INTERNACIONALES in their vast new *bodega*.

El Cid
Big-selling *amontillado* from DUFF GORDON.

Fiesta de la Vendimia

The famous wine festival held in Jerez de la Frontera in mid–September to celebrate the beginning of the vintage. Dedicated each year to a different country or city where sherry is popular, it embraces flamenco, bullfighting and horse shows, and culminates in the pressing of the first fruits on the steps of the Collegiate Church, a ceremony presided over by the Queen of the Vintage and her attendants in traditional costume, chosen from the prettiest girls in Jerez.

Fina

A light, dry MANZANILLA from Sanlúcar.

Fino

The lightest, driest and most delicate style of sherry, a pale straw colour and of 15·5–18 percent strength – the present tendency is to market lighter, less alcoholic *finos*. It develops beneath the FLOR until final fortification and is at its fragrant best when freshly bottled. Once opened, it should be served chilled and drunk within a few days.

Fino Quinta

Excellent *fino* from OSBORNE.

Flor

A film of yeasts of the genus *saccharomyces* growing spontaneously on the surface of certain types of sherry, especially *finos*, during maturation in SOLERA. It protects the wine from undue oxidation or conversion to vinegar and develops most thickly on wines aged in old butts.

Fortification

The addition to a wine of alcohol or brandy. When deficient in alcohol, *fino* sherries are lightly fortified at an early stage, and *olorosos* more strongly to kill the FLOR. *Finos* destined for export are further fortified before shipment or bottling with a 50 percent mixture of alcohol and mature sherry to prevent the reappearance of the *flor*.

Garvey

Jerez de la Frontera. Famous sherry house founded by William Garvey, who emigrated from Ireland in 1780 and set up business in Sanlúcar de Barrameda about 1797. His *bodegas* were for long among the biggest in Jerez and are impressive even by modern standards, with an *oloroso* SOLERA ranged along the side of an arcaded patio some quarter of a mile long.

The firm was taken over in 1979 by RUMASA, which fastidiously restored the old family mansion and also constructed a new vinification plant and further large *bodegas* for maturing the wine on the outskirts of Jerez. After the collapse of RUMASA the firm was for a time government-controlled, but was finally acquired by a German cooperative.

The wine is now fermented either in stainless steel or in cement *tinajas* (*see* Montilla-Moriles, page 148). Of its excellent sherries, the best known is the San Patricio *fino*, named by William Garvey after the patron saint of his native Ireland. Other wines include the aromatic and fully flavoured Tio Guillermo *amontillado*, the dry Ochavico and medium-dry Long Life *olorosos*, and the sweet Flor de Jerez cream sherry.

González Byass

Jerez de la Frontera. One of the largest and most important sherry firms, still family controlled, González Byass was founded in 1835 by Don Manuel María González Angel, who later took into partnership the firm's London agent, Robert Blake Byass. The head of the firm until his death some years ago, Don Manuel González Gordon, Marqués de Bonanza, was one of the most distinguished figures in Jerez, and wrote one of the best books on its wines: *Sherry, The Noble Wine* (1972).

The old *bodegas* in the centre of the town, alongside those of PEDRO DOMECQ, are vast in size: the famous 'La Concha', designed by Gustave Eiffel, houses 12,400 butts, and the more modern 'Tio Pepe' *bodega*, on three floors, a further 30,000; but even these are dwarfed by the modern vinification plant of 'Las Copas' on the road to Cádiz with its capacity of 60,000 butts. A quaint and human touch about one of the older *bodegas* is the small mice, carefully protected and fed – on sherry, of course.

TIO PEPE is the biggest-selling *fino* in the world, and deservedly so, since it remains one of the driest and most elegant. Other popular wines are the Elegante dry *fino*, La Concha medium *amontillado*, Alfonso dry *oloroso*, San Domingo pale cream and Nectar cream. González Byass also makes a magnificent old Amontillado del Duque and some superb old *olorosos* in limited quantity, such as the dry Apostoles Oloroso Muy Viejo and two very old dessert sherries, the Matusalem and Solera 1847 *oloroso dulce*, both almost black in colour with deep maderized nose and dryish bitter-sweet finish, since most of the sugar has been consumed over the years. *See also* page 275.

Guadalete, River

The Guadalete, flowing into the Bay of Cádiz, fairly closely follows the eastern boundary of the fan-shaped sherry-producing region.

Guadalquivir, River

Flowing into the Atlantic at Sanlúcar de Barrameda, the Guadalquivir forms the western boundary of the sherry region, dividing it from the salt marshes of the famous wildlife reserve of the Coto Doñana.

Harvey & Sons (España), John

Jerez de la Frontera. The old Bristol company of John Harvey & Sons had its origins in an earlier company founded in 1796, with which the Harvey family became associated in the early 19th century. Long famous as sherry shippers and particularly for its BRISTOL MILK and BRISTOL CREAM it is now a subsidiary of Allied Brewers, and it was not until 1970 that it established its own vineyards and *bodegas* in Jerez by buying the old-established firm of Mackenzie & Co. It later acquired the adjoining large *bodegas* of the Marqués de Misa and in 1973 began

developing much larger vineyards in association with
GARVEY and BARBADILLO. The continuous vinification plant
which it operates at the Gibalbin vineyards with Barbadillo
is one of the most modern in the region. More recently,
Harvey's have acquired the ex-RUMASA firms of PALOMINO
& VERGARA and Fernando A de TERRY, thus becoming the
largest concern in Jerez.

The old Misa *bodega* is one of the most impressive in
Jerez, and a perennial attraction for visitors in the beautiful
gardens of the old Mackenzie *bodegas* is the pool with its
Mississippi alligator.

Apart from the world-famous Bristol Cream, Harvey's
markets an extensive range of sherries, including the
inexpensive Luncheon Dry *fino*, Club Amontillado and
Tico, specially blended for drinking with ice and mixers
such as tonic and lemonade. At the top end of the range,
Bristol Milk is a better sherry than Bristol Cream, and the
1796 wines – Superior Fino, Fine Old Amontillado, Palo
Cortado and Rich Old Oloroso – are all first-rate.

Hidalgo y Cía, Vinícola

Old-established Sanlúcar firm and makers of the light and
graceful La Gitana *manzanilla*.

Infantes de Orleans-Borbon, Bodegas de los

Founded by the Duke of Montpensier in 1886, the firm is
now 50 percent owned by BARBADILLO. Among its well-
made sherries are the Alvaro *manzanilla* and first-rate
Botánico *amontillado*.

Internacionales, Bodegas

Jerez de la Frontera. Bodegas Internacionales is of the new
generation of sherry firms. The modern *bodega* was built by
RUMASA and completed in 1977. It occupies the largest
single building in Jerez and adjoins González Byass's new
vinification plant on the road to Cádiz, just outside Jerez.
After the expropriation of RUMASA in 1983 the company
was first administered by the government, then sold to the
Spanish industrialist Don Marcos Eguizábal in 1985. The

bodega, with its 63,000 butts, also houses the wines and *soleras* of the ex-RUMASA concerns of BERTOLA, DIESTRO, MARQUES DE MISA, Otaolaurruchi, PEMARTIN and VARELA. DIEZ-MERITO, engulfed by RUMASA shortly before the expropriation, is part of the same group, but possesses its own large vinification plant, and separate *soleras*.

Apart from the well-known brands of Bertola and the others, Bodegas Internacionales markets a good *fino* and other sherries under the label of The Duke of Wellington.

Jerez de la Frontera

Jerez (or Xérès) de la Frontera is the capital of the sherry region and, in corrupted English form, has given its name to the wine. The town was probably founded by the Phoenicians and was much fought over during the period of the Moorish occupation, hence the suffix of *de la Frontera* granted by King John I in 1380 (there is another Jerez de los Caballeros on the borders of Portugal). Its wines were well known in Roman times; but the trade greatly increased with the settlement of foreign traders, mostly English, after the expulsion of the Jews in 1492 and the massive participation of English, Scottish and Irish shippers, many of whom remained in the area, during the late 18th and 19th centuries.

With its old castle and walls, narrow streets and white Andalucian houses, its great roofed market and innumerable *bodegas*, often set in decorative gardens, it is a most attractive place to stay, especially in late spring or autumn. The best hotels are the modern four-star Hotel Jerez, whose amenities include a shaded garden, swimming pool and a spacious lounge, a crossroads for Jerez society before dinner; the Royal Sherry Park and the Avenida Jerez.

Many of its *bodegas* are described separately; the others on the official list of shippers are:

Tomás Abad	M Gil Luque
B M Lagos	Antonio Nuñez
José Bustamente	Luis Páez
José Estévez	Cayetano del Pino y Cía
M Gil Galán	Bodegas Rayón
Luis G Gordon	Juan Vicente Vergara
Emilio M Hidalgo	Viñas
José M Guerrero Ortega	

La Goya

First-rate *manzanilla pasada* made by DELGADO ZULETA.

La Guita

Classic *manzanilla pasada* made by PEREZ MARIN.

La Ina

PEDRO DOMECQ's big-selling, excellent *fino*, a shade less dry than some.

La Riva

Jerez de la Frontera. This well-known Spanish house was founded in 1776. It is now a subsidiary of PEDRO DOMECQ, but continues to make and sell wines under its own label. Tres Palmas has always been one of the best *finos*.

Los Tercios

Reputed vineyard area with ALBARIZA soil, to the southwest of JEREZ and adjoining that of BALBAINA.

Lustau, Emilio

Jerez de la Frontera. One of the leading independent, family-owned firms, Lustau occupies *bodegas* incorporating part of the old city wall. It also owns a large new *bodega* on the outskirts of Jerez and is one of the concerns which has best weathered the current recession through its policy of selling well-made own-brand sherries. Its Dry Lustau in various styles are first-rate wines, especially the *oloroso* and *palo cortado*. What has particularly caught the imagination of sherry drinkers is the ALMACENISTA range of sherries from small, individual stock-holders, rarely seen abroad until Lustau began selecting, bottling and shipping them for retail sale.

Macharnudo

Rated the best of the ALBARIZA areas, Macharnudo lies on high ground north of Jerez. At its centre is Macharnudo castle, familiar to enthusiasts of PEDRO DOMECQ sherries from its picture on their labels. Built during the 17th century, the firm still uses the castle for receptions.

Manzanilla

A pale, crisp and very dry *fina* with a salty tang from SANLUCAR DE BARRAMEDA, made in a SOLERA sometimes containing as many as fourteen SCALES. The word is also used in Spain for camomile tea, from which it is probably derived because of a certain similarity in flavour. *Manzanillas* owe their special characteristics to the atmospheric conditions and the special methods of operating the *soleras* in Sanlúcar. Not all the wines matured in Sanlúcar emerge as *manzanillas*, and *manzanilla* musts aged in Jerez develop as normal *finos*.

Manzanilla pasada

An old and mature *manzanilla*, resembling a light and very dry *amontillado*.

Marqués de Misa

Founded in the late 18th century, Misa became one of the

largest shippers during the 19th. The firm was bought out by RUMASA, while its impressive *bodega* was acquired by John HARVEY & Sons. The wines, now made at Bodegas INTERNACIONALES, are sold under the labels of Fino Chiquilla, Amontillado Abolengo, Oloroso La Novia and Brandy Royal.

Marqués del Real Tesoro, Herederos del

Jerez de la Frontera. The first Marquis gained the title ('Royal Treasure') by using his own silver to forge cannonballs while in command of a fleet for the Royal Treasury. The *bodega* was founded by a descendant in the late 19th century. One of the smaller family firms, it is particularly noted for an excellent *manzanilla* and a good, natural, unsweetened, nutty *amontillado*. It was fairly recently bought by José Estévez who, in a period of recession, has boldly constructed a brand new *bodega*.

Medina y Cia, José

Sanlúcar de Barrameda. The company was formed fairly recently following the acquisition of various *bodegas* in Sanlúcar de Barrameda and Jerez de la Frontera by the Medina family, who have complete control, and are now among the largest producers of *manzanilla* and large exporters, especially to the Low Countries. It markets a complete range of sherries under the Medina label and is also well known for the Alegría *manzanilla* and Jalifa *amontillado* from Hijos de Pérez Megia, a company within the group.

Medium sherry

An increasingly popular term used to describe a sherry akin to *amontillado* in style, but a little sweetened and made from a blend of wines rather than by ageing *fino*.

Mitad y mitad

A 50–50 mixture of alcohol and mature sherry which is used for fortification.

Oloroso

The darkest, softest, fullest-bodied and most fragrant of the styles of sherry, containing up to 24 percent alcohol. It is matured without FLOR and in its natural state is completely dry, but is often blended with Pedro Ximénez wine and VINO DE COLOR for making sweet dessert sherries.

Osborne y Cía

Puerto de Santa María. Founded in 1772, Osborne is the largest of the firms in Puerto de Santa María. As early as 1872 it bought the important firm of DUFF GORDON and has since launched sister concerns in Portugal, Mexico and the Rioja (see Montecillo, page 188). Its old *bodega* in Puerto de Santa María, built in 1837, is one of the most beautiful in the region; and the modern vinification plant, where the wine is fermented in horizontal rather than vertical tanks to approximate more closely to the traditional butt, is among the most advanced.

The wines include the excellent Fino Quinta, very dry, with a greenish cast and almond-like taste; the nutty Coquinero *amontillado*; the dry Bailen *oloroso*; and Osborne Cream. The firm is also the largest maker of Spanish brandy and spirits. *See also* page 278.

Pajarete, paxarete

Sweet Pedro Ximénez wine used for sweetening certain styles of sherry.

Palo cortado

A style of sherry between an *amontillado* and *oloroso*. Between 17·5 and 23 percent, it is classified as *dos* (the weakest), *tres* or *cuatro cortados* according to body and age. Genuine *palo cortado* is a beautiful wine with great depth and fragrance, but always expensive.

Palomino & Vergara

Jerez de la Frontera. This family firm, founded in 1765, occupies *bodegas* in the middle of Jerez, of which the centrepiece is the great glass-domed offices with the original mahogany and gilt counter and fitments. With its capacity of 40,000 butts, it was one of the largest of the firms taken over by RUMASA and now belongs to John HARVEY & Sons. Its strength has always been in the domestic market, though it possesses flourishing export markets in the Netherlands and Germany and is now exporting to Britain.

Its wines include a light, dry Tio Mateo *fino* with good *flor* nose and also medium, cream and pale cream sherries labelled as Palomino & Vergara. The firm is also well known for its Fabuloso and Eminencia brandies.

Pedro Domecq

Jerez de la Frontera. Pedro Domecq is the oldest of the large *bodegas* and the biggest single firm in the region, with extensive vineyards in MACHARNUDO and elsewhere, and dozens of *bodegas* between Jerez, Puerto de Santa María and Sanlúcar de Barrameda. In the oldest, 'El Molino', built in 1730, there are butts laid down centuries ago and dedicated to historical figures such as Pitt, Nelson and Wellington. The firm was founded by an Irish emigrant in 1730, but greatly expanded by the Domecq family from the Basses Pyrenées in association with its English agent, father of the writer John Ruskin. Its present head, Don José Ignacio Domecq, is one of the great sherry authorities of his generation; and the family maintains ties with Britain, among other things mounting one of the world's crack polo teams from among its members.

The firm has extensive interests in Mexico and has begun production of an excellent Rioja (*see* page 177). It is also one of the biggest makers of Spanish brandy in the world, and has built a huge new *bodega* in Jerez, modelled on the Great Mosque in Córdoba, to house the *soleras* for ageing it.

Apart from the famous *fino* LA INA, Domecq's other sherries include one of the best dry *olorosos*, Rio Viejo; a superb Sibarita *palo cortado*; the popular DOUBLE CENTURY cream; and an older and even richer Celebration Cream. *See also* page 279.

Pemartín y Cía, José

Jerez de la Frontera. The business was founded in 1819 by a French emigré, but thanks to the extravagances of Julian Pemartín, whose house in Jerez was constructed along the lines of the Paris Opéra, went bankrupt in 1857. It was for a time taken over by Sandeman, then became part of the RUMASA group and is now controlled by the reorganized Bodegas INTERNACIONALES. Its wines include Viña Pemartín *fino* and *amontillado*. *See also* page 279.

Pérez Marín, Hijos de Rainera

Sanlúcar de Barrameda. This small firm, founded in 1850, has long been known for making some of the best *manzanilla*. Its Bodegas La Guita took the name from the habit of a former member of the family, Domingo Pérez Marín, of refusing to sell his wine except for cash – *guita* in local slang. Its most famous wine is the delicious La Guita *manzanilla pasada*, an old and very fragrant *fina* on the point of conversion to *amontillado*. The other speciality is a *vinaigre de yema*, a sherry vinegar made in *solera* and of quite astonishing fragrance and fruitiness.

'Plastering'

The light dusting of the grapes with gypsum (calcium sulphate) before vinification, a process strongly attacked in Victorian times, but beneficial in its effects and leading to improved acidity in the musts.

Puerto de Santa María

Next in importance of the sherry towns to JEREZ, Puerto de Santa María is particularly noted for its *finos*, *amontillados* and brandy, and was the main port for shipping sherry until it was supplanted in the 1920s by its larger neighbour, Cádiz. It is a pleasant, open place with wide streets and houses with grilles and *miradors*. There are good beaches in the vicinity, served by resort hotels such as the luxurious Monasterio de San Miguel (a converted monastery) and the three-star Santa María and Meliá Caballo Blanco; and on the outskirts is the lush Casino Bahía de Cádiz.

Officially listed shippers in Puerto de Santa María without separate entries are:

Bodegas 501 (Carlos y Javier de Terry)	José Luis González Obregón
Miguel M Gómez	Jesús Ferris Marhanda
González y Cía	Portalto

PX

Abbreviation for the Pedro Ximénez grape, used mainly for sweet wines in Jerez, but for dry in Montilla (*see* page 141). There is a legend that it originated in the Canaries, was thence taken to the Rhine and brought to Jerez by one Pieter Siemens, a soldier of the Emperor Charles V, in the 16th century. Unfortunately, this seems more picturesque than true.

Raya

A term employed in classifying musts and also used to describe less delicate styles of *oloroso*.

'Refreshment'

The replenishment of the butts of a SOLERA with younger wine as the most mature is drawn off.

Rivero, J M

Founded in 1650 and reputedly the oldest of the sherry houses, the firm now belongs to Antonio Nuñez of Jerez de la Frontera, who continues to market the famous C–Z sherries, once bought by King Edward VII, and the old Trafalgar cream and brandy.

Rota

Village on the coast west of Jerez, once known for its red Rota tent wine, but now the site of a great US naval base.

Ruiz Mateos, Zoilo

Founded as a small wine company in ROTA in 1857, Ruiz Mateos was the springboard for the vast RUMASA empire, to which, in abbreviated form, it gave its name. The company moved to Jerez in 1930 and later acquired the handsome mansion of La Atalaya, formerly belonging to the Vergara family of Palomino & Vergara, as administrative headquarters both for itself and the whole of RUMASA's sherry group. La Atalaya also housed the magnificent Museum of Clocks and Watches founded by José María Ruiz Mateos, the President of RUMASA; the mansion is now a municipal museum.

Ruiz Mateos's *bodegas* and the *soleras* of its magnificent DON ZOILO sherries were taken over by DIEZ-MERITO and are now marketed under its label.

RUMASA

The early steps in the formation of RUMASA have been described under RUIZ MATEOS, and the company embarked on the highroad to fortune when it signed a contract with John HARVEY & Sons of Bristol for supplying all its large requirements of sherry. After breaking with Harvey's, José María Ruiz Mateos, the younger son of the founder, Don Zoilo, moved to Madrid and set about forming what was to become the largest grouping in Spain, embracing banks, insurance, shipping, chemicals, hotels and property.

However, RUMASA lost none of its early interest in wines and gained control of some 35 percent of the *bodegas* in Jerez: RUIZ MATEOS, Unión de Exportadores de Jerez, WILLIAMS & HUMBERT, PALOMINO & VERGARA, MARQUES DE MISA, PEMARTIN, VARELA, BERTOLA, Otaolaurruchi, DIESTRO, Lacave, Diez Morales, Valderrama & Gordon, Bodegas INTERNACIONALES, GARVEY and TERRY. In the Rioja, it took over Paternina, Bodegas Franco-Españolas, Lan and Berberana; in Montilla, Monte Cristo and Pérez Barquero; and in the Penedès, the sparkling wine firms of Castellblanch, René Barbier, Conde de Caralt and Segura Viudas. Its foreign acquisitions included the Augustus Barnett chain of off-licences in England.

RUMASA overstretched itself and in 1983 was expropriated lock, stock and barrel by the government, which took over the running of the different enterprises, finally selling them. This has been the subject of prolonged litigation, with José María Ruiz Mateos seeking refuge abroad for a time. The last of the companies to be returned to private ownership was Williams & Humbert, since Ruiz Mateos had maintained that the trade mark Dry Sack was his property and not that of the firm.

Sack

Old name for sherry (and also for Málaga and Canary wines), probably originating in the 15th century and derived from the Spanish *sacar* (to draw out).

San Patricio

One of the best-known *finos*, made by GARVEY.

Sánchez Romate Hermanos

Jerez de la Frontera. This old-established firm is supplier to the Spanish Royal family. Its sherries, which have long been noted for their quality, include the NPU *amontillado*, an unblended *solera* wine of great quality; Marismeño *fino*; Don Antonio *oloroso*; and Romate cream.

Sánchez Romate is, however, most famous for its Cardenal Mendoza brandy (*see* page 272).

Sandeman–Coprimar

Jerez de la Frontera. The firm was founded by a Scot, George Sandeman, who started business as a shipper in London about 1790, acting as agent for DUFF GORDON and later setting up his own establishments in Oporto and Jerez. Until its recent takeover by Seagram it remained a family firm. One of the largest concerns in Jerez, it makes its wines scrupulously and by traditional means, though the wines are no longer vinified in cask as they were until recently.

Big-selling wines are its DON FINO and Armada Cream, a first-rate dessert wine. In limited amount it also makes some quite exceptional wines, such as the Royal Ambrosante *palo cortado* and the Imperial Corregidor and Royal Corregidor *olorosos*, dry and sweet.

Sanlúcar de Barrameda

Sherry town west of Jerez at the mouth of the Guadalquivir estuary, famous for its dry *manzanillas*. A picturesque place with a wide beach opposite the wildlife reserve of Las Marismas, it possesses several good seafood restaurants and a few small but characterful hotels: Tartaneros; Los Helechos; and the Posada del Palacio.

Apart from *bodegas* with separate entries, the other firms in Sanlúcar are:

| Manuel de Argüeso | Hijos de A Pérez Megía |
| A Parra Guerrero | Pedro Romero |

'Scale'

Term used of a SOLERA to denote a row of butts containing wine of similar type and age.

Sobre tabla

Young wine which has been racked free of the lees and is ready for use in a CRIADERA.

Solera

Derived from the Latin *solum*, or Spanish *suelo* (meaning a floor), the word in its narrower sense applies to the BUTTS at floor level from which sherry is withdrawn for bottling or shipment. More loosely it is used for the whole assembly of butts in which sherry is matured, including those of the CRIADERA from which the *solera* proper is replenished. The butts are arranged in tiers or SCALES containing wine of identical type, but progressively younger in age. As wine in limited amounts is from time to time taken from the last row of butts, or *solera* proper, these are topped up with rather younger wine, and each scale is in turn 'refreshed' or replenished from that immediately preceding it in age. This procedure is known as 'working the scales', and is feasible because the younger wine rapidly takes on the characteristics of the older.

Soleras for producing *fino* require more scales, perhaps five, than those used for the fuller-bodied *oloroso*; and the most complicated are those used in SANLUCAR DE BARRAMEDA for making MANZANILLA, with up to 19.

Soto, José de

Jerez de la Frontera. Apart from its sherries, which include Fino Campero, Fino Soto, Amontillado la Uvita, Oloroso la Espuela and cream, the firm was the first to make a *ponche* (*see* page 279), and its brand remains one of the best.

Sunning

In the past it was standard practice to lay out the grapes on esparto grass mats and to sun them briefly. Thanks to improved methods of judging the optimum time for picking, sunning is now mainly used for grapes intended for sweet wines and the effect is to concentrate the amount of sugar in the must.

Terry, Fernando A de

Puerto de Santa María. This large firm, also brandy makers on a big scale, was founded in 1883 by the descendants of an Irish family which had settled in Spain as long ago as 1500. In 1981 the family sold both the *bodegas* and their famous establishment for raising the white Cartujano horses to a Catalan finance house, in fact acting for RUMASA; the company now belongs to John HARVEY & Sons. Most of the wine is made in a huge complex outside Puerto de Santa María, equipped with the latest in handling and pressing machinery, a modern vinification plant and some 40,000 butts. There are further large *soleras* in the atmospheric old *bodegas* in Puerto de Santa María itself.

In Spain, the sherries are labelled as Camborio *fino*, *oloroso* and cream. Some 90 percent of shipments to the UK go to Marks & Spencer, and are labelled as St Michael. *See also* page 281.

Tio Pepe

The world's largest-selling *fino*, made by GONZALEZ BYASS, and one of the driest, of consistently high standard.

Tres Palmas

Excellent *fino* from LA RIVA.

Valdespino, A R

Jerez de la Frontera. Old-established Spanish sherry house, whose *bodegas* and patios are among the most beautiful in Jerez – the older *bodegas* were once part of an ancient monastery. Valdespino makes a classic single-vineyard Inocente *fino*; a dry macho Tio Diego *amontillado*; an older

and superb Don Tomás *amontillado*; and a raisiny Pedro Ximénez Solera Superior.

Varela

Jerez de la Frontera. A company once within the RUMASA group, now part of Bodegas INTERNACIONALES and known particularly for its Varela Medium and Varela Cream sherries.

Venencia

An instrument used for withdrawing samples of sherry from the butt. In JEREZ, it consists of a small silver cup on a long whalebone handle; in SANLUCAR DE BARRAMEDA, where it is even more important not to disturb the FLOR, the cup is smaller and the *venencia* is made in one piece out of a bamboo cane.

Vino de color

A dark-coloured wine used for blending with certain brown and dessert sherries and made by fermenting a sugary boiled-down must (ARROPE) with a proportion of new must.

Williams & Humbert

Jerez de la Frontera. The firm was founded in 1877 by Alexander Williams, until then working as a clerk for WISDOM & WARTER. It subsequently became one of the most important in Jerez. A jewel in RUMASA's crown, it was the last of the sherry companies acquired by the expropriated colossus to be returned by the government to private ownership, when it was sold to Antonio BARBADILLO.

Its *bodegas* are among the most picturesque in Jerez; and points of interest for visitors are the splendid coaches and harnesses and the carefully preserved office of the British Vice-Consul, located within the *bodega* until the consulate was discontinued in 1979.

Its most popular wine is the DRY SACK *amontillado*; it also makes the well-known Canasta Cream and Walnut Brown, while Pando (sometimes, but wrongly, thought to have been named after the P & O shipping line) is a good *fino*.

Wisdom & Warter

Jerez de la Frontera. The company was founded in 1854 by two Englishmen, of whom *Punch* once wrote 'Wisdom sells the wine, Warter makes it.' The firm, now controlled by GONZALEZ BYASS, markets a wide range of sherries, including Fino Oliva, Manzanilla la Guapa, Amontillado Royal Palace, Tizón Oloroso and Wisdom's Choice cream.

Zapatos de pisar

The old-fashioned cowhide boots, studded with flat tacks and formerly used in crushing the grapes. Crushing is now carried out in horizontal presses, either of the mechanical or pneumatic type, or in yet more modern vinification plants by a continuous process, in which a first light crushing produces musts for *finos* and later, heavier pressing, for the fuller-bodied *olorosos*.

Wine and Food

On gastronomic maps of Spain, Andalucía is often labelled the *zona de los fritos* or 'region of fried food'; and high on the list of such dishes must come the fries of mixed fish, sometimes called *parejas* in Cádiz – this being the name of the dish cooked by the fishermen while at sea in their boats.

Cooking in the sherry region is very much oriented towards fish and seafood, available in great variety from the Bay of Cádiz and the nearby Atlantic coastline. In places such as Sanlúcar de Barrameda, the shellfish is magnificently fresh and the lobsters, for example, are large enough to serve a party of six. Another great speciality is the *gazpachos* or cold soups. Sherry vinegar is one of the best and fruitiest of vinegars – it is a great adjunct in salad dressing and other dishes. Apart from the delicious iced cakes and fruit tarts from the sweet trolley, by far the most popular sweet is *tocino de cielo* (*see* page 150).

Sherry is, not surprisingly, often used in cooking, and more than this it is usual to drink a chilled *fino* throughout the meal rather than a table wine.

Acedías fritas Fried baby soles.

Barbujitos Small fresh anchovies, fried.

Bistec salteado al Jerez Steak sautéed with sherry.

Boquerones de la Isla Fried fresh anchovies, locally caught.

Cañaíllas de la Isla A sea-snail typical of the coast. It is lightly boiled and eaten cold, the sharp tail of one snail being used to extract the meat from the others.

Cazón Baby shark, marinated with paprika and vinegar.

Consomé al Jerez Consommé with sherry, usually 'fortified' with an extra dose at the table!

Coquinas al ajillo Cockles in garlic sauce.

Dorada a la sal Gilthead baked in a thick paste of sea salt, which is removed by the waiter at the table.

Fritura gaditana A mixed fry of small fish.

Gazpacho andaluz Cold, uncooked soup containing chopped

tomatoes, cucumber and green peppers, together with olive oil, vinegar and garlic. Breadcrumbs may either be used in making it or served on the side.

Helado de pasas con PX A particularly delicious ice cream made with raisins and served by pouring sweet Pedro Ximénez sherry over it.

Jamón de Jabugo The best and most fully flavoured type of the highly cured *jamón serrano*, from a village near Huelva. Like Bayonne or Parma ham, it is eaten either on its own or with melon.

Macedonia de frutas naturales Fruit salad with sherry.

Naranjas acaramelizadas Fresh oranges, cut up and served in a syrup containing caramel.

Paire Scabbard fish, cut into steaks and grilled.

Pijotas A tiny fish fried like whitebait.

Pipirrana con gambas Prawns cooked with tomatoes and peppers.

Puntillitas Minute inkfish, dipped in a light batter and fried in olive oil.

Riñones al Jerez Calves' or pigs' kidneys, sliced and sautéed in olive oil and served in a tomato sauce containing sherry.

Salchichas al Jerez Fried sausages, flavoured with sherry and served with squares of fried bread.

Salpicón de mariscos Cold fish and shellfish salad with scampi, monkfish and lobster, dressed with sherry vinegar.

Sopa de pescado gaditana A rich fish soup akin to *bouillabaisse*.

Tortilla suflé A sweet soufflé omelette.

Urta a la roteña *Urta* is a fish for which there is no translation. It feeds on shellfish, acquiring great flavour, and is a speciality of Rota, on the coast west of Jerez, where it is cooked with a rich sauce of tomatoes and red peppers.

Restaurants

Arcos de la Frontera *Mesón del Brigadier* (near the Lake of Arcos with terrace and views; well known for its meat and charcuterie).

Cádiz *El Faro* (best in Cádiz, splendid range of locally caught fish and sophisticated cooking); *Ventorrillo del Chato* (period charm and well-cooked Andalucian dishes).

Jerez de la Frontera *La Mesa Redonda* (small sophisticated restaurant belonging to one of the Valdespino family, who does the cooking and marketing); *El Bosque* (charming surroundings, international cuisine and some well-cooked Andalucian dishes, good wine list); *Mesón del Duque*; *Tendido* (opposite the bullring, local fish dishes and good wine list).

Puerto de Santa María *El Faro del Puerto* (branch of the famous *El Faro* in Cádiz); *La Soleta* (spacious restaurant outside the town); *La Terraza* (luxurious restaurant of the Casino Bahía de Cádiz, international cooking).

Sanlúcar de Barrameda *Mirador Doñana* (beach restaurant serving *tapas* and the excellent local seafood); *Bigote* (superb and splendidly fresh seafood – essential to book in advance).

Valencia and Murcia

The eastern area along the Mediterranean coast, known in Spain as the Levante, embraces the three DO regions of Utiel-Requena, Valencia and Alicante within the autonomy of Valencia, and Jumilla and Yecla in Murcia. In terms of bulk production, the Levante is second in importance only to La Mancha. The city of Valencia is home to a number of large wineries with the very latest in equipment, drawing from the region in general for grapes or wine. Clean and drinkable light table wines are supplied to the world and its supermarkets, and the *bodegas* specialize in blending wines to the specification of their customers.

The traditional wines are of the Mediterranean type, full-bodied, spicy and high in alcohol. The alcoholic strength of the wines from Yecla and Jumilla may in part be explained by the fact that the black Monastrell grape so typical of the regions was largely unaffected by phylloxera, and the vines are not usually grafted on to American stocks as in other parts of Spain and the rest of Europe. The Monastrell is also the grape *par excellence* of Alicante, though a certain amount of white wine is made from the Verdil.

Perhaps the best of the Levante wines are the *rosados* from the upland region of Utiel-Requena, made from the black Bobal grape. These are among the very best rosés from Spain, pale, very light, fruity, fragrant and refreshing. The commercial *bodegas* in Valencia draw largely on the wine from Utiel-Requena for their blends – the Swiss firm of Schenk, for example, maintains a *bodega* there and buys from the cooperatives – and there is a gentlemen's agreement that wine from any of the three demarcated regions of the autonomy of Valencia may be labelled and shipped as DO Valencia. Not surprisingly, in a part of the country famous for its dessert grapes, there is also some luscious Moscatel from the coastal area.

Tourists in resorts such as Alicante, Benicasim, Benidorm, Calpe and Javea will certainly find it worthwhile to experiment with the local growths and the house wine in the restaurants, rather than choose Rioja.

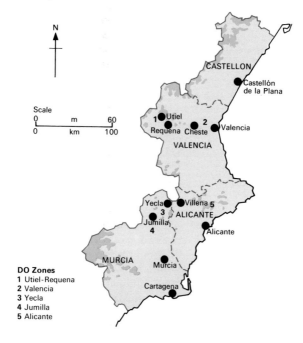

Alicante

Alicante, with its mild climate and marble-paved promenade, lined with palms and facing the port, is the best base for visiting the *bodegas* in its area and also those of the somewhat inaccessible regions of YECLA and JUMILLA in the mountainous hinterland of Murcia. The best hotels are the four-star Meliá Alicante and Grand Sol in the city itself, and the five-star Sidi San Juan Palace-Sol in the vacation resort of Playa de San Juan on its outskirts.

Alicante DO r p (w dr sw) ★→★★

This demarcated region, extending to 17,154 hectares and producing 20 million litres of wine in 1989, is divided into two subregions. The maritime zone on the coast around Calpe, Javea and Denia makes sweet Moscatel. The larger and more important central zone lies in the hills around Villena, Pinoso and Monóvar and produces a light rosé, a VINO DE DOBLE PASTA, and full-bodied reds high in alcohol, made with some 90 percent Monastrell. Small amounts of white wine are also made from some 85 percent of Verdil.

Alto-Turia DO w dr ★★

Subdivision of the DO VALENCIA in the high northwest of the province producing white wines of some quality: fruity, lightly acid with a greenish cast and containing some 11·5–13 percent of alcohol, they are made with the Merseguera grape.

Benicarló r ★

A prime favourite in the 19th century for lacing less robust French wines, the red wine of Benicarló has virtually disappeared owing to the expense of replanting with grafted vines after the disastrous phylloxera epidemic. The small town of Benicarló, with its comfortable seaside *parador*, is close to the picturesque and sea-girt Peñiscola, whose castle was the refuge of the last of the Anti-Popes, Pedro de Luna.

Bleda, Bodegas DO r p w dr g ★★

Jumilla (Murcia). DO Jumilla. The *bodega* was founded in 1917 by the father of the present owner and was the first in the region to bottle its wines (in 1936). The white Castillo Jumilla, made from 100 percent Airén, and the red and rosé containing 100 percent Monastrell, are worthwhile young wines for early consumption. There is also a rich and fruity Montesinos *crianza* and a fortified Oro Viejo.

Carcelén NCR, Asensio DO r p w dr ★→★★ 75, 78, 81, 83

Jumilla (Murcia). DO Jumilla. Maker of sound, but

typically full-bodied Jumilla wines high in alchol, labelled as Sol y Luna, Pura Sangre, Bullanguero and Acorde.

Casa de Calderón DO r p g ★★
Requena (Valencia). DO Utiel-Requena. Small *bodega*, islanded in its vineyards, owned by the Mompó family and making some superior Requena wines, among them a port-like *generoso*.

Castaño, Bodegas DO r p w dr ★→★★
Yecla (Murcia). DO Yecla. Well-equipped *bodega*, the best in Yecla, labelling its wines as Viña las Gruesas, Pozuelo and Castaño. The young red Castaño, made by carbonic maceration, is clean, very fruity and well structured.

Castellón de la Plana r w dr ★
The province of Castellón de la Plana, north of Valencia, was once a prolific producer of wines, including the famous BENICARLO. After the PHYLLOXERA epidemic it was replanted with HYBRIDS, yielding coarse, 'foxy' wines frowned on by INDO; because of the expense of replanting with grafted varieties its vineyards are being progressively abandoned.

Castillo de Liria w dr r p ★→★★
Label used by Vicente GANDIA PLA for its range of pleasant table wines.

Cheste w dr ★
Formerly a DO in its own right, Cheste, lying between VALENCIA and UTIEL-REQUENA, has been incorporated in the DO VALENCIA. It is a prolific producer of dry and somewhat earthy white wines of 12·5–15 percent, neutral and without a great deal of character.

Clariano DO r w dr ★
Subdivision of the DO VALENCIA in the extreme south of the province bordering Alicante. It produces both red and white wines of 11–13 percent, the best being the reds made from the Monastrell.

Egli, C Augusto w dr p r ★→★★
Valencia and Utiel-Requena. Large Swiss-owned exporter
founded in 1903. The red Casa Lo Alto *crianza*, made at its
modern *bodega* in Utiel-Requena, is full and fruity.

Eval, Bodegas DO r (p g) ★★ 83, 86, 88
Villena (Alicante). DO Alicante. Large modern *bodega*
making good López de la Torre reds, matured in oak, from
a blend of Monastrell and Cencibel (Tempranillo).

Fondillón g ★★★
Famous *generoso* from Monóvar, west of Alicante, copper-
coloured, aromatic and aged in cask for some 20 years.
Very little is now made; the 1959 vintage is legendary.

Gandía Pla, Vicente w dr r p ★→★★
Valencia. Large-scale exporter with huge state-of-the-art
plant at Chiva, west of Valencia, making inexpensive and
very drinkable Castillo de Liria wines.

García Carrión, Bodegas J DO r p w dr ★→★★
Jumilla (Murcia). DO Jumilla. Private firm making good
standard Jumilla wines, mainly red.

García Poveda, H L DO r (p w dr sw) res ★→★★
Villena (Alicante). DO Alicante. Sizable family concern
with *bodegas* at Villena in the hills behind Alicante. Costa
Blanca red, white and rosé; Marquesado red, white and
rosé; Costa Blanca Moscatel. The firm also makes a range
of vermouths, full-bodied in character like the other wines.
See also page 275.

Hybrids
The district around CASTELLON DE LA PLANA, BENICARLO and
Vinaroz was a large supplier of red wine to France during
the PHYLLOXERA epidemic of the late 19th century, but after
it had itself been affected, the vines were replaced with
American hybrids. Many survive on peasant plots, but
government regulations forbid their use in new plantations.

Irrigation

Because of the low rainfall, JUMILLA and YECLA are regions where irrigation is permitted, but only on a limited scale and during the winter.

Jumilla DO r (w dr) ★→★★

The demarcated region extends to 41,736 hectares with a production in 1989 of 53 million litres of wine, most of it a dark, full-bodied red containing up to 18 percent alcohol. Apart from the heat of its long summers, the other reason for this high alcohol content is that, because of the high content of chalk and organic material in the soils, the region was unaffected by phylloxera, and it is one of the few areas in Spain or in Europe where vines are still grown ungrafted. The best wines are made with the Monastrell and aged in oak, and efforts are being made to reduce the high alcohol content by earlier picking and blending with white wine.

La Purísima, Cooperativa Agrícola DO r p w dr g ★

Yecla (Murcia) DO Yecla. The livelihood of the thousands of smallholders in Yecla have depended on this huge cooperative which vinifies their grapes. In the mid-1980s it exported vast amounts of basic bulk wine but has undergone a severe crisis as the demand fell away, with consumers demanding something better. It is to be hoped that modernization will result in better wines and a revival of its fortunes.

Levante

Name given to the strip stretching along the Mediterranean coast of Spain from the Cabo de Gato, just east of Almería, to the delta of the Ebro in the north.

Murviedro, Cavas

Label for a range of very drinkable Valencian wines from Bodegas SCHENK. The white is made with Merseguera and Moscatel; the rosé with Bobal and Garnacha; and there are different *crianza* reds made with Monastrell and Garnacha,

100 percent Monastrell and 100 percent Tempranillo (from Utiel-Requena).

Ochoa Palao, Enrique DO r w dr p ★→★★
Yecla (Murcia). DO Yecla. Best for its red Barahonda and Ochoa, made from Monastrell and Garnacha.

Phylloxera
Certain areas of the Levante (JUMILLA and YECLA) were wholly or partially unaffected by this insect pest of the vine and still grow ungrafted vines, while others, like CASTELLON DE LA PLANA, were replanted with American HYBRIDS and have never fully recovered.

Poveda, Salvador DO r p g ★→★★★
Monóvar (Alicante). DO Alicante. Family concern with *bodegas* in the hills, making some of the best Alicante wine, albeit full-bodied and high in alcohol, notably the red and rosé Viña Vermeta and the outstanding FONDILLON *gran reserva* 1969.

San Isidro, Cooperativa DO r (p w dr) res ★→★★ 70, 80, 84
Jumilla (Murcia). DO Jumilla. Huge, well-equipped and well-run modern cooperative. Apart from its fresh young Sabatacha white and rosé, and a young red Casa Alta for immediate consumption, it also makes good oak-aged reds under the labels of Solera, Sabatacha and 50 Aniversario.

Schenk, Bodegas r p w dr sw res ★→★★
Valencia. This Spanish arm of the large Swiss concern buys wine from the whole Levante area and from as far afield as La Mancha, and apart from elaborating and shipping wines for supermarkets and own-label purchasers, bottles good standard Valencian wines under the label Cavas MURVIEDRO.

Señorío del Condestable, Bodegas DO r p w dr ★★
Jumilla (Murcia). DO Jumilla. An outpost of Bodegas y Bebidas (formerly Savin, *see* page 174) making a particularly pleasant red Condestable.

Yecla, in the hills of Murcia

Utiel, Cooperativa Agrícola de DO r ★ p ★★

Utiel (Valencia). DO Utiel-Requena. One of the best of the large cooperatives in the region making a thick black VINO DE DOBLE PASTA for blending, a normal red wine, and light, pale and fragrant Del Tollo and Sierra Negrete rosés.

Utiel-Requena DO r p ★→★★

At the western extreme of the province of Valencia, Utiel-Requena, with an area of 39,500 hectares and a production in 1990 of 142 million litres, is an upland extension of the central plateau. The typical wines, made from some 90 percent of the black Bobal grape with smaller amounts of Cencibel (Tempranillo) and Garnacha, are of three types: a thick, almost black VINO DE DOBLE PASTA for blending (of which progressively less is being produced); a pale, light and entirely delicious rosé; and a sturdy *tinto* or red wine. Another increasingly important activity is the large-scale production of grape juice.

Valencia

Valencia, the third city of Spain, surrounded by its orange
and lemon groves, is the queen of the Levante, and despite
the devastations of the Napoleonic and Civil Wars, there
still remain parts of the old walls with their gates and
turrets, and narrow streets flanked with balconied houses.
Its *fallas*, celebrated in mid-March, with bonfires and
processions of giant effigies in the streets, is one of the
liveliest Spanish fiestas.

Valencia is the headquarters of numerous huge export
houses, shipping wine in bulk all over the world; and its
Grao ships more wine than any other port in Spain.

The natural base for visits to the neighbouring vineyards
and to those of UTIEL-REQUENA, it has many luxury hotels –
such as the Astoria Palace, Meliá Valencia and Reina
Victoria – but my own favourite is the old-fashioned three-
star Inglés, opposite the best ceramic museum in Spain, in
the palace of the Marqués de Dos Aguas.

Valencia DO (r) w dr sw ★→★★

The demarcated region, extending to 18,566 hectares and
producing 54 million litres of wine in 1990, incorporates
the former DO CHESTE and the subregions of ALTO-TURIA,
CLARIANO and VALENTINO. They produce more white wine
than red, mostly of typical Mediterranean type, earthy, full-
bodied, strong and low in acid.

Valentino DO r dr (w) ★→★★

The largest of the subregions of the DO VALENCIA, to the
west of the city in the centre of the province and
incorporating the former DO CHESTE. The principal white
grapes are the Merseguera, Malvasía, Moscatel, Pedro
Ximénez and Planta de Pedralba; and the best wines are the
dry whites made from the Merseguera and Pedro Ximénez
and the sweet Moscatels. Reds from the Garnacha Tinta and
Tintorera.

Valsangiacomo, Cherubino w dr r p ★★

Valencia. Reputed exporter of regional wines including the

pleasant Vall de Sant Jaume range and superior Marqués de Caro wines.

Vinival, Bodegas r p w dr sw ★

Valencia. Vinival was founded in 1969 to handle bulk wines from various regions of the Levante from the old-established firms of Garrigos, Mompó, Teschendorff and Steiner; the majority shareholder is now Bodegas y Bebidas (formerly Savin, *see* page 174). It operates from a huge, brick-built, cathedral-like building near the port. With its capacity of 30 million litres, it ships huge quantities of sound, spicy Mediterranean-type wine. The best of the big-selling Torres de Quart range is the soft rosé; much the best of its wines are the rosé and red Viña Calderón.

Vino de doble pasta

Much of the wine from UTIEL-REQUENA and ALICANTE is made in an entirely individual fashion. The grapes are destalked and lightly crushed, and after a few hours in the vat to extract colour from the skins the must is pumped off into a fresh vat, where fermentation continues *en blanc* to produce a light, fragrant and delicate rosé. The original vat is then topped up with a further load of crushed grapes, and continued fermentation produces a *vino de doble pasta*, thick in extract, black in colour, with up to 18 percent alcohol; not for consumption, but for blending with thinner wines such as those from Galicia. With a demand for lighter wines, production is decreasing in favour of grape juice.

Vitivino, Bodegas DO r ★★→★★★ 88

Jumilla (Murcia). DO Jumilla. Jean-Louis Gadeau, a French oenologist married to a local girl, has created a stir in Jumilla with his peachy red Altos de Pío, a revelation as to what can be done with the Monastrell grape.

Yecla DO r (w) ★→★★

The demarcated region, extending to 7,000 hectares and producing 150,000 hectolitres of wine in 1990, neighbours that of JUMILLA in the hills of Murcia and produces very similar wines. As in Jumilla, the impact of phylloxera was far less severe than in other parts of Spain, and some 40 percent of the predominant Monastrell grapes are grown ungrafted. The typical wines are dark, full-bodied reds containing up to 18 percent of alcohol. With a drop in the demand for bulk wine, exports have fallen dramatically in recent years, and attempts are now being made to produce lighter wines.

Wine and Food

Like all the coastal areas of Spain, the Levante offers a magnificent variety of fish and shellfish; but the region in general, and Valencia in particular, is known above all for its rice dishes, especially the world-renowned *paella*. The *huertas* or gardens of Valencia are famous for their oranges and also for their vegetables, of which good use is made in cooking. Alicante almonds are used to make nougats or *turrones*.

It is one of nature's ironies that hot regions, where one most appreciates lighter wines, produce the strongest, and colder areas the lightest. At least in its rosés from Utiel-Requena the Levante has a wine that goes admirably with fish and light food. Oddly enough, a full-bodied red wine goes better with *paella* than a white, though one of the spicy Valencian whites will also stand up to its mixture of definite flavours.

Arroz abanda Fish and shellfish cooked with onions, bay leaf, saffron, olive oil and seasoning, and served with rice, boiled in the fish stock. It is accompanied with *alioli*, a thick garlic sauce.

Arroz 'Empedrat' Popular with the workers in the *turrón* factories of Jijona, this is also known as *arroz de fábrica* ('factory rice') and is made with haricot beans, garlic, tomatoes, parsley and rice.

Bacalao a la valenciana Dried cod cooked in the oven with rice, fish broth, tomato purée, onions, grated cheese, butter and hard-boiled eggs.

Conejo a la valenciana Young rabbit stewed with green peppers, black peppercorns, garlic, parsley and olive oil.

Empanadillas valencianas Small pasties filled with tuna mixed with tomato sauce, then fried crisp in olive oil or baked in the oven.

Faves al tombet Fresh broad beans cooked with lettuce, artichoke hearts, garlic shoots, red paprika, vinegar and bread.

Guisantes al estilo valenciano Fresh peas cooked with garlic, pepper, onions, thyme, white wine, bay leaf, olive oil and saffron.

Paella valenciana Saffron-flavoured rice, cooked simply with fish and shellfish or with a variety of other ingredients, such as chicken, meat and fresh vegetables. It is usual in Spain to drink red rather than white wine with *paella*.

Potaje valenciano A thick soup containing chickpeas, spinach, sweet paprika, lemon, parsley, onions, garlic and egg yolks.

Sopa a la valenciana Thick soup with a variety of fresh vegetables, rice, onions and parsley, cooked in ham stock.

Sopa de mariscos levantina Valencian version of *bouillabaisse* with shellfish, vegetables, saffron, bay leaf, tomatoes and garlic. It is served in two parts: first the broth with croûtons, and then the shellfish with a cold sauce.

Turrón Nougat, in two varieties. *Turrón de Alicante* is a hard, brittle tablet made of toasted and coarsely chopped almonds, honey and egg whites. *Turrón de Jijona* is softer and contains ground almonds, ground pine kernels, sugar, coriander and egg yolks.

Restaurants

Alicante *Delfín* (excellent rice dishes and outstanding baked bass); *Nou Manolin* (good *tapas*, reasonable prices and wonderful cellar).

Murcia *El Rincón de Pepe* (Murcia is a goodish drive from Jumilla and Yecla, but this is quite simply one of the best restaurants in Spain).

Utiel *La Abuela* (regional cooking at its best; try the *ajo arriero* – creamy *bacalao* cooked with garlic, eggs and potatoes – with the local rosé).

Valencia *La Hacienda* (good cooking and a long wine list); *Eladio* (frogs' legs with fresh broad beans); *Galbis* (sea bass in garlic and pepper sauce; fried kid with garlic shoots).

Sparkling Wines

Manufacture in Spain of sparkling wines by the champagne method was first begun by Don José Raventós, whose family firm of Codorníu is now one of the largest concerns in the world to make wines of this type. To begin with, the wines were known as *champaña*, but the producers in Reims rightly objected that the name should be applied only to wines produced in the Champagne district of France; and they are now referred to as *cava*, a word also used, rather than *bodega*, to describe the establishments in which they are made.

Since February 1986 *cava* has been the subject of a DO which, in deference to the pundits of the EC and unlike most of the others, demarcates a patchwork of dissimilar regions, municipalities and villages in different parts of Spain where it may be produced. These include areas, sizable or minuscule, in the provinces of Girona, Barcelona (including the whole of the area in the Penedès demarcated for still wines), Tarragona, Lleida (Lérida), Zaragoza, Navarra, La Rioja and Alava, with others in Valladolid, Valencia and Badajoz likely to follow. However, more than 95 percent of *cava*, and all the best of it, is made in Cataluña, and probably more than 90 percent in and around Sant Sadurní d'Anoia in the Penedès, where it originated.

The grapes used for the wines in Cataluña are mainly the white Xarel-lo, imparting alcoholic strength and colour; the Macabeo (or Viura), contributing freshness and fruit; and the Parellada, grown up the hill slopes, conferring acidity and delicacy of nose. Chardonnay is increasingly being grown and used for *cava*; outside Cataluña it is generally made with 100 percent Macabeo (Viura). Pink wines (never referred to as rosé when talking of sparkling wines) are made with a proportion of the black Cariñena or Garnacha Tinta.

In modern installations, the must is extracted in horizontal presses and vinified in temperature-controlled stainless steel tanks, and elaboration then follows the classical methods of champagne. The young wine is dosed with a solution of sugar and with cultured yeasts, filled into stout champagne-type bottles, temporarily corked and left for a period of years in deep underground cellars until such time as the sugar has been converted into carbon dioxide and alcohol. The bottles are then, over a period of months, gradually upended, so that the fine sediment falls towards the neck of the bottle, which is finally frozen and uncorked, and the plug containing the sediment is forcibly expelled by the pressure of gas inside. A *licor de expedición* containing a little sugar is added; and the bottles are then recorked and allowed to rest before being labelled and despatched.

The large *cavas* have rationalized the process by using *girasols* to promote the descent of the sediment, forklift trucks and pallets for stacking the bottles in the cellars, and ingenious electronic systems for locating batches of bottles and bringing them to the bottling line for *dégorgement* (removal of the temporary corks) and labelling; but none of these handling processes affects the elaboration or quality of the wine – as romantics would sometimes have one believe. Such differences as do emerge between champagne and *cava* result from the character of the grapes and soil and not from the method of manufacture.

Not all *espumosos* (or sparkling wines) are made by the champagne method. There are also sparkling wines whose second fermentation takes place, not in individual bottles, but in large pressurized tanks known as *cuves closes* or, in Spain, *gran-vas*. This process produces acceptable wines, albeit with a larger and shorter-lasting bubble, but still a great deal better than the *gaseosos*, made simply by pumping carbon dioxide into still wine. The *vinos de aguja* or 'green wines', which develop a more subdued bubble or *pétillance* as the result of a naturally occurring secondary fermentation, are described in the chapter on Galicia.

There has been endless discussion about the relative merits of *cava* and champagne. In my own experience, *cava* tends to be a little softer, fuller in flavour and fruitier in nose; and champagne to possess more edge and finesse. Conventional wisdom is that nobody of any experience can fail to tell the difference, but that most discriminating of Spanish winemakers, Miguel Torres, writes of a systematic series of comparative tastings that 'the *cava* wines of Sant Sadurní d'Anoia have frequently been judged superior to their French homologues.' They are certainly less than half the price; and the only sensible thing is to drink and enjoy Spanish *cava* as a sparkling wine in its own right.

In 1991 some 150 million litres of *cava* were made, of which 50 million were exported, so that its production is now a most important facet of the Spanish wine industry.

Styles of Sparkling Wine

In increasing order of sweetness, Spanish sparkling wines are labelled as:

Brut de Brut		Seco	Fairly dry
Brut Nature	Very dry	Semiseco	Semi-dry
Brut Reserva		Semidulce	Semi-sweet
Vintage		Dulce	Sweet
Brut	Dry		

Rosado or Rose indicates a pink wine.

L'Aixertell

Brand name for a big-selling *cuve close* sparkler made by the Unió de Cellers del Noya, a company jointly owned by FREIXENET and Bodegas y Bebidas (*see* page 174).

Ampurdán, Cavas del

Perelada (Girona). This is under the same management as the Castillo de PERELADA, well known for its *cava* wines, but since it produces still wines in Cataluña (*see* page 80) and sparklers made by the *cuve close* method, Spanish regulations require that it be housed in a separate building across a public highway. Its Perelada was the subject of the famous 'Spanish champagne' case.

Bilbainas, Bodegas DO

Haro (Logroño). DO Cava. One of the leading producers of Rioja (*see* page 173), Bodegas Bilbainas also makes limited amounts of Lumen, Royal Carlton Cuvée Especial and Royal Carlton Brut Nature by the champagne method, using Viura and Malvasía grapes. The wines are made in deep cellars beneath the *bodega* by the most traditional methods, clearance after second fermentation taking place in PUPITRES and *dégorgement* being effected manually. The wines are dry and of good quality, but rather fuller in flavour than those from Cataluña.

Castellblanch DO

Sant Sadurní d'Anoia (Barcelona). DO Cava. When Castellblanch was founded by Don Jerónimo Parera Figueras in 1908, it was a family concern with only three employees and an annual turnover of 100,000 bottles of sparkling wine. Expansion took place rapidly under Don Jerónimo's son, and after RUMASA (*see* pages 230–231) acquired the company in 1974, output was boosted to ten million bottles, made both by the champagne method and in *cuves closes*. The firm is now part of the FREIXENET group. In order of quality, its wines are sold as Brut Zero, Extra Brut, Gran Cremant and Gran Castell.

Castilla la Vieja, Bodega de Crianza

Producers of an excellent Brut Natural Palacio de Bornos made by the champagne method. It is one of the absurdities of the *reglamento* covering sparkling wines that because it is made with 100 percent Verdejo, this delicious wine may not be called *cava. See also* Castilla-León, page 56.

Cava

Meaning 'cellar', the word is used both to describe an establishment in which sparkling wines are made by the champagne method, and also such wines themselves, now the subject of a DO.

Champaña

Name long used for Spanish wines made by the champagne method until, in deference to the French protests, the Spanish government forbade it.

Chandon DO

It says much for the name *cava* (and also reflects the difference in price of grapes in Cataluña and Reims) that Moët & Chandon should have set up an establishment and

are making a good quality NV wine with a blend of
Chardonnay and the traditional native grapes.

Codorníu DO 73, 75

Sant Sadurní d'Anoia. (Barcelona). DO Cava. It was Don
José Raventós of the family firm of Codorníu, engaged in
winemaking since 1551, who in 1872 began the
manufacture of sparkling wine by the champagne method
in Spain, after studying practices in Reims. Today,
Codorníu is one of the two largest concerns in the world to
make wines of this type.

The *cavas* and family mansion are situated in decorative
gardens above 17 kilometres of underground cellars. The
original buildings, designed in *fin de siècle* style with echoes
of Gaudí and including an old press house converted into a
wine museum, have been declared a National Monument;

and the former labelling hall is now a reception area for the
160,000 visitors who descend on the *cavas* each year.

Codorníu has vineyards of its own, but obtains large
quantities of grapes from some 350 regular suppliers in the
area. They are pressed in a modern band press and vinified
in batteries of temperature-controlled stainless steel tanks of
20,000 litres capacity. Subsequent elaboration of the wine is
by the traditional champagne method.

The best of its wines are the Gran Codorníu Brut and
Non Plus Ultra and Anna de Codorníu. Others are the
Rosé Brut, Extra Dry, Semi Dry, Sweet, Grand Cremant
dry and semi-dry, and Delapierre, named in honour of a
former French oenologist at the *cavas. See also* Raimat.

Conde de Caralt DO 69, 78, 80, 82, 85, 86

Sant Sadurní d'Anoia (Barcelona). DO Cava. The Conde
de Caralt was making *cava* wines long before it embarked
on the production of still wine in Cataluña (*see* page 86).
The concern, once part of the RUMASA group (*see* pages
230–231), now belongs to FREIXENET. Its dry and light
sparkling wine is bottled under the label Conde de Caralt.

COVIDES (Cooperativa Vinícola del Penedès) DO

Sant Sadurní d'Anoia (Barcelona). DO Cava. Large
cooperative making and exporting good *cava* under the
labels of Duc de Foix and Xenius.

Espumoso

Spanish name for sparkling wine.

Ferret, Cavas DO 87, 88

Guardiola de Font-Rubí (Barcelona). DO Cava. The Cava
Brut Natural from this small firm was chosen as one of the
very best *cavas* by the Madrid Club de Gourmets in 1992.

Freixenet DO 69, 71, 73, 75, 78, 85, 87

Sant Sadurní d'Anoia (Barcelona). DO Cava. Freixenet,
founded in 1915, with its recent acquisitions of CONDE DE
CARALT, CASTELLBLANCH and SEGURA VIUDAS, is about equal
in size to CODORNIU and between them the two concerns
make at least 80 percent of all the *cava* from the PENEDES.

The plant at Sant Sadurní is one of the most modern in
the Penedès, and the wine is vinified at low temperature in
huge stainless steel tanks of 600,000 litres capacity. Freixenet
was also the first of the *cavas* to introduce GIRASOLS. Thanks

to these innovations and most advanced handling and bottling equipment, it has been able to hold down the price of its *cava* wines without detriment to quality. The Freixenet group is currently the largest exporter of Spanish sparkling wines to the USA, where it sold 17 million bottles in 1988. It also makes sparkling wine in Mexico and California, and owns the champagne house of Henri Abelé.

Apart from splendid vintage wines, such as the Cuvée DS 1969, named in honour of Doña Dolores Sala, widow of the company's founder Don Pedro Ferrer Bosch, the best of the wines are the Reserva Real, the very dry and light Brut Nature, and popular Cordon Negro. It also markets the less expensive Carta Nevada and Cremant Rosé.

Gaseoso

The cheapest (and nastiest) form of sparkler made by pumping pressurized carbon dioxide into still wines.

Girasol

A large octagonal metal frame on a faceted base holding 504 bottles, increasingly used in place of the traditional PUPITRE to effect the descent of sediment after completion of the second fermentation. The frame, with its complement of bottles, may be swung round in a few seconds by a couple of men; and Freixenet, which was the first of the *cavas* to introduce it on a large scale, claims that it gives more consistent results than the *pupitre*. Most of the *cavas* in Cataluña have begun to use the device, and it has also been tried out in Reims by the French champagne-makers.

Girona

This province in the northeast of Cataluña produces sizable amounts of sparkling wine, most of it made by the Castillo de PERELADA and Cavas del AMPURDAN.

González y Dubosc DO NV

Sant Sadurní d'Anoia (Barcelona). DO Cava. This well-known firm is owned by the sherry-makers González Byass. The *cava* wines, light, dry and fresh and very reasonably priced, are marketed in the UK under the name of Jean Perico.

Gran-vas

Spanish name for *cuve close*. With this type of sparkling wine, second fermentation takes place in large closed tanks pressurized to 8 atmospheres, and lasts for four to five months according to temperature, usually $-5°C$. The wine is then filtered and bottled under pressure. Although the wines do not possess such a fine or lasting bubble as those made by the champagne method, they are a great deal more acceptable than GASEOSOS and make pleasant party drinking. To avoid the possibility of such wine being passed off as *cava*, Spanish regulations require that it may not be made in the same building. Corks from *cava* wine bear a star on the bottom, and *gran-vas* a small black circle.

Grapa

A metal hook used for securing the temporary cork during the second fermentation. *Grapas* and corks have now been largely replaced by crown caps.

Hill, Cavas DO 85, 86, 87, 88

Moja-Vilafranca del Penedès (Barcelona). DO Cava. Apart from its still Catalan wines (*see* pages 88–89), the firm produces a range of *cavas*, including Reserva Oro, Brut de Brut, Brutísimo and Rosado Brut.

Juvé y Camps DO 86, 87

Sant Sadurní d'Anoia (Barcelona). DO Cava. Sparkling

wine makers of repute, producing limited amounts of a
superior *cava* made from free-run juice, a favourite of the
Spanish Royal family. Their labels are: Reserva de la
Familia, Gran Reserva, Grand Cru and Rosado.

Lavernoya, Cavas DO
Sant Sadurní d'Anoia (Barcelona). DO Cava. Well-known
cellars whose wines, sold under the name of Lácrima
Baccus, include Primerisimo and Summum.

Licor de expedición
A solution of sugar in brandy and old white wine used to
top up the bottles after completion of the second
fermentation and removal of the temporary cork. It is the
amount of sugar in the *licor* which determines the style of
the finished wine. A dry brut will contain only some two
percent, while the sweet sparklers, which tend to be
popular in South America, are dosed to the extent of 12–20
percent. In general, the best sparkling wines are the driest,
because defects cannot be masked by excessive sweetening.

Licor de tiraje
A solution of sugar in white wine added before second
fermentation. It is from the breakdown of this sugar into
alcohol and carbon dioxide by the action of special yeasts
that wines made by the champagne method derive their
sparkle in the bottle.

Lleida
The province of Lleida (Lérida) in the northwest of
Cataluña produces sizable amounts of *cava*. *See* Raimat.

Marqués de Monistrol DO 75, 86, 87
Sant Sadurní d'Anoia (Barcelona). DO Cava. The *cavas* at
Monistrol de Noya, just outside Sant Sadurní, are among
the most picturesque in the area, with a flagged patio and
old wine press overlooked by the parish church; and
although Martini & Rossi acquired a 51 percent holding
(recently taken over by the British Grand Metropolitan),

the company, which has been making *cava* wines since 1882, is still very much a family concern, ten of the families who work in the *cavas* and vineyards living on the estate. Monistrol owns 300 hectares of vineyards and makes three million bottles of wine annually, most of it *cava* and much of it exported to Italy. The driest and most elegant of its sparkling wines are the Gran Tradición and Reserva Numerada. It also makes a Brut and dry and semi-dry wines. *See also* Cataluña, page 90.

Masachs, Josep DO 85, 86, 87

Vilafranca del Penedès (Barcelona). DO Cava. A sizable family firm currently producing some three million bottles yearly in its ultra-modern plant. Best of its wines are the extra brut Carolina de Masachs and Josep Masachs.

Mascaró, Cavas DO

Vilafranca del Penedès (Barcelona). DO Cava. Small and old-established family firm with cellars in the heart of Vilafranca, making liqueurs and an excellent brandy (*see* page 278) as well as still and good *cava* wines. Its dry Cava Reservada and Brut wines contain a high proportion of Parellada and are correspondingly fresh and fruity. *See also* Cataluña, page 90.

Mestres Sagues, Antonio DO 85, 86

Sant Sadurní d'Anoia (Barcelona). DO Cava. One of the smaller family firms in the Penedès making good sparkling wine by the champagne method, now available in the UK under the labels Clos Damiana, Clos Nostre Senyor, Coquet and Mestres Rosado.

Mont Marçal (Manuel Sancho e Hijos) DO 86, 87, 88

Castellvi de la Marca (Barcelona). DO Cava. Made only from free-run juice and from the traditional grape varieties Parellada, Xarel-lo and Macabeo, Mont Marçal Brut Natural and Mont Marçal Brut are first-rate wines, elegant and very dry.

Muga, Bodegas DO 79, 87

Haro (Logroño). DO Cava. One of the most scrupulous in its methods of the *bodegas* of the Rioja (*see* page 188), Muga some time ago revived an old Riojan tradition by making a *cava* wine. Launched under the somewhat unfortunate name of Mugamart, it has been rechristened Conde de Haro and is a bone dry, fruity and characterful wine in its own right – though nobody would confuse it with champagne.

Nadal Giro, Ramón DO

Pla del Penedès (Barcelona). DO Cava. Small family firm with 110 hectares of vineyards, and a well-equipped modern winery making a clean and elegant Nadal Brut.

Parxet DO

Santa María de Martorelles (Barcelona). DO Cava. The only producer of *cava* within the tiny DO Alella (*see* Cataluña, pages 79 and 91), making a fresh and fruity Brut Nature Chardonnay and also a first-rate Parxet from a traditional blend of Macabeo, Parellada and Pansa Blanca (Xarel-lo).

Penedès

The Penedès as such is *not* demarcated for producing *cava* as it is for still wines (*see* pages 91–92). Nevertheless all the individual municipalities within the DO Penedès are also entitled to make *cava* by the *méthode champenoise* or *método tradicional*, as it is to be known in the future, and it is from this geographical area that 95 percent of *cava* originates.

Many of the scores of *cavas* in and around Sant Sadurní d'Anoia and Vilafranca del Penedès are small family firms which will sell direct to visitors, who descend on the area from Barcelona in their hordes at weekends to look around the *cavas* and taste.

Since in the last decade the number of *cavas* with DO has increased from 65 to upwards of 220, it is no longer practical to print the names of firms other than those included in the A–Z listing.

Perelada, Castillo de DO 85

Perelada (Girona). DO Cava. Traditions of winemaking at Perelada, on the verges of the Pyrenees, date from the 12th century, when the Carmelite monks planted the first vineyards. To this day, the cellars lie beneath the 14th-century church of Carmen de Perelada, with its delicately arcaded patio, and the crenellated castle built shortly afterwards. The old buildings house a splendid library, a museum of glassware and ceramics and an extensive wine museum. More recently, a casino has been opened in the castle – dare one suggest, to promote the consumption of its excellent sparkling wines?

As distinct from the associated Cavas del AMPURDAN, the Castillo de Perelada produces only *cava* wine. About 50 percent of the grapes are from its own vineyards, the rest being bought from local farmers; and the wine, carefully made by the champagne method, is binned away to undergo its second fermentation in deep cellars underneath the former orchard.

The Brut Castillo is a deepish yellow in colour with fruity nose, but, despite its name, it has a somewhat sweetish finish; the best of the wines is the Gran Claustro, which, with five to six years in the cellars, emerges dry, soft and flowery.

Pupitre

The traditional method of coaxing the sediment and fine suspended matter into the neck of the bottle after the second fermentation of a sparkling wine is to place the bottles, neck first, into the oval holes of a *pupitre*, a wooden frame in the form of an inverted V. The bottles are regularly given a shake and a slight angular twist by hand, and the inclination of the *pupitre* is gradually altered, so that the bottle ends up almost on its head, with the solid matter against the bottom of the cork.

Raimat DO

Raimat (Lleida). DO Cava. The Raimat Chardonnay made by a subsidiary of Codorníu with the grapes grown on its estate outside LLEIDA (*see also* pages 94–95) is one of the best of all *cavas*. There is also a good Blanc de Blancs made with a blend of Macabeo, Chardonnay and Parellada.

Raventós i Blanc, Josep Maria DO 85, 86

Sant Sadurní d'Anoia (Barcelona) DO Cava. Josep Maria Raventós left the family firm of CODORNIU to make his own *cava* on the basis of 130 hectares of inherited vineyards. The Raventós i Blanc Brut is aimed at the top of the market.

Rioja, La

In the full flush of the Rioja boom of the late 19th century, various of the newly founded *bodegas* set about making sparkling wine by the champagne process from the local white Viura and Malvasía grapes. The Compañía Vinícola del Norte de España (*see* page 176) was so successful that it actually started a sister establishment in Reims. Although this lasted only three years, CVNE for long continued to supply the French champagne makers with Rioja wine during the period when they were suffering from the after-effects of the phylloxera epidemic.

There has been a revival in the making of sparkling wine in La Rioja, where various areas are demarcated under the DO Cava; in addition to Bodegas BILBAINAS and Bodegas MUGA, Bodegas Olarra and Bodegas Faustino-Martínez are both making brut *cava* from 100 percent Viura.

Rovellats DO 85, 87

San Martí de Sarroca (Barcelona). DO Cava. Small family firm making limited amounts of exclusive and expensive *cava*, stocked by some of the leading restaurants in Spain. Its labels are Brut Especial, Brut Imperial and two *gran reservas*, Brut Nature and the Gran Cru – Masia S XV, produced in minuscule amount.

San Sadurní de Noya (Sant Sadurní d'Anoia)

Now spelt on roadsigns in the Catalan form of Sant Sadurní d'Anoia, this little town west of Barcelona is the headquarters of the Spanish sparkling wine industry, with *cavas* on every street. There is a new two-star hotel at nearby Covides, the Sol; otherwise one may stay either in Barcelona or in nearby VILAFRANCA DEL PENEDÈS.

Segura Viudas DO

Sant Sadurní d'Anoia (Barcelona). DO Cava. Flagship of the companies formerly within RUMASA (*see* page 230), but now part of the FREIXENET group, making sparkling wine by the champagne method. The nucleus of the modern winery is an old house picturesquely situated on the road from Sant Sadurní to Igualada, with Montserrat (*see* Cataluña, pages 90–91) as a backdrop. Part of the grapes are grown on the 110 hectares of surrounding vineyards, the rest being bought from local growers. The most delicate of its wines, dry, light and fresh, and among the best of all Spanish *cavas*, are the Reserva Heredad and Aria. Other marks are the Brut Vintage, Brut, Rosé, Dry and Medium Dry.

'Sunflower'

English translation of GIRASOL.

Vallformosa, Masia DO

Vilobí del Penedès (Barcelona). DO Cava. Family firm making stylish brut *cavas*. *See also* Cataluña, page 101.

Ventura, Jané DO

El Vendrell (Tarragona). DO Cava. Well-known for its still wines (*see* Cataluña, pages 101–102), the firm also produces good Brut Natural and Brut *cavas* from the traditional Xarel-lo-Parellada-Macabeo blend.

Vilafranca del Penedès

Vilafranca is primarily a centre for making still wines (*see* Cataluña, page 102) but a number of the *cavas* are located there; it is also the headquarters of the official regulatory body for sparkling wines, the Consejo Regulador de los Vinos Espumosos.

Wine and Food

Manufacture of sparkling wines centres on Cataluña, especially the Penedès, and details of regional cooking and restaurants are given in the chapter on Cataluña.

Spirits, Aromatic Wines and Liqueurs

Sherry is so much an image of Spain that foreigners are often surprised to learn that a great deal more of it is drunk outside the country than in, especially in Britain, the Netherlands and the northern European countries, and that in Spain itself brandy, most of it produced in Jerez, is much cheaper and more popular. Sales of sherry have, in fact, declined in recent years, a decline aggravated by the increasing fashion among the younger generation for imported spirits, vermouths and liqueurs, and brandy has been the salvation of some of the big sherry houses.

The Spanish learned about distillation from the Moors. Alcohol was first used in medicine by the Catalan-born Arnold of Vilanova, and Spanish brandy was first shipped from Cataluña in the 17th century. Until the early 19th century it was used in Jerez only for the fortification of sherry, and the first Jerez brandies were not made by the sherry houses until the mid-19th century.

The first brandies were made by what is now known as the Charentais method, perfected in Cognac, by distillation of wine in a simple pot-still, in effect a copper kettle with a coiled condenser. This takes place in two stages, and the raw spirit is then matured in oak casks. It is still the method employed for the best and most refined Spanish brandy; but the great bulk of inexpensive Spanish brandy is made by 'continuous' distillation of wine in tall, steam-heated columns in the manner of grain whisky, a more economical and productive industrial process. The resulting *holandas*, or 65 percent grape spirit, made in distilleries all over Spain, are then diluted with water and aged in oak casks.

In Jerez, which produces the great bulk of Spanish brandy, maturation takes place in a *solera* (*see* page 233), with the periodic 'refreshment' of the older spirit with younger; and because of the aeration and quicker maturation, this gives rise to brandies quite different in character from those made in Cataluña or France, where there is no such frequent transfer from cask to cask. Jerez brandy has an oaky charm of its own, but it is so distinctive that it is not sensible to make direct comparisons with cognac or armagnac.

In 1987 a new DO was set up for Brandy de Jerez and a Consejo Regulador established to administer it. The main provisions are that only brandy made in Jerez de la Frontera, Puerto de Santa María and Sanlúcar de Barrameda qualifies for DO and that it must be made by traditional methods from *aguardiente de vino* (grape spirit) and matured in *criaderas* and *soleras* as in making sherry or by static maturation in a single barrel as in making an *añada* or vintage sherry. In ascending order of quality and depending on the time of maturation and on the content of aldehydes, esters and higher alcohols the *reglamento* defines three types of Brandy de Jerez: *Solera*, *Solera Reserva* and *Gran Reserva*, the last of which must be matured for more than three years and contain more than 300 milligrams of non-alcohols per 100 centilitres of absolute alcohol.

Another popular spirit is *aguardiente*, made by distilling the pips and skins remaining from the fermentation of wine. Akin to the French *marc* or Portuguese *bagaceira*, this is a somewhat fiery liquid best left to those who have learned to stomach it.

Spain also produces a gamut of liqueurs, many of them household names marketed internationally by foreign companies and made under licence in Spain, by the maceration of fruits and herbs in alcoholic solution and subsequent distillation. A variety of firms in Jerez and Cataluña make very respectable gin and vodka by the traditional methods. Vermouth is made in large amounts, much of it under licence, by the preparation of herbal extracts and their blending with white wine. The native *anís* is first rate; and tonic wines and spirits containing quinine extract, of which the best known are Jerez-Quina and Calisay, are something of a speciality and are made in Jerez, Málaga and Barcelona.

Aguardiente

Aguardiente is defined by the Estatuto de la Viña, del Vino y de los Alcoholes as 'natural alcohol with a strength of not more than 80 percent' distilled from vegetable materials. It therefore constitutes a wide variety which includes the HOLANDAS used for the manufacture of brandy and known as *aguardiente de vino*, as well as other varieties distilled from fermented fruits and cereals.

However, over the counter of a bar, *aguardiente* means *aguardiente de orujo*, a popular and potent spirit distilled

from the grape skins and pips left over from the
fermentation of wine in the manner of the French *marc* or
Portuguese *bagaceira*. It is made all over Spain and is not
normally branded, but poured from an unlabelled bottle, a
fact which, combined with its well-deserved reputation for
strength, intimidates many tourists.

Alvear

Apart from making Montilla (*see* page 143), Alvear also
produces brandy, made from HOLANDAS and matured in
solera after the fashion of the Jerez brandies and the fortified
wines of the area. The inexpensive Secular is fruity, with a
raisiny nose and peppery finish. The more refined Senador
and PRESIDENTE are oakier and more aromatic, and the finish
of the Presidente Alvear Gran Reserva is extremely dry.

Amer Picon

The well-known orange-flavoured bitters, manufactured
under licence in Spain.

Anís

Aniseed-flavoured liqueur corresponding to the French
anisette. The best Spanish *anís*, such as CHINCHON and ANIS
DEL MONO, is of excellent quality.

Anís del Mono

One of the best and most popular brands of ANIS, made by
Bosch y Cía, a subsidiary of OSBORNE, in Badalona near
Barcelona.

Barceló, Luis

A Málaga firm, whose speciality is VINOS QUINADOS.

Bénédictine

Famous French liqueur made under licence in Spain.

Bertola

Sherry firm which makes Tudor and Gran Reserva
brandies.

Bilbainas, Bodegas

About the only *bodega* in the Rioja to produce that *rara avis*, a Riojan brandy to stand alongside its still and sparkling wines. Its Imperator has a vinous, oaky nose, is completely dry, but it tastes of little except oak, and the finish is short. *See also* pages 173 and 255.

Blázquez, Hijos de Agustín

Well-known sherry firm, makers of FELIPE II, one of the drier and least manipulated of the Jerez brandies.

Bobadilla

Sherry firm best known for its brandies: Solera 103 White Label, aged for six months, pale and delicate; Solera 103 Black Label *reserva*; and Gran Capitán *gran reserva*, a blend of brandies between three and eighty years old.

Brandy

As has been explained in the introduction to this section, most Spanish brandy is made from HOLANDAS, produced by distilling wine (in the manner of grain whisky) in a continuous still and maturing the raw spirit in *solera* (*see* Sherry, page 233). The better Catalan brandies, as also a few of the premium Jerez marks, are, however, made by the Charentais method in pot-stills. Most commercial Spanish brandies are sweeter and more caramelized than the French and have therefore made less impact to date in international markets other than Latin America.

Brandy 103

Popular Jerez brandy made by the sherry firm, BOBADILLA.

Caballero, Luis

Sherry concern located in Puerto de Santa María and maker of one of the best brands of PONCHE, Caballero, sold in eye-catching silvered bottles.

Calisay

Quinine-based liqueur, a speciality of the Barcelona area,

which may be drunk either as a *digéstif* or, with ice and
with or without fruit (such as lemon, orange and
maraschino cherries), as an apéritif. A dash of Calisay much
enlivens fruit salads. *See also* Mollfulleda.

Capa Negra

Jerez brandy made by the sherry firm of Sandeman-
Coprimar in Jerez de la Frontera.

Cardenal Mendoza

Jerez brandy made by the sherry firm of Sánchez Romate
and labelled 'Cardinal' in the USA. First produced in 1887,
this *gran reserva* brandy is aged in *oloroso* casks and is one of
the best from Jerez, exceptionally smooth and fragrant.

Carlos I

The most refined of the brandies made by PEDRO DOMECQ
in Jerez, and though very slightly on the sweet side, it is
light and spirituous, more resembling a French cognac than
most Jerez brandies and more suited to northern tastes.

Chartreuse

Although many well-known French liqueurs are made
under licence in Spain, Chartreuse was more firmly rooted,
since from 1903–40, during the exile of the monks from La
Grande Chartreuse, it was made exclusively in Tarragona.
The distillery was directly supervised by the three fathers
who share the closely guarded secret of its recipe and who
spent January to May in Tarragona and the rest of the year
in Voiron, in the French Alps.

It is said that 130 herbs (many procured locally) were
used for making Green Chartreuse, and rather fewer for the
Yellow. The difference between the French and Spanish
versions was minimal, though in my experience the Spanish
was slightly drier – and also, of course, like all Spanish-
made liqueurs, vastly less expensive.

I write in the past tense, since the Tarragona distillery
was closed in 1991.

Chinchón

One of the best brands of ANIS, made by a subsidiary of
González Byass in the small town of Chinchón, southeast of
Madrid. It was named after a 17th-century Marquesa de
Chinchón, wife of a governor of Peru, who in 1638
discovered the medicinal properties of quinine, giving her
name to the cinchona tree from the bark of which it is
obtained and, indirectly, inspiring the fabrication of VINOS
QUINADOS, drunk as tonics.

Cinzano

Cinzano, in its different varieties, is made under licence in
Vilafranca del Penedès and, with Martini, is the most
widely drunk VERMOUTH in Spain.

Cointreau

This famous orange-flavoured liqueur was formerly made
for the house of Cointreau by Cavas MASCARO in Vilafranca
del Penedès. It is still made in Vilafranca, but by a Spanish
subsidiary under the close supervision of the French firm.

Coñac

To the legitimate discomfort of producers in Cognac,
Spanish brandy is almost universally known in Spain as
coñac. This is no fairer than labelling sherry-type wines
from Cyprus and elsewhere as 'sherry', a practice the Jerez
houses are vehement in denouncing; and the makers of
Spanish brandy are careful to label their product as 'brandy'
or Brandy de Jerez.

Cuarenta y Tres

A sweet, light yellow, vanilla-flavoured liqueur, rather
resembling Southern Comfort in taste, made by Diego
Zamora in Cartagena. Its name means 'forty-three'. Sweet
as it is, Spaniards often drink it as an apéritif.

Don Narciso

Delicate and aromatic brandy, a blend of seven- and ten-
year-old spirits and one of the best from Spain, made and

matured by the Charentais method by Cavas MASCARO in Vilafranca del Penedès.

Dubonnet

The popular French apéritif, made under licence in Barcelona and differing little from the original.

DYC

Spanish-made whisky produced in a distillery near Segovia, where the water and grain are considered to be most like those of the Scottish Highlands. It is not of the quality of the original and has made little headway against the imported Scotch widely obtainable in Spanish supermarkets and grocers.

Escat

Barcelona firm making a wide range of spirits, including vodka, gin, *anís*, *pastís*, advocaat, kirsch, rum (known in Spain as *ron*), together with crème de menthe, cherry and apricot brandies, and a liqueur made with bananas from the Canary Islands.

Espléndido

The youngest of the range of brandies from the sherry firm of GARVEY.

Fabuloso

Jerez brandy made by Palomino & Vergara, an old family sherry firm acquired by Allied-Lyons after having suffered badly at the hands of RUMASA (*see* pages 230–231).

Felipe II

Pleasant and inexpensive Jerez brandy made by Agustín BLAZQUEZ in Jerez de la Frontera.

Fontenac

One of the best brandies from Miguel TORRES in Vilafranca del Penedès. It is made by the Charentais method and is aged in French style rather than in *solera*; it is hence less oaky than its Jerez counterparts, and more along the lines of an armagnac.

Fundador

Fundador was one of the first Jerez brandies and was put on sale to the public by PEDRO DOMECQ in 1874, some 20 years after Don Pedro Domecq Lustau had been so struck with the quality of a batch of HOLANDAS accidentally left in cask that he decided on systematic production of a brandy. To foreign tastes, it remains one of the most agreeable of the inexpensive brandies, since it is grapier and less sweetened than many of its competitors. The trend in Spain has, however, been to smoother and sweeter brandies in the medium-price bracket; and domestic sales of Fundador, for long one of the biggest-selling brand names, have declined.

García Poveda, H L

Makers, apart from table wines from the Alicante area (*see* Valencia and Murcia, page 244), of a range of Costa Blanca vermouths, fully flavoured and spicy in comparison with those from France and Italy.

Garvey

Famous sherry house and producer, in ascending order of age and refinement, of Espléndido, Gran Garvey and RENACIMIENTO brandies.

González Byass

Apart from sherries, González Byass makes three brandies: SOBERANO, the medium-priced INSUPERABLE and, in very limited amount, the exquisite LEPANTO *gran reserva*.

Gordon's Gin

This is made under licence in Spain by PEDRO DOMECQ with close supervision from London.

Gran Duque de Alba

Premium quality *gran reserva* Jerez brandy made by Diez-Merito.

Holandas

Grape spirit containing 65 percent alcohol and made by the
continuous distillation of wine in various districts of Spain,
especially La Mancha, Extremadura and Huelva. This spirit
is subsequently diluted with water and aged, either in *solera*
or cask, to make brandy.

Honorable

An exceptional brandy made by Miguel TORRES in
Vilafranca del Penedès by double distillation in copper pot-
stills and long maturation in French oak.

Independencia

Dark, velvety and sweet, and sold in a curious distorted
bottle to emphasize its age, this is a premium *gran reserva*
brandy from the sherry house of OSBORNE.

Insuperable

The big brother of SOBERANO from GONZALEZ BYASS,
smoother and more aromatic.

Jerez-Quina

Popular tonic wine, made with sherry, macerated cinchona
bark and the peel of Seville oranges, and regularly
administered to Spanish children and convalescents.

Larios

Larios makes good Málaga (*see* page 136), but in Spain it is
a household word for its gin, sold in bottles with a red and
yellow label with a marked likeness to that of the export
Gordon's. Though not of quite the same quality as good
London gin, it is entirely acceptable with mixers. The firm
also produces the 1866 Gran Reserva brandy, Triple Seco
orange liqueur, and rum.

Lepanto

Soft, mellow and fragrant, but entirely Jerezano in
character, this expensive *gran reserva* brandy from GONZALEZ
BYASS, sold in a cut-glass decanter, is exceptional.

Liqueurs

Most of the best-known French liqueurs are made under licence in Spain (*see* Cointreau, Bénédictine, Marie Brizard) and differ little from the originals – except that they are much cheaper and therefore a popular purchase with travellers. There are also numerous separately listed firms making fruit brandies, crème de menthe, kirsch and also some native liqueurs with a foreign following (*see* Ponche, Cuarenta y Tres, Pacharán).

Lustau, Emilio

Sherry firm whose brandy is sold as Señor Lustau.

Magno

Made by osborne in Puerto de Santa María, Magno, which spends four to five years in *solera*, is dark in colour, smooth, aromatic and on the sweet side, very much to the Spanish taste and a nice brandy. It currently commands some half of the domestic market in the increasingly popular medium-price range.

Marie Brizard

Perhaps the most famous of French *anisettes*, this is made under licence at Pasajes in the Basque country.

Martini

Martini, especially in the sweet and bitter-sweet varieties, is extremely popular in Spain and is made in Barcelona.

Mascaró, Cavas

Mascaró, a small family concern in Vilafranca del Penedès (*see* page 90), has for long provided some of the best Catalan brandy. Made by the Charentais method and aged along French lines, it is more akin to cognac or armagnac than to the Jerez-style brandies. The regular Mascaró, light, smooth and fragrant, is in my own opinion much superior to most three-star cognacs and a great deal less expensive. The older DON NARCISO is produced from Macabeo, Xarel-lo and Parellada grapes vinified in the *cava* itself.

Mascaró also produces a vodka and a superior gin, made with alcohol distilled from sugar beet and juniper berries from the Penedès. For many years the firm made Cointreau for sale in Spain and now produces its own curaçao, the Gran Licor de Naranja, a pleasant liqueur made by steeping dried orange peel from Spain, Algeria, Haiti and Italy in alcoholic solution and then distilling it.

Mollfulleda, Distilerías

Large firm with its distillery in Arenys de Mar near Barcelona, specializing in the quinine-based CALISAY. Apart from this, it also produces rum, gin, kirsch and a range of liqueurs – orange, peppermint, coffee, cocoa, and others.

Montulia, Bodegas

Apart from Montilla (*see* page 146), Montulia also makes ANIS and a range of *solera* brandies.

Orujo

Popular name for the fiery *aguardiente de orujo* distilled from grape skins and pips (*see* Aguardiente).

Osborne y Cía

This famous sherry firm is the largest producer of spirits in Spain, making VETERANO, MAGNO and INDEPENDENCIA brandies. All tend to be dark in colour and somewhat sweetened and caramelized to the Spanish taste. Its Conde de Osborne *gran reserva* is even older and mellower than Independencia and is sold in distinctive white ceramic bottles designed by Salvador Dali. Osborne also makes a PONCHE and produces RIVES Gin in a new plant outside Puerto de Santa María, and ANIS DEL MONO in Barcelona.

Pacharán

A delicious liqueur with a base of ANIS made from sloes in Navarra. The most widely available brand is ZOCO.

Pedro Domecq

One of the first firms to make brandy in Jerez, Pedro Domecq maintains a huge store for ageing its brandies in *solera* and, taking into account its vast Mexican operation, is probably the biggest manufacturer in the world. In ascending order of age and quality its labels are: FUNDADOR, Carlos II and CARLOS I. Domecq also makes an Anís Dulce and a sweet lime liqueur, the Crema de Lima.

Pemartín y Cía, José

In ascending order of age and refinement, the brandies from this old-established sherry firm are Pemartín, Brandy 1810 and VOG. It also markets a rum.

Pernod

The well-known aniseed-flavoured drink is made under licence in Tarragona.

Ponche

First produced by the sherry firm of José de Soto in 1888, *ponche* is a blend of brandy and herbs; often flavoured with orange, it is a most satisfactory drink for those with a taste for something sweeter than brandy but less sticky than a liqueur and fills an uncluttered gap in the market. It stands out on the shelves of a bar because of its silvered bottles. De Soto's *ponche* remains one of the best since it is more aromatic and less sweet than some. Other Jerez producers are Osborne, Diestro, Bobadilla, Caballero and J Ruiz y Cía, makers of the excellent Ponche Español.

Presidente
The best of the brandies from the Montilla firm of ALVEAR.

Queimada
Galician speciality made by setting alight AGUARDIENTE in a white chinaware bowl. When the blue flame subsides, the liquid is, surprisingly, stone cold. More elaborate versions are made, especially at Christmas, by pouring the spirit into an earthenware *cazuela*, adding roasted coffee beans, slices of fresh lemon and maraschino cherries, burning off some of the alcohol and ladling the potent concoction into glasses.

Quinine
Quinine-based apéritifs and liqueurs are widely produced and popular in Spain. *See also* Jerez-Quina, Calisay, Vinos Quinados and Chinchón.

Renacimiento
Smooth and very old *gran reserva* brandy made by GARVEY of Jerez and sold in a cut-glass decanter.

Ricard
The well-known French *pastís* made under licence in Reus in Cataluña.

Rives
A good-quality Spanish gin made by OSBORNE.

Soberano
One of the biggest-selling of Spanish brandies, made by GONZALEZ BYASS in Jerez. Like FUNDADOR, it is less sweetened and caramelized than many and will thus appeal to foreign visitors more than the darker varieties popular with the Spaniards themselves. An honest-to-goodness young Jerez brandy, remarkably inexpensive, especially when bought in litre bottles, the taste for it grows!

Sol y sombra

Literally 'sun and shade', a mixture of brandy and ANIS.
Aficionados usually mix one part of brandy with two of *anís*.

Terry, Fernando A de

Less caramelized than it once was, the regular Terry, in a
bottle with a yellow net, is extremely popular in Spain. The
older and more refined Solera 1900 is still on the sweet side.

Torres, Miguel

Together with MASCARO, Torres produces the best Catalan
brandy. The range, in order of age, comprises Torres 5 and
Torres 10 made by the *solera* system; FONTENAC, Miguel
Torres Black Label and HONORABLE premium brandies,
made by the Charentais method on the premises and
subsequently aged in oak for long periods. I have attended
blind tastings where it proved extremely difficult to
distinguish the Black Label from good VSOP Cognac. Se
also pages 99–101.

Vermouth

Vermouth, much of it made under licence in Cataluña (for example CINZANO and MARTINI), is produced on a large scale in Spain. The only way in which these Spanish-made vermouths differ from their Italian namesakes is in the local white wine used for their manufacture – a relatively unimportant factor in comparison with the herbal extract – and in price. There is also a wide variety of purely Spanish vermouths, produced mainly in Cataluña and along the east coast. These tend to be heavier and fuller in flavour.

Veterano

Jerez brandy made by OSBORNE and known the length and breadth of the country, if only because of the roadside hoardings with their large black bull. Dark in colour and somewhat sweetened and caramelized, it is one of the biggest-selling brandies in Spain.

Vinos quinados

Tonic or medicated wines containing quinine extract, drunk either for pleasure or given to children and invalids. *See also* Jerez-Quina and Luis Barceló.

Vodka

Spanish vodka, like gin, is produced in sizable amounts in Jerez and the Barcelona area, and is inexpensive and of acceptable quality – certainly when drunk with mixers.

Whisky

It is now more chic among Spaniards to drink whisky than sherry. Most of the best-known brands of Scotch are readily obtainable – and no more expensive than in their homeland – as also some American and Canadian whiskeys. Although attempts have been made to produce whisky (*see* DYC) in Spain, the home-made product has not caught on.

Zoco

Best known of the brands of PACHARAN, the sloe liqueur from Navarra.

Index

The following abbreviations are used in the index: Bod. *Bodega*; Cía *Compañía*; Coop. *Cooperativa*; DO *denominación de origen* area; Hnos *Hermanos*; (H) entry which includes hotel recommendation; (R) restaurant recommendation